PRIMACY OF CHRIST

PRIMACY *of* CHRIST

The Patristic Patrimony in
Joseph Ratzinger/Benedict XVI's
Analogy in Theology

VINCENT C. ANYAMA

◆PICKWICK *Publications* • Eugene, Oregon

PRIMACY OF CHRIST
The Patristic Patrimony in Joseph Ratzinger/Benedict XVI's Analogy in Theology

Copyright © 2021 Vincent C. Anyama. All rights reserved. Except for brief quotations in critical publications or reviews, no part of this book may be reproduced in any manner without prior written permission from the publisher. Write: Permissions, Wipf and Stock Publishers, 199 W. 8th Ave., Suite 3, Eugene, OR 97401.

Pickwick Publications
An Imprint of Wipf and Stock Publishers
199 W. 8th Ave., Suite 3
Eugene, OR 97401

www.wipfandstock.com

PAPERBACK ISBN: 978-1-7252-6156-3
HARDCOVER ISBN: 978-1-7252-6155-6
EBOOK ISBN: 978-1-7252-6157-0

Cataloguing-in-Publication data:

Names: Anyama, Vincent C., author.
Title: Primacy of Christ : the patristic patrimony in Joseph Ratzinger/Benedict XVI's analogy in theology / Vincent C. Anyama.
Description: Eugene, OR : Pickwick Publications, 2021 | Includes bibliographical references and index.
Identifiers: ISBN 978-1-7252-6156-3 (paperback) | ISBN 978-1-7252-6155-6 (hardcover) | ISBN 978-1-7252-6157-0 (ebook)
Subjects: LCSH: Benedict XVI, Pope, 1927–. | Catholic Church—Doctrines—History—21st century.
Classification: BX1378.6 .A64 2021 (print) | BX1378.6 .A64 (ebook)

Dedicated to my Parents,
Magnus and Mary Anyama

Table of Contents

Acknowledgments ix
Abbreviations xi

Introduction 1

PART ONE: PATRISTIC PATRIMONY

Chapter 1: Patristic Consensus on Analogy 17
    Faith and Reason 17
    Image and Participation 29
    God-Talk 51
    Conclusion 65

Chapter 2: The Fathers whom Ratzinger Quotes 68
    Truth in Faith, Philosophy, and Politics 68
    The Original Man and the Priority of Love 89
    Pneumatic and Ecclesial Participation 95
    Primacy of Christ in God-Talk 123
    Conclusion 132

PART TWO: RATZINGER'S PRIMACY OF CHRIST

Chapter 3: Analogy of Faith and Reason in Ratzinger's Theology 135
    Fourth Lateran Council 135
    Bonaventure 137
    Joseph Ratzinger 148
    Conclusion 169

Chapter 4: Ratzinger's Image and Participation Analogy 171
  Image 171
  Participation 179
  Conclusion 204

Chapter 5: Ratzinger's Primacy of Christ in God-Talk 206
  The Limitation of Human Nature and Divine Transcendence 206
  Naming God 209
  Human Words Become Divine Word 215
  Primacy of the Incarnate Word in Christian Prayer 225
  Evangelization 231
  Conclusion 234

General Conclusion 235
  The Patristic Patrimony in Ratzinger's Primacy of Christ 235
  Answers to the Analogy Questions in Ratzinger 243
  Points for Further Consideration 248
  Conclusion 252

Bibliography 253
Index 261

Acknowledgments

WRITING A DOCTORAL DISSERTATION is not an isolated work of the *doctorandus* but the product of a collaborative effort of a network of support often unnoticed. My first word of thanks goes to Cardinal Kevin Farrell, the former bishop of the Catholic Diocese of Dallas and the current Prefect of the Dicastery for the Laity, Family and Life, whose initiative to send me to study set this work in motion. Many in my home Diocese of Dallas have been very helpful in my writing of this dissertation, especially the Most Reverend Edward Burns, Most Reverend Gregory Kelly, and the parish communities of St. Francis in Frisco, All Saints in Dallas, and St. Joseph in Richardson.

My immense gratitude must also be expressed to those who helped me through the long and arduous process of study, research and writing. Most particularly, my special gratitude rightly goes to my *Moderator*, Father Joseph Carola, SJ, who is a great mentor, a talented theologian, and a true friend. His seminars and classes ignited in me a deep appreciation for the Church Fathers, and for the theology of Joseph Ratzinger/Pope Benedict XVI. During the course of this study, he has diligently guided me with critical suggestions, fraternal encouragements, research materials and professional rigor. I cannot thank him enough for his dedication and diligence. I also wish to thank Father Joseph Xavier, SJ, my second reader, for the assistance he offered in the later stages of this process. I would like to thank Father Amaury Begasse de Dhaem, SJ, who guided me in the first six months of my research on the Bonaventurian foundations of Ratzinger's theology.

There are many others whom I should thank, but I will name only a few. I would like to thank Father Justin Kizewski, who encouraged me to pursue the theme of Analogy in the theology of the Church Fathers and Joseph Ratzinger. I am grateful to the faculty and staff of Mundelein Seminary in Chicago as well as the faculty and staff of Herzogliches Georgianum Seminary in Munich for their hospitality during my summer research work in the United States and during my German language studies in Germany respectively. My immense gratitude also goes to my brother priests at the Casa Santa Maria of the Pontifical North American College for their friendship and fraternal support. I am mindful of those friends whose prayers accompanied me through this project, especially the Religious Sisters of Mercy of Alma, Michigan, and my friends from the various Dioceses of South-East Nigeria.

I want to thank my seminarian and lay students of St. Thomas University at St. Mary's Seminary in Houston, Texas. I hope that my classes offer a little aid toward their deeper love for the mysteries of our faith in Christ. Finally, I wish to extend a special word of thanks to my family for their love, support, and prayers in these years of my study abroad. May God reward them abundantly and sustain them in His love.

Rev. Vincent C. Anyama
St. Mary's Seminary, Houston, TX
January 12, 2020
The Baptism of the Lord

Abbreviations

ANF	*Ante-Nicene Fathers*
CCSL	Corpus Christianorum: Series Latina
CCSG	Corpus Christianorum: Series Graeca
CSEL	Corpus Scriptorum Ecclesiasticorum Latinorum
GCS	Griechischen Christlichen Schriftsteller
LCC	Library of Christian Classics
NPNF	Nicene and Post-Nicene Fathers
PG	Patrologia Graeca
PL	Patrologia Latina
Prol.	Prologue
PTS	Patristische Texte und Studien
GNOS	Gregorii Nysseni Opera Supplementum
SC	Sources Chrétiennes
ST	Aquinas, *Summa theologiae*

Augustine

Civ.	Augustine, *De civitate Dei*
Conf.	Augustine, *Confessiones*
Div. quaest.	Augustine, *De diversis questionibus LXXXIII*
Doctr. chr.	Augustine, *De doctrina christiana*
Enarrat. Ps.	Augustine, *Enarrationes in Psalmos*
Gen. Man.	Augustine, *De Genesi contra Manichaeos*
Mag.	Augustine, *De magistro*
Ord.	Augustine, *De ordine*

Retract.	Augustine, *Retractationes*
Serm.	Augustine, *Sermones*
Solil.	Augustine, *Soliloquiorum*
Tract. Ev. Io.	Augustine, *In Iohannis evangelium tractatus*
Trin.	Augustine, *De Trinitate*
Util. cred.	Augustine, *De utilitate credenda*
Ver. rel.	Augustine, *De vera religione*

Bonaventure

Apol. Paup.	Bonaventure, *Apologia Pauperum*
Brev.	Bonaventure, *Breviloquium*
Hex.	Bonaventure, *Hexaemeron*
Itin.	Bonaventure, *Itinerarium mentis in Deum*
Red.	Bonaventure, *De reductione artium ad theologiam*
Sent.	Bonaventure, *Sententiarum*

INTRODUCTION

> He is the image of the invisible God, the first-born of all creatures. . . . It is he who is the head of the body the Church, he who is the beginning, the first-born of the dead, so that primacy may be his in everything.
>
> —COLOSSIANS 1:15–18

It is our basic Christian claim that Christ who is Lord of the universe, infinitely surpasses all human greatness. This claim finds its magisterial expression in number ten of the Second Vatican Council document, *Gaudium et Spes*: "The key, the center and the purpose of the whole of man's history is to be found in its Lord and Master."[1] At the opening of the second session of the Council, Pope Paul VI acknowledges this "Lord and Master" as the "real president of this council."[2] As a young *Peritus* to Cardinal Joseph Frings of Cologne for the Second Vatican Council, Fr. Joseph Ratzinger was "most impressed" by how the Pope's address drew from "the early Christian awareness of *Christ's primacy*" to direct the Council's interpretation of the present age.[3] As a theologian and as Pope Benedict XVI, the same theme of Christ's primacy remains the single thread that weaves together all of his life's work.

In his book *Salt of the Earth*, Joseph Cardinal Ratzinger describes his theology as bearing "the stamp of the Fathers, especially Augustine."[4] Ratzinger's seminal work on Augustine's ecclesiology, *Volk und Haus*

---

1. Flannery, *Vatican Council II*, 910.
2. Benedict XVI/Ratzinger, *Theological Highlights*, 67.
3. Benedict XVI/Ratzinger, *Theological Highlights*, 67.
4. Benedict XVI/Ratzinger, *Salt of the Earth*, 66.

Gottes in Augustins Lehre von der Kirche[5] lays the patristic foundation of his theological career. Under the direction of his mentor and *Doktorvater* Göttlieb Söhngen, Ratzinger discovered in the writings of the Church Fathers and Bonaventure, the primacy of Christ as the context for all philosophical discussions concerning the human person. Very early on in his academic carrier, Ratzinger's Christ-centered approach to natural theology took on an ecumenical preoccupation.[6] He considers his ecumenical sensibility as something he inherited from Söhngen, who came from a mixed marriage.[7] In his *Last Testament*, Pope Benedict XVI fondly recalls how Söhngen's lectures "were never only about the Catholic tradition, but rather always in dialogue with Protestantism too, particularly at that time with Karl Barth."[8]

As a young student, Ratzinger would have been immersed in his mentor's intense involvement in the analogy debate between the prominent German Jesuit Erich Przywara and the protestant Karl Barth. Barth sharpened the Reformation's antagonism to philosophy by his blistering attack on the theory of *analogia entis* or analogy of being, which he considered "the invention of Antichrist" and an obstruction to the possibility of his becoming Catholic.[9] He rejected the possibility of man's natural knowledge of God outside of biblical revelation as the road to secular misery. Ratzinger's mentor, Söhngen, saw a possibility of ecumenical dialogue based on Barth's language of *analogia fidei* (analogy of faith). As Thomas Joseph White explains, Söhngen's analogy of faith consists in the notion whereby "the ontological and philosophical discourse (the *analogia entis*) was always contextualized by Christology and a higher and more ultimate understanding of the Christian mystery."[10] Essentially, Söhngen argued for a Christocentric "*analogia entis* within an *analogia*

---

5. Benedict XVI/Ratzinger, "Volk und Haus Gottes."
6. Benedict XVI/Ratzinger, *Last Testament*, 98.
7. Benedict XVI/Ratzinger, *Last Testament*, 98.
8. Benedict XVI/Ratzinger, *Last Testament*, 98.
9. See Barth, *Church Dogmatics*, 1/1:x: "I can see no third possibility between play with the *analogia entis,* legitimate only on Roman Catholic ground, between the greatness and the misery of a so-called natural knowledge of God in the sense of the *Vaticanum,* and a Protestant theology self-nourished at its own source, standing upon its own feet, and finally liberated from such secular misery, I can therefore only say No here. I regard the *analogia entis* as the invention of Antichrist, and think that because of it one cannot become Catholic."
10. White, *Analogy of Being*, 18.

fidei," which seemed to appease Barth.[11] Ratzinger's writings such as *Introduction to Christianity*, and *In the Beginning* testify to how he imbibed his mentor's Christocentric synthesis of the analogy of faith and reason.[12] However, what opened the door for the uniqueness of Ratzinger's contribution to the synthesis of faith and reason was his encounter with the process of the intellectual conversion of Augustine, which confronted him with the significance of Greek philosophy in the Christian synthesis of faith and reason.[13] As Benedict XVI recalls,

> Augustine had not at first been able to start with the God of Abraham, Isaac, and Jacob.... He turned his attention to philosophy, then fell into Manicheism, and only after that discovered what would remain his modus operandi for the rest of his life: "In the Platonists I learned 'In the beginning was the Word.' In the Christians I learned, 'The Word became flesh.' And it is only thus that the Word came to me."[14]

What constitutes the ingenuity of Ratzinger's contribution to the analogy debate is the question we seek to investigate in this dissertation, in such a way that is respectful of his intellectual background, which he says is fundamentally patristic and biblical.

Status Quaestionis

In other to build on the foundations laid by previous scholarship, a survey of their questions, concerns, and limitations related to the use of analogy in Ratzinger, is necessary for our study. The survey shows that no attempt has been made to adequately consider the broad patristic foundations of the primacy of Christ per se and its relationship to the use of analogy in Ratzinger's theology. What is notable among scholars is their focus on the Christocentric Augustinianism and the primacy of truth in Ratzinger's theology. While their contributions are significant, their insights are often less comprehensive.

---

11. Betz, "Translator's Introduction," in Przywara, *Analogia Entis*, 93: "By 1940 Barth seemed to be appeased by Göttlieb Söhngen's argument for an *analogia entis* within an *analogia fidei*."

12. See White, *Analogy of Being*, 18.

13. Benedict XVI/Ratzinger, *Last Testament*, 104–5.

14. Benedict XVI/Ratzinger, *Last Testament*, 104–5.

Walter Kasper criticizes the theological synthesis in Ratzinger's *Introduction to Christianity* as undergirded by Platonic idealism, in the sense that the synthesis does not begin with the existential but with the Platonic dialectic of the visible and the invisible.[15] Following Kasper, James Corkery considers Ratzinger's primacy of the *Logos* to bear a Platonic primacy of the "idea." In Ratzinger's theology, Corkery sees how the *Logos*-love, which contains the universal "idea" of creation, takes primacy over the *particular* facts of creation.[16] Corkery insists that Ratzinger's idealistic presentation of the primacy of the *Logos* lends itself to a pessimistic and anti-world view that is not "praxis-centered," but conditions our encounter with God to the necessity of *turning around* from the world instead of *turning to* it.[17]

Rejecting Kasper's criticism of Ratzinger, Peter McGregor claims that when Ratzinger speaks of the invisible as "more real,"[18] the context is the "the difficulty confronting coming to faith in God, given the nature of human knowing."[19] McGregor sees Ratzinger as attempting a balancing act between two biblical truths that are beyond human synthesis: "The knowability and unknowability of God by human beings."[20] He does so by demonstrating the double concealing modes of God's self-revelation, which Ratzinger calls the "law of disguise."[21] On the one hand, as the creative *Logos*, God surpasses all thought and yet encompasses it. On the other hand, under the sign of the lowly, he made himself accessible through the failure of the crucified one in a way that supersedes all expectations. While the Cross remains "the point at which one can actually touch God,"[22] it shows God to be entirely other. Contrary to Corkery's identification of Ratzinger's *Logos*-Christology as anti-world and non-praxis centered, McGregor insists that Ratzinger's theological synthesis proposes a praxis of *metanoia*, which is distinct from the idealism of the Platonic analogy of the Cave and consistent with the Christian analogy of how we correspond with the truth. There is a turning away

---

15. See Kasper, "Das Wesen Des Christlichen," 182–88; "Theorie und Praxis," 155.
16. Corkery, *Joseph Ratzinger's Theological Ideas*, 31–32.
17. Corkery, *Joseph Ratzinger's Theological Ideas*, 31.
18. Benedict XVI/Ratzinger, *Introduction to Christianity*, 74.
19. McGregor, *Heart to Heart*, 91.
20. McGregor, *Heart to Heart*, 93.
21. Benedict XVI/Ratzinger, *Introduction to Christianity*, 254–55.
22. Benedict XVI/Ratzinger, *Introduction to Christianity*, 256.

from the "world" in a Johannine sense of primordial human rebellion against God. Then, unlike the Platonic proposal of turning to the facets of truth, Ratzinger proposes a turning *to* truth completely revealed in the biblical command, "repent and believe in the Gospel" (Mark 1:15).[23] Thus, in favor of a non-idealistic character of Ratzinger's primacy of the *Logos,* McGregor's brief comments on Ratzinger's discussions on man's correspondence to the truth leave room for a more focused development of analogy in Ratzinger's theology of the relationship between God and man.

Robert Krieg claims that Ratzinger's reliance on Max Scheler's idealism conflates Christology and anthropology.[24] However, Joseph Lam dismisses Krieg's criticism as "lacking a solid basis."[25] Lam argues that Ratzinger mentions Scheler only three times in his earlier works, and "in all three times, Ratzinger rejects both Scheler's separation of the metaphysical from religious cognition, and Scheler's interpretation of the Augustinian epistemology as fundamentally based on the primacy of love."[26] With this response to Krieg's criticism, Lam returns the focus of Ratzinger's Logos-Christology to the question of the relationship between faith and reason, theology and metaphysics.[27] According to Lam, part of Krieg's problem is his reference only to "Ratzinger's *Glaube, Geschichte*

---

23. McGregor, *Heart to Heart,* 94: "The question of the knowability and unknowability of God by humans, which is a question of how we correspond with the revealed truth by faith, hinges on the use of analogy."

24. Investigating what he calls "the accuracy of Kasper's analysis," Krieg dismisses the reconciliatory qualities of Ratzinger's theology and holds that it is historical and christologically impersonal enough: "[Ratzinger's] approach to the Christian faith loses sight of the individuality of its founder. . . . His meditations on the life of Jesus of Nazareth fail to distinguish Jesus from those who call themselves Christian" (Krieg, "Cardinal Ratzinger," 205).

25. Lam, *Theological Retractations,* 110.

26. Lam, *Theological Retractations,* 110.

27. Related to Ratzinger's Christological arguments for the "reasonableness of faith" is his insistence on the "reasonableness of love," a synthesis of the spiritual-intellectual sense of Christ's primacy. We see this in Ratzinger's rejection of Scheler's view as "alien to Augustine" because it places love before knowledge as though faith does not bring reason and will together: "Seit Max Scheler hat man sich vielfach angewöhnt, von einem Primat der Liebe im Denken Augustinus zu sprechen, so wie man vorher schon von einem Primat des geredet hatte, ja selbst die Lehre, dass die Liebe dem Erkennen vorangeht, wurde auf Augustin zurüruckgeführt. Wer Augustin selbst kennt, weiß indessen, dass solche Gedanken in seinem Werk keinen Platz haben" (Benedict XVI/Ratzinger, *Habilitationsschrift und Bonaventuras-Studien,* 553).

und Philosophy, page 543" as his proof of our theologian's dependence on Scheler.[28]

In conclusion, while Kasper, Corkery, and Krieg approach the theology of Ratzinger from the angle of idealism, McGregor and Lam propose an alternative approach, which is more comprehensive and spiritual. In agreement with McGregor and Lam, we contend that a more comprehensive and spiritual approach is in harmony with the fundamentally patristic and biblical intellectual background of Ratzinger's theology.

Eschatology and Platonism

In his work on *Resurrection Realism*, Patrick Fletcher's investigation of Augustine's influence on Ratzinger's eschatology places "Platonism" at the center of his comparison between Augustine and Ratzinger. Highlighting areas of discontinuity between Augustine's Platonism and Ratzinger's anti-Platonic position, he says:

> One could say that Ratzinger rejects some of those elements of Platonic anthropology that Augustine accepts (e.g., the body-soul schema), and even appears close to accepting the immateriality of beatitude (a Platonic idea rejected by Augustine). It is clear from Ratzinger's discussion in *Einführung* that his understanding of Platonic anthropology in that work has little in common with Augustine's understanding of it. For Augustine, the existence of a body and a soul need not automatically lead to the notion that the body is the soul's prison. Augustine freely used these concepts, and distinguished them in order to unite them in the resurrection.[29]

In some areas of continuity between Augustine's and Ratzinger's eschatology, Fletcher claims that "Ratzinger began as a suspicious "anti-Platonist," but gradually came to embrace the contributions of Greek philosophy to a Christian understanding of the resurrection."[30] Fletcher's focus on the "Platonic" dimension of eschatology does not adequately consider eschatology as a question of analogy of participation between God and man, which places Christ the God-man at the center of the discussion.

---

28. Lam, *Theological Retractations*, 109.
29. Fletcher, *Resurrection Realism*, 83–84.
30. Fletcher, *Resurrection Realism*, 72.

Integrity of Human Nature in Divinization

Commenting on Ratzinger's exegesis of the baptism of Christ in the second volume of *Jesus of Nazareth*, Gabino U. Bilbao of the Spanish school observes that Ratzinger's Christology obviates the development of a theology of anointing grounded on the Trinitarian manifestation at the baptism of Christ.[31] Anointing Christology, which emphasizes the anointing of the humanity of the Son facilitates a positive and robust presentation of the integrity of human nature. In relation to the lack of anointing Christology in Ratzinger, Bilbao accuses our theologian of inadequate treatment of the integrity of the human nature in his volitional Christology.[32] Bilbao observes in Ratzinger's commentary on the union of Christ's two wills during his prayer on the Mount of Olive, the disappearance of "the consistency proper to the freedom of the humanity, which corresponds with the human will."[33] Bilbao then presents his concern as a question of the meaning of "divinization" in Ratzinger's volitional Christology: "In Ratzinger's reading of the influence of the *Logos* on humanity, its work of divinization on humanity tends not to emphasize that to speak of divinization neither means a change in substance nor an alteration of the same humanity."[34]

Bilbao's concern about the integrity of human nature in Christ's work of divinization of man is precisely a question of the relationship between the primacy of Christ and the analogy of man's participation in

---

31. Bilbao, "Neocalcedonismo," 84: "Qué puede estar en el trasfondo de la postura de Ratzinger, obviando el tema de la uncion?"

32. Bilbao suggests that Ratzinger's concern with the modern Nestorianism and liberal exegesis limits capacity to speak positively of the anointing of the humanity of the Son because it would suggest a non-personal approach to Christology: "Ratzinger estádirigiendo su interpretacion del bautismo en primera línea contra la exegesis liberal, que hacía de Jesús un mero hombre. Es decir, está desenmascarando una de las raíces del modern nestorianismo, que reduce la escena del bautismo a un acontencimiento que nos dice algo sobre la humanidad de Jesús.... Desde esta impostación antinestoriana y antiliberal tan arraigada en Ratzinger, parece difícil que se pudiera abrir la puerta hacia una lectura positive de la unción de la humanidad del Hijo" (Bilbao, "Neocalcedonismo," 101–2).

33. Bilbao, "Neocalcedonismo," 93: "La consistencia propria de la libertad de la humanidad, que se correspondería con su voluntad humana, tiende a desaparecer."

34. Bilbao, "Neocalcedonismo," 93: "En la lectura de Ratzinger del influjo del Logos sobre la humanidad, la divinizacíon que en ella se opera, se tiende a no subrayar que dicha divinizacíon no supone un cambio sustancial ni una alteración en la misma."

the divine. Therefore, Bilbao's question demands an analogical study on Ratzinger's primacy of Christ.

Ratzinger's Spiritual Christology

McGregor recognizes the absence of a well-developed interrelationship between pneumatology and Christology in the early writings of Ratzinger. However, he found a resolution in our theologian's spiritual Christology of the heart and the Eucharist. Yet his discoveries on the spiritual Christology of Ratzinger present new questions on analogy regarding our theologian's use of the "image of the heart."

Against Kasper's and Corkery's more Platonic interpretation of Ratzinger, McGregor emphasizes the "stoical" and more spiritual perspective.[35] McGregor's analysis of the patristic influence on Ratzinger's "Heart to heart" Christology led to a comparison between Pius XII's and Ratzinger's use of the Fathers on this topic, which ends up drawing contrasts more than it demonstrates the parallels. By so doing, he falls short of conveying the message that Ratzinger's patristic method wishes to convey, i.e., the Fathers are our common patrimony, where the philosophical variations undergirding the various theological approaches to faith in tradition find a common ground, and a symphonic continuity of the faith: "The Fathers . . . were the theological teachers of the undivided Church; their theology was, in the original sense of the word, an "ecumenical theology" that belonged to all; they were "Fathers" not only of a part but also of the whole."[36]

McGregor questions the precise way—whether metaphorical or analogical—in which Ratzinger intends his application of the image of the heart to the divine and the human:

> As we have seen, the term "heart" is constantly employed by Ratzinger in his "personal search for the face of Jesus." It is used to refer to three different "hearts"—the heart of God the Father, the heart of Jesus, and the hearts of human persons. This raises two immediate questions. First, what kind of meaning is Ratzinger seeking to communicate through the use of this term? Is he simply mimicking in an unreflective or equivocal way the use of the term in Sacred Scripture? Second, if the term has a definite meaning, is it univocal, whether it is applied to the

---

35. McGregor, *Heart to Heart*, 346–47.
36. Benedict XVI/Ratzinger, *Principles*, 147.

Father, the Son, or to human persons; or does it have a different meaning when applied to human hearts, including the human heart of Jesus, than when it is applied to the heart of the Father, and are these meanings related in a metaphorical or analogical manner?[37]

To the first question pertaining the definite meaning of the term "heart," McGregor clearly answers that Ratzinger "regards the human heart as the "place" of integration of the intellect, will, passions and senses, of the body and the soul."[38] To the second question, McGregor finds in the Eucharist, a *communio* of both the "symbolic or metaphorical value" and the "analogical value" of Ratzinger's Stoical-anthropological use of the image of the heart, which conveys that the Spirit as "gift" flows from the heart of Christ as the Church: "The Eucharist is the *symbolon* of . . . the believer's heart, the Father's heart and the heart of Jesus in the heart of the Church."[39] The Eucharist becomes both the symbolic expression of the Father's invisible love in the pierced heart of Christ, and the analogical center of knowing and speaking well in love of the truth.

However, McGregor does not adequately deal with the analogical part of the question. In this quotation, McGregor raises questions that are beyond the limits of his work on two major fronts. Firstly, Ratzinger largely uses patristic and biblical foundations in his reflections on the "image of the heart." A focused investigation on the patristic influence on Ratzinger's Stoic image of the heart will shed more light into the spiritual analogy in Ratzinger's Christology. Secondly, the second part of McGregor's question as to whether Ratzinger uses the term "heart" in a *univocal* way when he applies it to Christ and to the believers, still remains unanswered. We consider McGregor's question as crucial to understanding the place of analogy in Ratzinger's spiritual Christology.

Analogy in Ratzinger

In his survey of the modern debates on the use of analogy, Justin Kizewski identifies three ways in which Ratzinger contributes to the analogy debate. For Kizewski, Ratzinger highlights "what is at stake" in the analogy discussion: "Understanding of truth, the importance of prayer, and

---

37. McGregor, *Heart to Heart*, 172.
38. McGregor, *Heart to Heart*, 172.
39. McGregor, *Heart to Heart*, 371.

the analogy of the faith (Scriptures)."⁴⁰ However, he does not discuss what constitutes the three contributions.

Commenting on Gottlieb Söhngen's, Erich Przywara's, and Hans Urs von Balthasar's influence on Ratzinger's use of analogy, Peter Kucer describes how Ratzinger's Christological synthesis of *analogia entis* and *analogia fidei* maintains the distinction between the two movements of analogy. With regard to the distinction between analogy of being and analogy of faith, Kucer says:

> Despite Söhngen's formative influence on Ratzinger, when it comes to his definition of an analogy of faith, Ratzinger leans more in the direction of Przywara, who more clearly distinguishes the analogy of faith from analogy of being by defining the analogy of faith as referring to a correct reading of Scripture, where scriptural passages ought always be seen in relationship to other passages, in particular regarding the relationship of the Old Testament to the New Testament.⁴¹

Aligning our theologian with Söhngen's and Balthasar's Christocentric approach, Kucer describes Ratzinger's synthesis as follows: "Although Ratzinger sides more with Przywara's concept of the analogy of faith, he nonetheless agrees with Söhngen's and Balthasar's more explicit Christological presentation of the analogy of being."⁴² While Kucer finds a similarity between Söhngen's, Balthasar's, and Ratzinger's Christocentric synthesis of analogy, he neither confirms nor denies explicitly that "*analogia entis* within *analogia fidei*" is a constitutive element of Ratzinger's Christocentric synthesis.⁴³ Finally, Kucer discusses the influence of Augustine's and Bonaventure's illumination theory in Ratzinger's use of analogy. However, he does not consider the broader patristic patrimony operative in Ratzinger's use of analogy.

---

40. Kizewski, "God-Talk," 128.

41. Kucer, *Truth and Politics*, 57.

42. Kucer, *Truth and Politics*, 58.

43. Benedict XVI/Ratzinger, *Beiträge zur Christologie*, 1057: "Die analogia entis in der analogia fidei." Analogy of being within the analogy of faith refers to the knowledge of the ontological similarity between God and creation by the light of divine revelation. Cf. Kucer, *Truth and Politics*, 57.

Conclusion

Four main analogy questions emerge from our *status quaestionis*. The first involves Peter McGregor's question as to whether Ratzinger uses the term "heart" in a univocal way when applied to Christ and when applied to believers. The second involves Justin Kizewski's comments on Ratzinger's contribution to the modern analogy debate; namely, the explanation of what the threefold contribution of Ratzinger's analogy consists in is yet to be addressed. The third question pertains to Kucer's attempt to synthesize *analogia entis* and *analogia fidei* in Ratzinger's primacy of Christ. Finally, the fourth question derives from Bilbao's concern about the integrity of the human nature in Ratzinger's volitional notion of divinization. In the survey above, we concluded that Bilbao's concern is a question of analogy of participation in Christ.

Finally, Patrick Fletcher limits his study of the patristic foundation of Ratzinger's eschatology to Augustine. Peter Kucer discusses the influence of Augustine's and Bonaventure's illumination theory in Ratzinger's use of analogy. However, while Ratzinger's theology is primarily Augustinian, the patristic patrimony present in his theology is not merely Augustinian. Our study explores the broad spectrum of the Fathers whom Ratzinger quotes. Contrary to Fletcher's Platonic approach to the study of Ratzinger's eschatology, our study of the patrimony of the ancient authors on Ratzinger's use of analogy offers an alternative approach to his eschatology. The patristic categories, which we employ for the study of Ratzinger's primacy of Christ in analogy provides the opportunity for more insights on the theology of Ratzinger.

Aim

The primary aim of our thesis is to study Ratzinger through the lens of the Church Fathers and ancient ecclesiastical writers. The *status quaestionis* illustrates the need to achieve this goal through the trajectory of analogy in theology. Some Ratzinger scholars prefer a Platonic approach to our theologian's primacy of Christ and considered it idealistic. Others consider his spiritual Christology as the way to resolve the apparent idealistic tendencies in his theology, while raising questions that require further examination of our theologian's use of analogy. The goal of this thesis is to offer a systematic study that addresses these analogy questions in Ratzinger's theology. Central to the claim of this thesis is how the Fathers and other ancient ecclesiastical writers facilitate the interpretation of the use of analogy in Ratzinger's primacy of Christ.

Limits

With such a broad scope of research, some limits come to mind. This thesis does not claim an exhaustive treatment of Ratzinger's primacy of Christ or his analogy in theology. The structure of this thesis benefits from Justin Kizewski's work on *God-Talk*.[44] We use his patristic categories on the use of analogy—faith and reason, image and participation, and God-Talk—to set the limits of our study of analogy in Ratzinger's theology. Our concern is strictly with the relationship between the patristic patrimony and Ratzinger's theology on analogy. While we draw from our theologian's studies on Bonaventure's theology of history, the consideration of Bonaventure's thought *per se* or any other medieval use of analogy, is beyond the limits of our investigation. Our study does not engage the classical primacy debate between the Thomistic and Scotistic schools. While we indicate possible influence of Söhngen's and Balthasar's synthetic approach to analogy, our concern is not with the influence of Ratzinger's contemporaries on his use of analogy, but on the patrimony of the Church Fathers present in our theologian's synthetic method.

With regard to Ratzinger's writings selected for this study, we are not particularly interested in the documents he wrote as the Prefect of the Congregation for the Doctrine of faith. In his *Last Testament with Peter Seewald*, our theologian acknowledges that a document like *Dominus Jesus*, which he signed and defended as the Prefect of the Congregation for the Doctrine of Faith does not strictly represent his private theology: "I deliberately never wrote any of the documents of the office myself, so that my opinion does not surface; otherwise I would be attempting to disseminate and enforce my own private theology. . . . I did not write any documents myself, including *Dominus Jesus*."[45]

---

44. The expression "God-Talk," as used by Justin Kizewski, recapitulates Gregory of Nyssa's description of "God's relation to us in terms of a mother's baby-talk to her infant and the infant's loving return of a most imperfect form of communication" (Kizewski, "God-Talk," 4; cf. Gregory of Nyssa, *Contra Eunomium* 2.419 [SC 551:378]).

45. Benedict XVI/Ratzinger, *Letzte Gespräche*, 200 [*Last Testament*, 172].

Methodology and Structure

The methodology we employ is a "hermeneutic of continuity" in the way we demonstrate the inner unity of thought between the broad patristic tradition and the theology of Ratzinger. The hermeneutic of continuity helps us to avoid a fragmented reading of Ratzinger. To establish the continuity between the ancient authors and Ratzinger on analogy, the method by which this study advances firstly considers Ratzinger's collective and specific references to the ancient authors on the analogy of faith and reason, image and participation, and God-Talk. Secondly, we use the three patristic categories to explain the primacy of Christ in Ratzinger's theology.

Hence, this study consists of two main parts. The first two chapters constitutes Part 1 entitled, "The Patristic Patrimony." The first chapter, which is propaedeutic, serves as a way of introducing the three patristic divisions we employ. While the bulk of the research in chapter 1 is mostly unoriginal, however, our demonstration in this chapter, of the "the collective referential continuity" between the ancient authors and our theologian, is original. By "the collective referential continuity" we mean the concepts of analogy present in the Fathers and the other ancient ecclesiastical writers that Ratzinger references with the collective term "the Fathers." Chapter 2 contains the bulk of the originality in our research. This chapter, which serves as the immediate link between the first and the second part consists in the Church Fathers and ancient ecclesiastical writers whom Ratzinger quotes, thus demonstrating a "specific referential continuity" between the ancient authors and our theologian. The result is an identification of the principles and concepts that shape the inner trajectory of the subsequent chapters.

Chapters 3, 4 and 5, which make up Part 2, constitute further significant originality in the way we use our findings from Part 1 to explain the notion of the primacy of Christ in Ratzinger. As alluded to earlier, the patristic categories of faith and reason, image and participation, and God-Talk determine the organizational structure of our study of Ratzinger in Part 2. Thus, this second part has three chapters with each chapter dedicated to each patristic category. We will consider the intervening developments of the patristic use of analogy according to how they help establish the inner unity of thought between the Fathers and our theologian. Chapter 3 considers "Ratzinger's primacy of Christ in faith and reason" and addresses the question of truth in our theologian's use of analogy. Chapter 4 focuses on the analogy of "image and participation" in Ratzinger and responds to the concerns of McGregor, Fletcher, and Bilbao on Ratzinger's theology. Chapter 5 uses the category of "God-Talk" to interpret Ratzinger's biblical and liturgical theology.

Finally, a concluding chapter offers a summary of the fruit of our investigation and an appraisal of the claims of our thesis. In the general conclusion, we look for answers to the questions on primacy of Christ and the use of analogy raised in the *status quaestionis*. An evaluation of our discoveries based on the driving theological questions demonstrates an application of the claim of our thesis: it is more fitting to read the theology of Ratzinger through the lens of the Church Fathers. Our general conclusion includes modest suggestions regarding areas for further development, which would require some studies beyond the limits of our work.

PART ONE

Patristic Patrimony

Chapter 1

Patristic Consensus on Analogy

ON NUMEROUS OCCASIONS, RATZINGER references the Fathers and ancient ecclestical writers with the collective expression "the Fathers."[1] The patristic concepts in which Ratzinger finds a concensus among the Fathers, constitutes the focus of this introductory study on the use of analogy as indications of the continuity between the theology of Ratzinger and patristic thought. What determines the trajectory of this investigation is our concern for identifying the synthesis of the descending and ascending movements of Christian analogy in patristic thought.[2]

Faith and Reason

Faith and reason are the two analogous ways of knowing God and speaking about Him, which are constitutive of the ontological convergence of the divine and human nature. How do the Fathers speak of the existing similarities and dissimilarities between faith and reason in relationship to God?

---

1. Applying the logic of "referential continuity," we also make a further distinction between a "collective referential continuity" and a "specific or singular referential continuity" to the Church Fathers. On "referential continuity," see Kizewski, "God-Talk," 272.

2. See Kizewski, "God-Talk," 264. Kizewski agrees with Erich Przywara that the "ascending nature of analogy anticipates what will be called *analogia entis*, while the descending nature of analogy reflects what is called the *analogia fidei*."

Clement of Alexandria

For Clement, "wisdom" is the fundamental common ground that embraces both Scripture and philosophy. By wisdom, he means the "true philosophy," which he defines as follows:

> We define wisdom to be certain knowledge, being a sure and irrefragable apprehension of things divine and human which the Lord has taught us, both by his advent and by the prophets. And it is irrefragable by reason, inasmuch as it has been communicated. And so it is wholly true according to [God's] intention, as being known through the means of the Son. . . . This wisdom, then—rectitude of soul and of reason, and purity of life—is the object of the desire of philosophy, which is kindly and lovingly disposed towards wisdom, and does everything to attain it.[3]

In other words, the measure of wisdom or true philosophy is its harmony with the knowledge of Christ. His comparative juxtaposition of Greek philosophy and biblical wisdom identifies natural wisdom as "seeds of knowledge," not the knowledge of wisdom *per se*. He says "that knowledge, which is the scientific demonstration of what is delivered according to the true philosophy, is founded on faith."[4] Prior to the understanding of the relationship between philosophical and theological knowledge of truth is a clarity of their distinct integrity.

For Clement, philosophy considered in itself perceives a portion of the one truth as though it is the whole truth: "The sects both of barbarian and Hellenic philosophy . . . vaunts as the whole truth the portion, which has fallen to its lot."[5] He speaks of philosophical wisdom as the natural gift of the "spirit of perception [*semina cognitionis*]."[6] Thus, as one considers the integrity of philosophy, its limitations become more apparent. For Clement, before the coming of Christ, philosophy could not conduct the Greeks to the entirety of justification.[7]

Clement anchors the relationship between faith and philosophy in Christ. For him, there is only one way of truth, and Christ is the one Perennial River into which all other preparatory streams of wisdom (such

---

3. Clement of Alexandria, *Strom.* 6.7 (SC 446:170).
4. Clement of Alexandria, *Strom.* 2.11 (SC 38:73).
5. Clement of Alexandria, *Strom.* 1.13 (PG 8:753, 756).
6. Clement of Alexandria, *Strom.* 1.2, 4 (PG 8:709C, 715).
7. See Clement of Alexandria, *Strom.* 1.20 (SC 30:124). Clement does not attribute a salvific element to philosophy. Salvation remains in the order of Grace.

as philosophy) flow.⁸ Philosophical wisdom flows into this stream of the truth in an analogous way because the divine causality of philosophical wisdom is "consequential"; whereas, the wisdom of Old and New Testament faith pertains to Christ's wisdom in a "primary" way.⁹

Philosophy as Co-operating Cause

Clement explains the right relationship between faith and philosophy with the distinction between perfect and co-operating causes. His analysis on causes considers more than these two categories.¹⁰ We focus only on the binaries: "perfect—co-operating" and "joint—co-operating" causes.

Concerning philosophy as co-operating cause, Clement says, "And if, for the sake of those who are fond of fault-finding, we must draw a distinction, by saying that philosophy is a concurrent and co-operating [συνεργόν] cause of true apprehension, being the search for the truth, then we shall avow it to be a preparatory training for the enlightened man."¹¹ For him, philosophy as a co-operating cause is not a *sine qua non* in the way that a fire is the immediate necessary cause of the burning of the log. Co-operating cause is a *sine qua non* only as the material cause of a thing is a necessity, such as "the brass in reference to the production of the statue."¹² To the extent that co-operating cause is necessary for the effect of an acting, it is that *without which* the effect takes place, but not an absolute cause. Therefore, co-operating cause is necessary to the extent that "everything that acts produces the effect, in conjunction with the aptitude of that which is acted on. For the cause disposes. But each thing is affected according to its natural constitution."¹³ The necessity of

---

8. See Clement of Alexandria, *Strom.* 1.5 (PG 8:720A).

9. Clement of Alexandria, *Strom.* 1.5 (PG 8:724–25).

10. See Kizewski, "God-Talk," 163–67. Kizewski considers Clement's complicated analysis of the different types of causes as one of the contexts in which he explicitly refers to analogy. One can find a more detailed analysis on these causes in Kizewski's work.

11. Clement of Alexandria, *Strom.* 1.20 (SC 30:123).

12. Clement of Alexandria, *Strom.* 8.9 (GCS 2/3:102; PG 9:601).

13. Clement of Alexandria, *Strom.* 8.9 (GCS 2/3:102; PG 9:601). According to Osborn, "[Clement's] logic notebook which is preserved as Book VIII of the *Stromateis* differs from the other seven books and . . . contains private notes, which either Clement took from lectures and written sources or which a later copyist has extracted from Clement." With regard to the sources of his tools of logic, Osborn says, "These notes on logic represent an important blending of Aristotle and Stoicism which may be traced

a co-operating cause is as a co-efficient cause in the sense that the disposition dependent on the nature of the thing acted upon, is a necessary determinant factor for the effect of the act of the cause.

Distinct from philosophy, faith is for Clement, a perfect and/or synectic cause of knowing the truth for two reasons. First, as a perfect cause, "it is of itself sufficient to produce the effect" of the knowledge of truth.[14] Second, as a synectic cause, it "is that, which . . . being removed, the effect is removed."[15] The knowledge that faith offers is sufficient for producing the effect of true knowledge of God, while the wisdom of philosophy co-operates with knowledge in three ways: as preparatory, intensifying, and articulatory aid for knowing the truth.

As a *preparatory* cause, philosophy, "reaches after" the knowledge that is very proximate to the truth. While incapable of causing the knowledge of the truth, however, philosophy is capable of remotely "reaching after the knowledge which touches close on the truth."[16] Paul's illumination of the Areopagites's "Altar to the Unknown God," which illustrates the limits and possibilities of Hellenic philosophy, shows the capacity of philosophy for attaining some portion of truth in a way open to the whole truth.[17] But only faith can open someone's eyes to the whole truth contained and revealed by the Son.

As an *intensifying* factor to theological knowledge, Clement says that "the co-operating cause further aids the synectic (perfect), in the way of intensifying what is produced by it. . . . The co-operating cause, while effecting nothing by itself, co-operates with it, toward the production of the effect in the most intense degree."[18] What aids in further distinct clarification of how philosophy co-operates with faith by intensifying its effect of knowing, is Clement's finer distinction between joint-causes and co-operating causes. About joint-causes, he says,

> The joint-cause also belongs to the genus of causes, as a fellow soldier is a soldier, and as a fellow-youth is a youth. . . . For a thing may be a Joint-cause, though it be not a Synectic cause.

---

to Antiochus of Ascalon, who may be seen as the first Middle Platonist" (Osborn, *Clement of Alexandria*, 206–7).

14. Clement of Alexandria, *Strom.* 8.9 (GCS 2/3:102; PG 9:601).

15. Clement of Alexandria, *Strom.* 8.9 (GCS 2/3:102; PG 9:601). A synectic cause produces a direct and immediate effect such that its removal also removes the effect.

16. Clement of Alexandria, *Strom.* 1.20 (SC 30:123).

17. See Clement of Alexandria, *Strom.* 1.19 (PG 8:805).

18. Clement of Alexandria, *Strom.* 8.9 (GCS 2/3:102; PG 9:601).

> For the Joint-cause is conceived in conjunction with another, which is not capable of producing the effect by itself.[19]

As an intensifying aid to faith, philosophy does not relate to faith as a joint-cause because it co-operates with faith as something that is self-sufficient. While philosophy helps to intensify faith's knowledge of God, it adds nothing to the integrity of its content. Commenting on Clement's notion of the intensifying relationship of philosophy to faith, Kizewski says, "philosophy does not make the teaching of Christ more powerful, but rather it renders powerless the attacks against that faith."[20] Thus, the philosophical and theological causes of knowledge are neither univocal nor strictly equivocal, but are analogical. They are not univocal because "truth" or "wisdom" does not pertain to philosophy and faith as the common name "animal" belongs to both ox and man.[21] Nor are they strictly equivocal as though they speak of two incomparable or incompatible definitions of the truth.[22] In comparison to the perfect causality of faith, philosophy is a co-operative cause by analogy to the extent that the God of philosophy is the God of faith.

Finally, for Clement, philosophy co-operates with faith in its *self-articulation* and human knowledge is necessary for understanding Scripture. Philosophy helps to guard the faith against the assault of heresies by aiding the wisdom that comes with the ability to "distinguish the spurious from the genuine gold."[23] We shall discuss in greater detail under "God-talk" category, this aid of philosophy in the self-expression of faith and the consideration of the meaning of terms employed by faith.

In conclusion, Clement's distinction between the perfect causality of knowledge by faith and co-operating causality of apprehending truth

---

19. Clement of Alexandria, *Strom.* 8.9 (GSC 2/3:102; PG 9:601).

20. Kizewski, "God-Talk," 164.

21. Clement of Alexandria, *Strom.* 8.8 (GSC 2/3:95; PG 9:592): "And, again, of the things contained under these ten [Aristotelian] Categories, some are *Univocal*, as ox and man, as far as each is an animal. For those are Univocal terms, to both of which belongs the common name, animal; and the same principle, that is definition, that is animate essence."

22. According to Clement, "Equivocal terms have the same name, but not the same definition, as man—both the animal and the picture." Clement talks about "analogy" as a kind of equivocal term "as the foot Mount Ida, and our foot, because they are beneath." In other words, analogy is not a strict equivocation in so far as it indicates a *comparison* or similarity of beneathness of the human foot and that of the foot of Mount Ida. See Clement of Alexandria, *Strom.* 8.8 (GSC 2/3:95; PG 9:592).

23. Clement of Alexandria, *Strom.* 1.9 (PG 8:741A).

by philosophy, is an argument for the analogical nature of both modes of knowledge. The distinction also clarifies that the nature of the similarity between them. The preparatory character of philosophy finds its perfectibility in our faith in Christ. Thus, their relationship is founded on Christ, who is the true wisdom, the One Truth, and true philosophy in flesh. Kizewski noted that Clement's distinction between joint and co-operating cause introduces what will later be identified as univocity and analogous causes.[24] The distinction indicates that philosophy relates to faith as analogous cause, not as univocal cause.

Philosophy *within* Scripture

Another way in which Clement describes the nature of the relationship between faith and philosophy is by identifying the place and role of philosophy within Scripture. He describes the philosophical character of Scripture by identifying a certain barbarian philosophy within the true philosophy.

According to Eric Osborn, "Clement's account of philosophy . . . identified the biblical message as the 'barbarian philosophy' and Moses as a philosopher."[25] For Clement, this "Barbarian philosophy, which we follow, is in reality perfect and true."[26] Following Philo, he considers Moses a bringer of philosophy into the Hebrew faith: "Having reached the proper age, [Moses] was taught . . . the philosophy which is conveyed by symbols, which they point out in the hieroglyphical inscriptions. The rest of the usual course of instruction, Greeks taught him in Egypt as a royal child, as Philo says in his life of Moses. . . . And betaking himself to their philosophy, he increased his wisdom."[27] For him, among other things that Moses and Plato share in common, they both also drew from the ancient barbarian philosophy of the Egyptians. According to Clement, "Plato does not deny that he procured all that is most excellent in philosophy from the barbarians; and he admits that he came into Egypt."[28] Clement considers the philosophical heritage of the Jewish race to be older

---

24. Kizewski, "God-Talk," 167.

25. Osborn, *Clement of Alexandria*, 92. Barbarian philosophy pertains to Old Testament faith.

26. Clement of Alexandria, *Strom.* 2.2 (SC 38:35).

27. Clement of Alexandria, *Strom.* 1.23 (PG 8:900).

28. Clement of Alexandria, *Strom.* 1.15 (PG 8:768B).

than that of the Greeks: "of all these, by far the oldest is the Jewish race; and that their philosophy committed to writing has the precedence of philosophy among the Greeks, the Pythagorean Philo shows at large."[29] Thus, arguing from superior antiquity, the biblical barbarian philosophy is more excellent than Greek philosophy. The barbarian philosophy borrowed by the Greeks belongs, as it were, to the Hebrew Scriptures. We learn from Osborn that Clement's modification of Philo's account of philosophy, includes the fact that "philosophy studies the law and the interpretation of nature through the law."[30] Like Philo, Clement considers Moses "an interpreter of the sacred laws."[31]

There is even "a higher truth which [Clement] specifically calls the "true philosophy."[32] It has already been mentioned that Clement attributes true philosophy to the wisdom revealed by the Son.[33] While for Philo, the authentic philosophy is the Law of Moses, for Clement, it is the true wisdom of the Son. Christ perfects what is philosophically true and present in a veiled form within the barbarian philosophy of the Old Testament.[34]

From this consideration of Clement on philosophy and faith, we have discovered how Clement identifies the presence of philosophy *within* the bible in a Christocentric way. In the figure of Moses, which is a *type* of Christ, philosophy migrated from Egypt to the Hebrews, evident in his role as the exegete of the law and interpreter of nature through the law. He depended heavily on Philo, whose "thought was centered not on Plato but Moses, whose law is a copy of the law of nature and the authentic philosophy."[35] Through the typological presence and relationship between the biblical barbarian philosophy and true philosophy, we see indication of what will later be identified as *analogia entis* within the *analogia scripturae*.[36]

---

29. Clement of Alexandria, *Strom.* 1.15 (PG 8:768B).

30. For Clement, "Moses is a . . . philosopher" (Osborn, *Clement of Alexandria*, 91; cf. Clement of Alexandria, *Strom.* 1.24).

31. Clement of Alexandria, *Strom.* 1.22 (PG 8:896A).

32. Osborn, *Clement of Alexandria*, 92.

33. See Clement of Alexandria, *Strom.* 6.7 (SC 446:178); 8.1(PG 9:560).

34. See Clement of Alexandria, *Strom.* 2.1 (SC 38:32–34); 5.8 (PG 9:68–69).

35. Osborn, *Clement of Alexandria*, 93.

36. By analogy of Scripture, we simply mean the inner unity of the Old and New Testament according to the logic of faith.

Origen

Origen, though not a Church Father, contributes significantly to the insights of the patristic era on the relationship of faith and reason. Like Justin and Clement, he anchors faith and reason on the primordial Word. He acknowledges the limited capacity of natural knowledge of God unaided by faith. For him, some knowledge of the truth or meaning of creation is available to us through philosophy. He says, "there are some even of them [philosophers, whether of Greek or barbarian race] who appear to have held a belief in his existence, for they admit that all things were created by the word of reason or God."[37] To some level, philosophy is able admit that all things are created by the word of reason or of God, "it is possible to gain some notion of [the word of reason or God] from our experience of the visible creation and from the instinctive thoughts of the human mind."[38]

What Clement more explicitly indicated as "philosophy within Scripture," is what Origen implicitly describes with the metaphor of the "spoils of the Egyptians." According to Kizewski, "Origen is certainly the first to use the phrase 'Spoils of the Egyptians,' as a metaphor for the contribution of secular disciplines such as philosophy" toward Christianity.[39] He speaks of the *spolia Aegyptiaca* as he encouraged Gregory the Wonder-worker (Thaumaturgus) to use philosophy and other tools of natural sciences to explain the Scriptures: "I wish to ask you to extract from the philosophy of the Greeks what may serve as a course of study or a preparation for Christianity."[40] Regarding the spoils of the Egyptians, he says,

> Perhaps something of this kind is shadowed forth in what is written in Exodus from the mouth of God, that the children of Israel were commanded to ask from their neighbors, and those who dwelt with them, vessels of silver and gold, and raiment, in order that, by spoiling the Egyptians, they might have material

---

37. Origen, *De Principiis* 1.3.1 (SC 252:144) [*On First Principles*, 29]: "The doctrine of the Logos, the reason or Thought of God immanent in creation, was first expressed by Heraclitus (c. 500 BC). Plato, in the *Timaeus*, 34B, describes the Word-soul which the Creator put within the body of the universe to be the source of life and reason."

38. Origen, *De Principiis* 1.3.1 (SC 252:144).

39. Kizewski, "God-Talk," 177.

40. Origen, *Epistula ad Gregorium* 1 (SC 148:188) [ANF 4:393–94].

for the preparation of the things which pertained to the service of God.[41]

For Origen, the spoils of the Egyptians, which were "useful to the children of Israel . . . for God's service," includes philosophy.[42] While he does not go as far as Clement to say what kind of philosophy it is, he suggests that it is good philosophy since the spoils of the Egyptians are a metaphor for the best of human knowledge, culture and philosophy. Origen indicates that philosophy as "ancillary to Christianity"[43] is operative in a metaphorical way within the Scriptures themselves. What constitutes the communication of the wisdom of God in Scripture includes within it the instrumental and preparatory element of natural gifts of human knowledge.

Philosophy, though at the preparatory level of wisdom, nevertheless comes from the same creative Logos through the natural mediation of reason. For Origen, this philosophical knowledge originates from Christ, the Firstborn of all creation, but only as "the doctrine of the first principles of Christ" and "the elementary principles of knowledge."[44] However, while faith and reason find common ground in the primordial Logos, yet they are distinct forms of access to the truth. Distinct from philosophy is the "wisdom which is spoken to the perfect," which Origen says "is manifested both through the Scriptures and through the appearing of our Lord and Savior Jesus Christ."[45] Describing this wisdom of faith, he insists that the "knowledge to be confirmed from the Holy Scriptures," both of the Old and New Testaments, are more certain and credibly upheld than that of reason:

> We, however in conformity with our faith in that doctrine which we hold for certain to be divinely inspired, believe that there is no possible way of explaining and bringing to man's knowledge the higher and diviner teaching about the Son of God, except by means of those scriptures which were inspired by the Holy Spirit, namely, the gospels and the writings of the apostles, to

---

41. Origen, *Epistula ad Gregorium* 2 (SC 148:188).
42. Origen, *Epistula ad Gregorium* 1 (SC 148:188).
43. Origen, *Epistula ad Gregorium* 1 (SC 148:188).
44. Origen, *De Principiis* 4.1.7L (SC 268:290).
45. Origen, *De Principiis* 4.1.7G (SC 268:290).

which we add, according to the declaration of Christ himself, the law and the prophets.[46]

The reason for the greater certainty of faith over that of natural reason is due to reason's incapacity to receive on its own a knowledge that is essentially beyond its nature, "except by means of those Scriptures which were inspired by the Holy Spirit." The wisdom contained in the Bible is not merely a part of the whole, but the one Logos, communicating the meaning and truth of creation as a whole, presented in an embodied way in the letter of the one Bible, just as he presents himself in the flesh of Jesus. Origen says,

> The Logos of God, who was in the beginning with God, is not πολυλογία, he is not λόγοι. He is one, unique Word, formed of multiple sentences, each of which is a part of the same whole, of the same Logos. . . . Outside of him, even if one speaks of the truth, there is not truth, there is no unity, no harmony, no tending toward a same Whole. . . . He, on the contrary, who speaks the truth, even if he says everything without omitting anything, always pronounces a single Logos: the saints do not fail into the multiplicity of words, having always as their goal, a single Logos. . . . Thus, while profane words are multiplicity, all the Holy Books together are but a single Book.[47]

Origen's argument for the greater credibility of the truth of faith is its access to the totality of the truth contained in Christ. In Christ, there is no "multiplicity of words" but "a single Word," such that in his person, the multiple books of Scriptures becomes a single Book. As the abbreviation of the revealed truth, the rational participation of philosophical wisdom in Christ is only a partial wisdom in comparison to wisdom of faith in him. Just as we have seen in Justin and Clement, Origen presumes a fundamental Christocentric harmony that exists between faith and reason. The harmony consists in their mutual origination from the divine Logos, thus, the primacy of the *Logos*. We can say that for Origen, the reasonableness of biblical faith consists in the fact that the one and same Word is the origin of both the wisdom of the words of natural reason and the Wisdom of the *Verbum abbreviatum* of biblical faith. Thus, the analogy employed by Origen in his expression of the relationship between faith and reason is that of "Word and words," *Logos* and *logoi*.

---

46. Origen, *De Principiis* 1.3.1 (SC 252:144) [*On First Principles*, 29].
47. Origen, *Commentary* 5.4 (GCS 4:102) [Lubac, *History and Spirit*, 386].

Gregory of Nyssa

Echoing Origen's *spolia Aegyptiaca,* Gregory of Nyssa speaks of moral and natural philosophy, and other riches of reason, as useful gifts for understanding faith:

> Our guide in virtue commands someone who "borrows" from the wealthy Egyptians to receive such things as moral and natural philosophy, geometry, astronomy, dialectic, and whatever else is sought by those outside the Church, since these things will be useful when in time the divine sanctuary of mystery must be beautified with the riches of reason.[48]

Gregory's particular contribution to our discussion on patristic analogy of faith and reason is his emphasis on the "moral" or tropological value of reason's co-operating causality toward the life of virtue. Faith and good conscience are for him two distinct ways of acquiring virtue: "[there] are the two pursuits through which virtue is acquired, namely, faith toward the divine and conscience toward life."[49] However, to underscore the harmony between both, he says, "moral and natural philosophy may become at certain times a comrade, friend, and companion of life to the higher way, provided that the offspring of this introduces nothing of a foreign defilement."[50] Gregory describes how "the use of reason" aids growth in virtue:

> If, then, one should withdraw from those who seduce him to evil and by the use of reason turn to the better, putting evil behind him, it is as if he places his own soul, like a mirror, face to face with the hope of good things, with the result that the images and impressions of virtue, as it is shown to him by God, are imprinted on the purity of his soul.[51]

For him, reason plays a crucial role in the moral disposition of the soul in anticipation of the grace of faith. Reflecting on the Egyptian plague involving the death of their firstborn sons, he interprets the triple-anointing on the doorpost of the Israelites as metaphors for the presence of the harmony between the three faculties of the soul—the rational, appetitive and spiritual. Israel was protected by their faith (symbolized by

---

48. Gregory of Nyssa, *De vita Moysis* 2.115 (SC 1:114) [*Life of Moses*].
49. Gregory of Nyssa, *De vita Moysis* 2.192, 198 (SC 1:236, 242).
50. Gregory of Nyssa, *De vita Moysis* 2.37 (SC 1:126, 128).
51. Gregory of Nyssa, *De vita Moysis* 2.47 (SC 1:132).

the blood) from the plague because unlike the Egyptians, they possessed moral virtue. For Gregory, it was not faith alone that protected Israel from the destruction of their firstborn, but the harmony of their moral conscience with faith: "If the rational falls from above and the appetitive and spirited disposition makes it the part trampled on, then the destroyer slips inside. No opposition from the blood resists his entrance, that it to say, faith in Christ does not ally itself with those of such disposition."[52] He considered the Egyptians' lack of rational moral virtue as the primary cause of the plagues: "The Egyptians' free will caused all these things . . . and the impartial justice of God followed their free choices and brought upon them what they deserved."[53] Thus, one way that reason relates to faith is by moral integrity of the conscience in co-operation with the grace of faith; and both paths of virtue stand on the same rock who is "Christ the absolute virtue."[54]

Conclusion

While establishing a clear distinction between faith and reason, the different ways in which the Fathers and ancient ecclesiastical writers apply the words "wisdom" and *logos* to both philosophy (in a preparatory way), and Christian faith (in a more perfect way) suggest analogy. They ultimately refer to Christ as the fundamental source of the best of philosophical wisdom that serves as ancillary to faith's wisdom. Gregory of Nyssa helps us to recognize the moral compass of Christian virtue as the function of reason. We saw in Origen an indication of Christ's primacy with the abbreviation of biblical words in the Word—*Verbum abbreviatum*. Identifying the formula of *Verbum abbreviatum* as a "patristic and medieval tradition," Benedict XVI describes the concept as follows: "It says that Jesus is the *Verbum abbreviatum* (cf. Rom 9:28, with a reference to Isa 10:23), the abbreviated Word, the short and essential Word of the Father who has told us all about him. In Jesus the whole Word is present."[55] Clement's idea of the migration of philosophy into the Hebrew faith is what Origen saw as part of the effects of *spolia Aegyptiaca*. Their indication of the presence of philosophy within the Scriptures is already

---

52. Gregory of Nyssa, *De vita Moysis* 2.97, 98 (SC 1:165).
53. Gregory of Nyssa, *De vita Moysis* 2.86 (SC 1:156).
54. Gregory of Nyssa, *De vita Moysis* 2.244 (SC 1:274).
55. Benedict XVI/Ratzinger, *Transforming Power of Faith*, 81.

the budding of what is later known in modern theology as *analogia entis* within the *analogia fidei*. Ratzinger describes how the primacy of Christ underlies the analogical synthesis of the patristic and biblical metaphor of *spolia Aegyptiaca*: "Almost all the Fathers loved the slogan of the *spolia Aegyptiaca*, of the treasures of Egypt that the new Israel of believers rightly from its pagan past carried off into its Christian future. . . . Creation and the deeds of Christ are not two different or even opposite works but only two stages of a single divine plan."[56]

Image and Participation

In this section, we investigate the patristic analogical use of image and participation, and how these terms helped them to articulate the primacy of Christ. These two notions, which are critical aspects of both the patristic and medieval analogy, allow us to interpret Ratzinger's theology in continuity with tradition. While we discuss how each of the selected Fathers and ancient ecclesiastical writers uses image and participation to demonstrate the relationship between God and creature, our concern is primarily to discover what their consensus on this category consist in.

Image

Our particular interest on the patristic notion of image is how its ontological structure grounds analogy. We seek to understand the role of their Christological interpretation of this concept and how it shapes the reasonableness of biblical talk about God and man. How the ancient authors reflect on their exegesis of "image" illuminates the metaphysical foundation of the anthropological realities of the soul, spirit and body.

Irenaeus

For Irenaeus, the terms "image" and "likeness" connote analogy between God and creation. In his anti-Gnostic polemic, Irenaeus uses these terms both in a disjunctive and yet inseparable way, thus highlighting the analogous meaning they bear. Scholars consider the meaning of image and likeness in Irenaeus to be ambiguous. But the dynamic relationship

---

56. Benedict XVI/Ratzinger, *Glaube in Schrift und Tradition*, 237.

between the two is significant to his insights on the analogical concepts, image and participation.

IMAGE

For Irenaeus, image conveys the natural man (flesh and blood),[57] while likeness is the spiritual man that comes from the Son and the Spirit.[58] However, we need to consider Irenaeus's understanding of image in the context of his polemics against the Gnostics, who fragment the integrity of human nature by compromising its material aspect. According to Eric Osborn, Irenaeus speaks separately of image and likeness mainly as an argumentative tactic for exposing the false teaching of the Gnostics by "taking [their] position in order to destroy it."[59] Battling for the cohesive inclusion of the material aspect of man in salvation by Christ, he resists the Gnostic separation of the body as it would pertain to the image, and the spirit as it would pertain to the likeness.

In agreement with Jacques Fantino, Fredrick McLeod describes *similitude* as affirmation of "the general analogous correspondence that can be said to be present between human beings and God."[60] Acknowledging that the analogy between human nature and divine nature remained after Adam's fall up to the time of the Incarnation, Irenaeus says, "Those therefore, who allege that [the Word] took nothing from the Virgin do greatly err, [since] in order that they may cast away the inheritance of the flesh, they also reject the analogy [between man and God]."[61] For him, the birth of Christ through Mary confirms the preservation of the similitude of the image between the first and the second Adam.[62] Here he affirms the

---

57. See Irenaeus, *Adversus Haereses* 5.10.1, 2 (SC 153:124, 126).

58. See Irenaeus, *Adversus Haereses* 5.6.1 (SC 153:72): "Per manus enim Patris, hoc est per Filium et Spiritum [Irenaeus commonly uses the image of the Son and the Spirit as the *two hands* by which the Father creates the world], fit homo secundum similitudinem Dei, sed non pars hominis."

59. Osborn, *Irenaeus of Lyons*, 213: "He is arguing *against* the possibility that either the image or the lines might be saved alone. If it were the case that the image could be saved alone, we should be speaking about the body, and if it were the case that the likeness could be saved alone, we should be speaking about the spirit."

60. McLeod, *Image of God*, 55. See Fantino, *L'homme*, 91, 106–7. For Fantino, an example of such similitude would be the analogous correspondence between the reasonable and free nature of human beings and how God acts.

61. Irenaeus, *Adversus Haereses* 3.22.1 (SC 211:430).

62. Irenaeus, *Adversus Haereses* 3.21.10 (SC 211:428, 430): "Si autem ille de terra

integrity of image as the human nature, which the Word took from the Virgin in order to perfect it.

Image as Recapitulation

Irenaeus's notion of image as recapitulation, which explains how Christ is the first born of all creation, is an explicit evidence of patristic use of analogy to express their sense of the primacy of Christ.[63] According to Kizewski, "Irenaeus reveals how dependent recapitulation is on an analogous notion of image."[64] He did so by considering the summation of what came before, in light of the priority of the Incarnation over the creation of Adam. In other words, characteristic of the Irenaean primacy of Christ is the idea of the beginning appearing at the end.[65] Commenting on the complexity of the term "recapitulation," Osborn says that "recapitulation does four things: it corrects and perfects mankind; it inaugurates and consummates a new humanity."[66] What concerns us at the moment is the ways in which the Incarnation has offered "a new intelligibility" for a more meaningful articulation of "image" in Irenaeus via recapitulation as "correction and perfection" of the image.[67] In his humanity, Christ revealed the true Image of God, which in turn reveals man as the imperfect image in need of perfection:

> For in times past, it was said that man was created after the image of God, but it was not [actually] shown; for the Word was as

---

quidem sumptus est et Verbo Dei plasmatus est, oportebat idipsum Verbum, recapitulationem Adae in semetipsum faciens, euisdem generationis habere similitudinem [what is translated as 'an analogy' in the *ANF* is more precisely 'similitudinem']. Quare igitur non iterum sumpsit limum Deus, sed ex Maria operates est plasmationem fieri? Ut non alia plasmatio fieret neque alia esset plasmatio quae saluaretur, sed eadem ipsa recapitularetur, seruata similitudine."

63. Later, we also discuss the patristic use of image as analogous expression of primacy of Christ under Tyconius.

64. Kizewski, "God-Talk," 198.

65. According to this Eastern Orthodox theologian, "perhaps the most striking and the most characteristically Irenaean point . . . is that the beginning appeared at the end" (Behr, *Irenaeus of Lyons*, 145).

66. Osborn, *Irenaeus of Lyons*, 98.

67. Kizewski, "God-Talk," 185: "If, as Irenaeus suggests, the Incarnation made manifest the meaning of being made according to the image of God, then it is not false to say that the Incarnation made possible the discovery of a new intelligibility concerning his image."

yet invisible, after whose image man was created. Wherefore he did easily lose the similitude. When, however, the Word of God became flesh, He confirmed both these: for He both showed forth the image truly, since He became Himself what was His image; and he re-established the similitude after a sure manner, by assimilating man to the invisible Father through the means of the visible Word.[68]

The revelation of the imperfect image in turn reveals its dependence on the true Image for its perfection. The perfection of the diminished image was made visible at the Incarnation because "perfection for Irenaeus lies at the end, not at the beginning of man's education by God."[69] The Incarnation, as the end and perfection of the diminished image, sums up what came before: "But if the former was taken from the dust, and God was his Maker, it was incumbent that the latter also, making a *recapitulation* in Himself, should be formed as man by God, to have an *analogy* with the former as respects his origin."[70] This Christological analogy with respect to human origin is properly that of image of the Image, which expresses how Christ recapitulates what came before. Regarding the question of the primacy of Christ, which involves God's intention to create the world, Irenaeus depicts Adam as the scheme or preliminary disposition of the Incarnation:

> So the Lord, summing up [recapitulation] afresh this man, reproduced the scheme [*dispositionem*] of his incarnation, being born of a virgin by the Will and Wisdom of God, that He too might copy the incarnation of Adam, and man might be made, as was written in the beginning, *according to the image and likeness of God*.[71]

Thus, image in light of the recapitulation introduces a dynamism of similarity and dissimilarity between the scheme and the real or the provisional

---

68. Irenaeus, *Adversus Haereses* 5.16.2 (SC 153:216).

69. Osborn, *Irenaeus of Lyons*, 219.

70. Irenaeus, *Adversus Haereses* 3.21.9; see also 3.16.6; 5.14.1–2.

71. Irenaeus, *Demonstration apostolicae praedicationis* 32 (SC 406:128) [*Proof of the Apostolic Preaching*, 16]: "Igitur hominem hunc recapitulans Dominus, eandem ipsi carnationis (σάρκωσις) accepit dispositionem (οἰκονομία) ex Virgine nascens voluntate et sapientia Dei, ut et ipse (eam quae) ad Adam (erat) similitudinem carnationis ostenderet et fieret (is qui) scriptus (erat) in initio homo secundum imaginem et similitudinem Dei."

and the perfect, which enables us to articulate the Incarnation in terms of an analogy between God and man.

Clement of Alexandria

Like Irenaeus, Clement of Alexandria identifies image with human nature. However, while Irenaeus helped us to see image as the whole of nature, Clement's emphasis is on image in the soul. For Clement, the capacity for doing good does not pertain to man's corporeality but to his ruling or best part, which is his soul:

> Conformity with the image and likeness is not meant for the body (for it were wrong for what is mortal to be made like what is immortal), but in mind and reason, both in respect of doing good, on which fitly the Lord impresses the seal of likeness, both in respect of doing good and of exercising [the] rule.[72]

Doing good and living ethically, which pertains to "mind and reason" is a function of the image: "Image of God is really the [rational soul] who does good."[73] For Irenaeus, while image is nature, likeness is related to the unity of nature (body, soul, and spirit) through participation in the Spirit of God. For Clement, however, image is *nous* (mind and reason) and likeness is related to proportionality participation in God.[74] McLeod claims that Clement and "the Alexandrian school were heavily influenced by Philo's Platonic views regarding the human being as a soul existing in a body."[75] In Clement's defense, Kizewski says, "as Clement is less restricted by the polemic against the Gnostics, he can focus on the image in what is the best part of us without sounding as if he is disparaging our corporeality."[76] Nevertheless, Osborn claims that one of Clement's chief contributions to Christian theology is his distinction between image and likeness in such a way that it demonstrates his greater loyalty to the New Testament than to Greek philosophy.[77] For Clement, everyone possesses the image, but only those who imitate Christ by assimilation has both the image and likeness: "Man straightaway on his creation receives what

---

72. Clement of Alexandria, *Strom.* 2.19 (SC 38:113).
73. Clement of Alexandria, *Strom.* 2.19 (SC 38:109).
74. See Osborn, *Clement of Alexandria*, 234–35.
75. McLeod, *Image of God*, 51.
76. Kizewski, "God-Talk," 185.
77. See Osborn, *Clement of Alexandria*, 233.

is 'according to the image' but what is 'according to the likeness' he will receive afterwards on his perfection."[78] The measure of one's perfection depends on the proportionality of his likeness to God.

Clement's indication of how "image" conveys Christ's primacy is more apparent in his discussions on the contrast between the Greek pagan images and the Christian image of God:

> But your Olympian Jove, the image of an image, greatly out of harmony with truth, is senseless work of Attic hands. For the image of God is his Word, the genuine Son of Mind [Father], the Divine Word, the archetypal light of light; and the image of the Word is the true man, the mind which is in man, who is therefore said to have been made "in the image and likeness of God," assimilated to the Divine Word in the affections of the soul, and therefore rational.[79]

There are two primacy notions present in this quotation. First, the Word of God who is the Son of the Father, is the Image while man, by virtue of his rational soul, is image of the Image. The necessity of the soul's assimilation to the *Logos* for perfection, is evidence of the Word's primacy. Secondly, the Word as "archetypal light of light" expresses with the analogy of illumination, how Christ is the perfect correspondence to the divine prototype as the primordial light. Both "image" and "light" confirms multiple ways of using human words and concepts to speak about God's relation to man on account of Christ's primacy.

Origen

According to Osborn, "Origen sees man as created in the image of God with the purpose of gaining the likeness of God."[80] In other words, image is the beginning and likeness is the end. Much like Clement's identification of image with the best part of man, Origen associates image with the interior man:

> In the beginning of the words of Moses, where the creation of the world is described, we find reference to the making of two men, the first *in the image and likeness of God* (Gen 1:26), and the second *formed of the slime of the earth* (Gen 2:7). . . . Of

---

78. Clement of Alexandria, *Strom.* 2.22 (SC 38:134).
79. Clement of Alexandria, *Cohortatio ad Graecos* 10 (SC 2*bis*:166).
80. Osborn, *Irenaeus of Lyons*, 212.

these two men he tells us that the one, namely, the inner man, is renewed from day to day; but the other, that is, the outer, he declares to be corrupted and weakened in all the saints and in such as he was himself.[81]

Unlike Irenaeus's comprehensive sense of image, Origen insists on the "invisible, incorporeal, incorruptible and immortal" qualities of the image of God.[82] Nevertheless, what underscores Origen's characterization of image as human nature is his understanding of man's dominion over the earth as a function of the image, which distinguishes human nature from other lower animals. He says,

> And God said: "Let us make man according to our image and likeness" . . . Consequently, in accordance with those things which we explained above, God wishes such a man as we described to have dominion over the previously mentioned beasts, birds, creeping creatures, four-footed creatures, and all the rest.[83]

For him, dominion, which pertains to man as image is what distinguishes human nature from the nature of other lower animals. Origen demonstrates dominion and image as references to human nature. This human nature is for him what Christ assumes in the form of a "servant." Christ's assumption of human nature corresponds with the logic of his primacy:

> Therefore, what other image of God is there according to the likeness of whose image man is made, except our Savior who is "the firstborn of every creature (Col 1:15)." . . . Moved with compassion for man who had been made according to his likeness, seeing him, his own image having been laid aside . . . he himself moved with compassion, assumed the image of man and came to him.[84]

In this citation, we find echoes of Irenaeus's and Clement's expression of the primacy of Christ with notion of "image of the Image." The analogy of image allows us to be able to speak about acts common to God and

---

81. Origen, *Canticum Canticorum*, Proem. c.2.4–5 (SC 375:92). On the theme of a double creation of man by Philo, who influenced the Alexandrian Origen, see Crouzel, *Théologie de l'image*, 54–55, 148–53.

82. Origen, *Homiliae in Genesim* 1.13 (SC 7bis:62) [*Homilies on Genesis and Exodus*, 63].

83. Origen, *Homiliae in Genesim* 1.12 (SC 7bis:60).

84. Origen, *Homiliae in Genesim* 1.13.5–6 (SC 7bis:62–63).

creatures, or the proportional merits of creatures precisely because of the fundamental relationship between creature and its archetype.

Basil

Basil comments on the epistemic dimension of the biblical "image," i.e., the significance of the analogy of image for understanding how creation comes to know God. For him, Christ as the "express image of the Father" grounds this epistemic perspective of image.

In his *Hexaemeron,* Basil begins with a premise directed to the close relationship between man's knowledge of himself and his knowledge of God: "The beholding of heaven and earth does not make us know God better than the attentive study of our being does."[85] For Basil, if man is made in God's image, and image indicates the analogous correspondence between God and man, then man's knowledge of himself as image invariably is directed toward his knowledge of God. Basil finds in the Johannine and Pauline Christological concept of image, the interpretative key to man's knowledge of himself as image:

> To whom does He say, "in our image," to whom if it is not to Him who is "brightness of His glory and the express image of His person" (Heb 1:9), "the image of the invisible God" (Col 1:15). It is then to his living image, to Him who has said "I and my Father are one" (John 10:30), "He that hath seen me hath seen the Father" (John 14:9).[86]

Man's knowledge of God through his study of what it means to be his image, depends upon the light of the Father's self-revelation of his image in the Son who alone is the "express image" of the Father. According to Basil, "he, who with the soul's eyes fix his gaze earnestly on the express image of the Only-begotten, is made perceptive also of the hypostasis of the Father."[87] Christ the "express image" is prior to the application of image to human nature because in the Son is contained the original image as it exists in the mind of the Father.

---

85. Basil, *Homiliae in Hexaemeron* 9 (SC 26:512) [NPNF² 8:106].

86. Basil, *Homiliae in Hexaemeron* 9 (SC 26:518).

87. Basil, *Epistolae* 28 (PG 32:335). While scholars like Anna Silvas considers this letter attributed to Basil as belonging to his brother Gregory, our interest is to highlight the inner unity between his theory of image in the *Hexaemeron,* and that of this letter. See Silvas, *Gregory of Nyssa,* 247.

John Chrysostom

According to Kizewski, "John [Chrysostom] describes image primarily in terms of dominion.... So 'image' refers to the matter of control, not anything else, in other words, God created the human being as having control of everything on earth, and nothing on earth is greater than the human being, under whose authority everything falls."[88] For John, image as dominion is analogous to the dominion that God enjoys over all his creation. However, likeness points to man's resemblance of God's gentleness and mildness. He says, "As the word 'image' indicated a similitude of command, so too 'likeness,' with the result that we become like God to the extent of our human power—that is to say, we resemble him in our gentleness and mildness and in regard to virtue."[89] Therefore, "image and likeness" is a more comprehensive notion of the analogy between human and divine nature. Image and likeness complement each other as dominion and mildness complement each other. The harmony of dominion and gentleness manifests in man's ability for self-control, which is a function of reason. For John, self-control is a result of the rule of reason, which tames creation into the likeness of the gentle God. What is unnatural to reason is ferocity, violence, and savagery.[90]

Self-control comes ultimately through the grace of the imitation of Christ, the creative Word. For John, it is in the person of Christ that Scripture demonstrates the perfect harmony of dominion and gentleness, of image and likeness. God's intention for creating us in his image and likeness corresponds with Christ's invitation to "Learn from me that I am meek and humble of heart, and you shall find rest for your soul (Matt 11:29)."[91] So, Christ's dominion and meekness are for John, the foundation of man's image and likeness to God. His indication, that Christ is the "foundation" of man is evident in his commentary on the Pauline primacy of Christ, the *Image of God* and *firstborn* of all creation (Col 1:15–18). As "God's Son, God's image, [Christ] shows the exact likeness."[92] The completion of image by likeness is Christ, who is the exact image and likeness. John interprets the Pauline teaching on the primacy of Christ

---

88. Kizewski, "God-Talk," 195; John Chrysostom, *Homiliae super Genesim* 8.9 (PG 53:69).

89. John Chrysostom, *Homiliae super Genesim* 9.7 (PG 53:76).

90. See John Chrysostom, *Homiliae super Genesim* 9.7 (PG 53:76).

91. John Chrysostom, *Homiliae super Genesim* 9.14 (PG 53:81).

92. John Chrysostom, *In epistolam ad Colossenses* III (PG 53:317) [*Homilies*].

in terms of Christ as the "foundation." He says, "The word 'firstborn,' [is said] in the sense of a foundation."[93] In other words, the as "firstborn" of all creation, Christ is their "foundation."

Ambrose

In his *Hexaemeron*, Ambrose begins his consideration of how man is the image and likeness with a Christological hermeneutic of Gen 1:3: "The 'image' of God is He alone who has said: 'I and the Father are one,' thus possessing the likeness of the Father so as to have a unity of divinity and of plenitude."[94] Like other patristic writers, he anticipates the primacy of Christ at the creation of the world by identifying him as "the image," "the beginning," and "the firstborn."[95]

He makes the distinction between Christ "the image of God" and the human soul made "to the image of God."[96] For him, the soul is "man's entire essence,"[97] and "is made in form like the Lord Jesus."[98] The soul is made according to the form of Christ. Ambrose describes the similitude of the human soul to Christ with the soul's ability to reflect all things. For him, the limitations of our corporeal vision is evident because with it, "I am unable to see what is behind me."[99] But the soul's vision transcends the limitations of corporeal vision because "our souls are able to envisage and reflect on all things."[100] The soul's vision that "crosses boundaries and gazes intently on what is hidden" also makes it possible that "God is attained and Christ is approached."[101] According to Kizewski "by attaining to that which "reflect on all things," [the soul] even in a sense *becomes* all things, becomes like God."[102] To the extent that the human soul bears such a resemblance to God, it is capable of self-transcendence by becoming more and more like God.

---

93. John Chrysostom, *In epistolam ad Colossenses* III (PG 53:319–20).
94. Ambrose, *Hexaemeron* 6.7.41 (CSEL 32.1:232) [*Hexamaron, Paradise*].
95. Ambrose, *Hexaemeron* 6.7.41 (CSEL 32.1:232).
96. Ambrose, *Hexaemeron* 6.7.43–6.8.44 (CSEL 32.1:234–35).
97. Ambrose, *Hexaemeron* 6.7.43 (CSEL 32.2:234).
98. Ambrose, *Hexaemeron* 6.8.46 (CSEL 32.2:237).
99. Ambrose, *Hexaemeron* 6.8.44–45 (CSEL 32.2:236).
100. Ambrose, *Hexaemeron* 6.8.44–45 (CSEL 32.2:236).
101. Ambrose, *Hexaemeron* 6.8.45 (CSEL 32.2:236).
102. Kizewski, "God-Talk," 197.

Thus Ambrose highlights the self-transcendence of the soul, its capacity for something beyond itself, as constituted by the Son, in whose image it was made. We can speak analogously about the soul's capacity for becoming like God on account of "the image," Christ, in whose form he was made.

Tyconius

In his *Book of Rules,* Tyconius includes image or likeness as part of the reason for the reality of recapitulation. He considers recapitulation as something that "goes from the beginning to the end" of time in a continuous way. Explaining recapitulation with the principle of synecdoche of time (the parts indicate the whole and vice versa), he points to something earlier in time as a likeness of what is to come. For instance, he indicates that there is the primacy of Christ in God's intention to create the world: "This world was constructed in the likeness of the Church" the body of Christ.[103] The sign of this likeness of the Church is man: "Man is therefore the 'sign of likeness' and the 'crowning of splendor,' of which a part perseveres in this splendor of divine likeness and in the 'delights of paradise,' i.e., the Church."[104] For him, particular figures in biblical history are shadows of the bipartite nature of this Church. Some represents the good and others the evil parts of it.

For Tyconius, the children of the promise, who freely live according to the image and likeness of God according to his original intention, are members of Christ's body, while those who are slaves to evil belong to the devil's body. He describes the children of the promise as those that "serve God freely and live according to the image and likeness of God and of Christ. They are good because that is what they want."[105] He characterizes the evil part of the church as the one "whose splendor has been corrupted . . . who does not respond to his origin by showing its likeness in his works."[106] As Kizewski rightly observes, "likeness and image are what distinguishes one member of the Lord's Body, which is the [true] Church, or that of the devil [the false church]."[107] The appearance of the body of

---

103. Tyconius, *Liber de septem regulis* 7.4.2 (SC 488:334) [*Book of Rules*].
104. Tyconius, *Liber de septem regulis* 7.14.1 (SC 488:358).
105. Tyconius, *Liber de septem regulis* 3.20.2 (SC 488:198–200).
106. Tyconius, *Liber de septem regulis* 7.17.1 (SC 488:368).
107. Kizewski, "God-Talk," 200.

Christ is essentially the appearance of the truth about who man is: one made in the image and likeness of Christ's body. Thus, like Irenaeus, Tyconius uses image as recapitulation to articulate the primacy of Christ.

Conclusion

Our study of the patristic understanding of "image" demonstrates how the notion of image is critical to understanding their teaching on the primacy of Christ. In Clement, man is "image of the Image" and the "archetypal light of light." What Basil depicts as the "express image," Chrysostom articulates as the "foundation of man." Grounded on the analogy of image, Ambrose highlights the capacity of the soul for self-transcendence toward becoming like Christ, the God-man.

However, it is the Irenaean and Tyconian "image as recapitulation" that articulates more explicitly the primacy of Christ. Regarding God's intention to create the world, Irenaeus points to the making of Adam as the "scheme of [Christ's] Incarnation." For Tyconius, "this world was constructed in the likeness of the Church," the body of Christ. Ratzinger's reference to the patristic sense of primacy of Christ is also grounded in their unique use of the analogy of image. He says, "There is a unique sense in which Christ is the 'image of God.' *The Fathers* of the Church therefore say that when God created man 'in his image,' he looked toward the Christ who was to come, and created man according to the image of the 'new Adam,' the man who is the criterion of the human."[108]

Participation

According to Hans Urs von Balthasar, "The intimacy of the connections that were already created by the Platonic structure of 'participation' is increased by the Stoic contribution of kinship with the divine nature, on the one hand, and by the contribution of the gospel on the other hand."[109] Plato's concept of participation—μετέχω, κοινωνία, μίμησις—describes how particulars participate in forms while retaining their identity. According to Osborn, "Aristotle rejected Plato's forms but retained the notion of participation to describe the difference between the imperfect and

---

108. Benedict XVI/Ratzinger, *Jesus of Nazareth*, 1:138.
109. Balthasar, *Presence and Thought*, 113–14.

perfect possession of a quality."[110] Nevertheless, both Plato and Aristotle offer a more ontological view of participation, which is fundamental to the integrity of nature. However, it is the stoic anthropology that indicates a more Pneumatic philosophical intuition of participation, whereby the exact correspondence of man as the microcosm, to the macrocosm of the entire cosmos, is a function of the divine primal fire or the *pneuma*.[111] The Stoic pneumatic anthropology offered the Fathers, an opportunity to articulate with a new synthesis, the metaphysical and historical dimensions of biblical notion of participation.[112] Our investigation is concerned with tracing what this patristic synthetic concept of participation consists in.

Justin Martyr

Eric Osborn indicates the two ways in which Justin Martyr uses the concept of participation. First, "all men share the spermatic logos in varying degrees."[113] Second, "the soul finds life only by participation in God who is life."[114] The first kind of participation emphasizes the metaphysical grounds while the second, presupposing ontology, looks to faith or spiritual analogy.

Participation by Reason

Identifying the presence of the "seeds of the logos" in the teachings of philosophers, poets, and historians, Justin Martyr presents participation as founded on reason. He says,

> I am proud to say that I strove with all my might to be known as a Christian, not because the teachings of Plato are different from those of Christ, but because they are not in every way similar;

---

110. Osborn, *Irenaeus of Lyons*, 259.

111. See Benedict XVI/Ratzinger, *Behold*, 66.

112. See Osborn, *Irenaeus of Lyons*, 259. Scripture expresses its notion of participation most frequently as μετέχω and κοινωνία. Μετέχω is used for Christ's assumption of human nature and man's participation in the divinity of Christ (Heb 2:1; 3:14). This participation is a sharing in Christ's suffering and glory (Phil 3:10; 2 Cor 1:7). Scripture uses κοινωνία as spiritual, and ecclesial participation in divine life, both now and at the end of salvation (cf. 1 Cor 10:16–18; 2 Cor 13:13; 1 Pet 1:4).

113. Osborn, *Irenaeus of Lyons*, 259.

114. Osborn, *Irenaeus of Lyons*, 259.

neither are those of other writers, the stoics, the poets, and the historians. For each one of them, seeing, through his participation of the seminal Divine Word, what was related to it, spoke very well.[115]

As we mentioned earlier, Justin uses the notion of participation [to] explain how it is that certain philosophers spoke well of God.[116] By the use of reason, the human mind participates in God in a way limited to human nature. This participation allows the philosophers and poets to use human words to communicate well, what the mind perceives about the Word. While Justin takes rational participation of creature to God for granted, however, he emphasizes the limits of this participation in comparison to Christ. Participation as a member of the body of Christ and participation through philosophical excexercise "are not in every way similar." The ontological distinction in Justin's concept of participation is particularly Christian because Christ is the center of the analogy.

What helps us to better understand Justin's Christian distinction is Joseph Carola's explanation of how the Martyr distinguishes between *logos spermatikos* (the Seminal Word) and *sperma tou logou* (the seeds of the word):

> Justin distinguishes between the *logos spermatikos* and the *sperma tou logou* (Seed of the Logos) present in all human beings. They are not identical. The term *logos spermatikos* ... refers specifically to the Divine Word. ... The *logos spermatikos* is not disseminated but rather actively disseminates or sows his seed (*sperma tou logou*), which is other than himself.[117]

Justin uses *logos* neither univocally nor in a strictly equivocal way, but by analogy, with Christ as the primary analogate. The difference between "logos spermatikos" and "sperma tou logou" is not only in degree but in kind. His distinction between Christ the "whole *logos*" (τοῦ παντὸς λόγου)[118] and the "seeds of logos" implanted in all mankind recapitulates an essential distinction between participation in the truth and the truth itself.[119] The Martyr says, "Indeed, all writers, by means of the engrafted

---

115. Justin Martyr, *Dialogus cum Tryphone* 6 (PTS 47:82).

116. Kizewski, "God-Talk," 204.

117. Carola, "Non-Christians in Patristic Theology," 36.

118. Justin Martyr, *Apologia* 2.8.10 (SC 507:340).

119. Kizewski, "God-Talk," 205: "A participation in the seed of Wisdom is not that Wisdom; a glimpse of the truth is not the truth."

seed of the Word which was implanted in them, had a glimpse of the truth. For the seed of something and its imitation, given in proportion to one's capacity, is one thing, but the thing itself, which is shared and imitated according to [God's] grace, is quite another."[120] So, what we have here is an ontological distinction necessary for the Christian comprehension of participation as an analogy.

Justin also speaks of "persecution" as significant to the moral dimension of participation. He recognizes that on account of a life lived according to reason, "the followers of the stoic teaching, because they were praiseworthy at least in their ethics, as were also the poets in some respects . . . were hated and killed."[121] He goes on to say that "The demons always brought it about that everyone, who strives in any way to live according to right reason and to avoid evil, be an object of hatred."[122] The love of wisdom, introduces on the philosophical level, an element of suffering on account of a life of virtue in accord with reason. For the Martyr, the element of persecution is indispensable for moral life because such a life, which practically affirms the rational harmony between the two ontologically distinct realities (God and creature), is bound to attract irrational oppositions. This basic conflict between a virtuous and malicious life, explains in part, the reason for an even greater hatred for Christians, who participate in the Whole Logos: "Nor is it surprising that the demons are proved to be the cause why they are much more hated who do not live according to only a part of the seminal word, but by the knowledge and consideration of the whole Word, which is Christ."[123]

The significance of "persecution" in the moral dimension of participation analogy, consists in the way it offers a preliminary philosophical foundation for the reasonableness of Christian sacrifice. According to Clement of Alexandria, it is on the account of "the sacrifice which is acceptable to God [as] unswerving abstraction from the body and its passions . . . that philosophy [is] rightly called by Socrates, the practice of death."[124] Therefore, reason, when considered as fundamental to moral life, is the grounds for the sacrificial element of participation.

---

120. Justin Martyr, *Apologia* 2.13 (SC 507:364).
121. Justin Martyr, *Apologia* 2.8.1 (SC 507:338).
122. Justin Martyr, *Apologia* 2.8.5 (SC 507:340).
123. Justin Martyr, *Apologia* 2.8.5 (SC 507:340).
124. Clement of Alexandria, *Strom.* 5.11 (PG 9:101B).

PNEUMATIC PARTICIPATION

With regard to the spiritual dimension of participation, Justin incorporates elements of the Stoic Pneumatic concept of the creative logos, into his articulation the biblical idea of Pneumatic participation. He finds a connection between the "ordering of the universe," which the stoics consider to be the function of the "spirit" (pneuma), and the significance of the name "Christ" or "the anointed one":

> As for his son, of who alone is properly called Son, the Word, who is with Him before all creation and is begotten [before all things] when in the beginning he created and ordered (ἔκτισε καὶ ἐκόσμησε) through him all things, is called Christ for having been anointed and for having been the one through whom God ordered all things.[125]

According to José Granados, "Justin considers an anointing of the world in such a way that it complements its constitution, just as things receive anointing after they have been formed. Justin intended the ordering of the world as its anointing. A presence of the spirit in this anointing would find support in Stoic concepts."[126] For the stoics, the "original fire" also called the "spirit" (pneuma), is the principle that penetrates the world and gives cohesion (order) to all things;[127] a concept akin to Justin's ἐκόσμησε.[128] Pneumatic ordering of the cosmos is a "power" or "dynamism" (dunamis) towards its finality through Christ's possession of the Spirit in his anointing.[129] The dynamic character of a cosmic Pneumatic ordering suggests a process, a becoming, or a vision of a living and moving universe. Justin's distinction between creating (ἔκτισε) and ordering (ἐκόσμησε), and his connection of ordering to anointing of Christ, indicates a parallel distinction between analogy of created nature and that of the power, anointing or ordering of nature. The former, which pertains to

---

125. Justin Martyr, *Apologia* 2.6 (PG 6:453A).

126. Granados, *Los Misterios*, 45.

127. See Colish, *Stoic Tradition*, 24. "Se trataría del Pneuma diekon o περιέχον, principio que penetra el mundo dando cohesion a todas las cosas. El fuego original es tambien llamado espíritu (pneuma) por los estoicos" (Granados, *Los Misterios*, 45n51).

128. See Granados, *Los Misterios*, 44. For Granados, Justin's connection of the ἐκόσμησε to the name of the anointed one (Christ), could not have come from the semitic anointing, which was particularly a religious ritual. Rather, a more amplified cosmic meaning of anointing was used by the Greeks towards profane objects.

129. Granados, *Los Misterios*, 48.

nature indicates the static form of nature, while the latter, which pertains to the inner Pneumatic power of created nature, indicates dynamic or spiritual movement of the analogy of participation.

However, for Justin, this Pneumatic dimension of participation through Christ's anointing is not only cosmic but is also concretely historical in the way that it is revealed in the *history of salvation* and prefigured in the reality of ecclesial participation. While Christ possesses the totality of the Spirit, creation participates in it to various degrees:

> Also, we have demonstrated . . . how to Him is referred all anointing, one of oil, one of myrrh, or some other composed of balsam, for the word says: "for this I anointed you, oh God, your God, with the oil of gladness, with preference for your companions (μετόσχους)" (Ps 44[45]:8). And thus made the kings and the anointed to be called kings and to be *anointed through participation* in him (οἱ χριστοὶ ἀπὸ τούτου μετέσχον καὶ βασιλεῖς καλεῖσθαι καὶ χριστοί); in the same way He himself received from the Father, being King, Christ, Priest, Messenger, and all other titles he has or had.[130]

The "companions" (μετόσχους) of Christ are anointed by way of participation (μετέσχον) in the one anointing of the Logos. Commenting on this text, Granados says "there is no doubt the anointing relates to the Spirit that possessed the figures of the Old Testament," thus presenting Christ as the "giver of the Spirit to the people of Israel through an anointing prior to his Incarnation."[131] He also speaks of the "Church" the new Israel, as an establishment of the Anointed One and as those called Christians or partakers in the Anointing One.[132] Therefore, the concrete experience of the Christian notion of participation, emerges from the teachings of Justin as an ecclesial reality through Pneumatic participation. With this synthesis of the stoic and biblical of Pneumatic activity, Justin introduces the ecclesial dimension of participation, as essential to it spiritual character. As a spiritual analogy, participation, which takes on a synthetic meaning, allows us to use analogy both in a cosmic and concrete way. Indication of the primacy of Christ consists in Justin's position that, the

---

130. Justin Martyr, *Dialogus cum Tryphone* 86.3–4 (PG 6:681A).

131. Granados, *Los Misterios*, 42: "No hay duda de que la unción se relaciona con el Espíritu que poseyeron los personajes del Antiguo Testamento. Se Presenta a Cristo como dador del Espíritu en el pueblo de Israel por una unción anterior a su venida en carne."

132. Justin Martyr, *Dialogus cum Tryphone* 63.5 (PG 6:621).

one anointing of the Logos, which orders the cosmos through the original fire of the pneuma, also gathers in biblical history, the companions of Christ, through prophecy and gift of the Spirit.

Irenaeus

While Justin Martyr applies participation to either the ontological or the Pneumatic relation between God and creation, Irenaeus presumes ontology as he uses participation to indicate the spiritual perfection of creation. According to Osborn, "salvation" in Irenaeus "presupposes creation and ends in participation."[133] Irenaeus defines participation in terms of the actualization of creation through its vision of God: "It is impossible to live without life, and the actualization of life comes from participation in God, while participation in God is to see God and enjoy his goodness."[134] Participation as "actualization of life" and the capacity to "see God" points to a life of perfection; a life filled with grace. There is sense of participation as the completion of creation, without which creation cannot transcend its limitations. The perfection, which Irenaeus speaks of as a condition of participation, is spiritual in the sense that perfection is the gift of the Spirit: "Those, then, are the perfect who have had the Spirit of God remaining in them, have preserved their souls and bodies blameless, holding fast to the faith of God."[135] He uses three synonymous terms to highlight what is necessary for a creature's participation in God: similitude, likeness and assimilation.

For him, the Spirit's restoration of our lost "similitude" is necessary for perfection. He says, "But if the Spirit be wanting to the soul, he who is such is indeed of an animal nature, and being left carnal, shall be an imperfect being, possessing indeed the image [of God] in his formation (*in plasmate*), but not receiving the similitude through the Spirit."[136] Similitude, as what is lost with the fall, is synonymous to likeness. In reference to the lost spiritual relationship of the creature to God, he uses *likeness* as

---

133. Osborn, *Irenaeus of Lyons*, 216.

134. Irenaeus, *Adversus Haereses* 4. 20.7 (SC 100:640–642): "Quoniam vivere sine vita impossible est, subsistentia autem vitae de Dei participatione evenit, participatio autem Dei est videre Deum et frui benignitate eius."

135. Irenaeus, *Adversus Haereses* 5.6.1 (SC 153:80).

136. Irenaeus, *Adversus Haereses* 5.6.1 (SC 153:76): "Si autem defuerit animae Spiritus, animalis est vere qui est talis et carnalis derelictus imperfectus erit, imaginem quidem habens in plasmate, similitudinem vero non assumens per Spiritum."

a distinct concept from *image*. He says, "Man's likeness to God was given by the Spirit, and restored by the pouring out of the Spirit on the faithful, which gives man back his lost innocence; it is the Spirit who leads man back to God."[137] In addition to similitude and likeness, Irenaeus also speaks of the restoration of what was lost as a process of "assimilation": "He re-established the similitude after a sure manner, by *assimilating* man to the invisible Father through the means of the visible Word."[138]

Similitude, likeness and assimilation express what is necessary for the perfection of man. Irenaeus uses them as concepts that considers the descending movement of the Spirit of God as prior to man's ability to ascend to perfection. Since participation for Irenaeus is about the perfection of creation, his description of likeness or similitude indicates a Spirit-centered correspondence of the fallen creature to God. Out of the three synonymous terms, it is *likeness* that brings out the synthetic meaning of Irenaeus's analogy of participation. As a spiritual notion, *likeness* understood as *assimilation* of creature into God, then articulates in a full and comprehensive way, the Christian anthropology of Irenaeus, which claims that even "the flesh is capable of . . . *participating* in incorruption," as evident in Christ's resurrection.[139] As we saw in his theory of recapitulation, it is the new intelligibility offered by the Incarnation of the Word that allows Irenaeus to speak of corporeal participation as a spiritual analogy.

Origen

Like Justin, Origen uses "seeds of reason" to explain the ontological foundation of participation: "All rational beings are partakers of the word of God, that is, of reason, and so have implanted within them some seeds, as it were, of wisdom and righteousness, which is Christ."[140] By virtue of reason, "participation in God the Father extends to all, both righteous and sinners" and "Christ is 'in the heart' of all men, in virtue of his being the word or reason, by sharing in which men are rational."[141]

---

137. Irenaeus, *Proof of the Apostolic Preaching*, 32.
138. Irenaeus, *Adversus Haereses* 5.16.2 (SC 153:216) (my emphasis).
139. Irenaeus, *Adversus Haereses* 5.3.3 (SC 153:54).
140. Origen, *De Principiis* 1.3.6 (SC 252:154).
141. Origen, *De Principiis* 1.3.6 (SC 252:154).

However, Origen's idea of participation also involves its concrete or personal dimension. He speaks of "diversity of participation" according to "proportionality" as follows:

> Nevertheless, just as in our illustrations we acknowledged some diversity in the reception of the light, when we described the individual power of sight as being either dim or keen, so also we must acknowledge a diversity of participation in the Father, Son and Holy Spirit, varying in proportion to the earnestness of the soul and the capacity of the mind.[142]

Proportionality suggests diverse capacities (*capacitate diversitas*) of participation, which harkens upon the particularity of each individual's unique participation to God. Elsewhere, he then connects the diversity of participation to the function of the "free-will," thus indicating what Ratzinger will later associate with the *personal* as distinct from the natural. He says,

> [Christ] granted invisibly to all rational creatures whatsoever a *participation* in himself, in such a way that each obtained a degree of participation *proportionate* to the loving affection with which he had clung to him. But whereas, by reason of the faculty of *free-will*, variety and diversity had taken hold of individual souls, so that one was attached to its author with a warmer and another with a feebler and weaker love, that soul of which Jesus said, "No man taketh from me my soul," clinging to God from the beginning of creation and ever after in a union inseparable and indissoluble.[143]

The degree of participation, which is proportional to an individual's "loving affection" to God, involves the faculty of freewill. Origen differentiates this kind of created participation from the kind of union existing between Christ's (human) soul and his divinity. The union of Christ's human soul with God is in a pre-eminent way, a union of oneness of spirit, such that "[his] soul, acting as a medium between God and the flesh, is the God-man."[144] What Christ pre-eminently has in the union of his humanity and divinity, which is his Sonship, we possess according to the

142. Origen, *De Principiis* 4.4.9 (SC 268:424, 426).
143. Origen, *De Principiis* 2.6.3 (SC 252:314).
144. Origen, *De Principiis* 2.6.3 (SC 252:314). We shall later discuss how Origen sees the significance of this detail—about the pre-eminence of the union of God and man in Christ—in the Christian argument for names of Jesus, especially as the "Son of God."

degree of participation as adopted sons.¹⁴⁵ Thus, for Origen, participation is also a spiritual relationship through which Jesus joins believers to himself in the one bond of the Spirit uniting his humanity to his divinity: "As the apostle promises to them whose duty it is to imitate Jesus, that 'he who is joined to the Lord is one spirit.'"¹⁴⁶

Origen's understanding of participation as a spiritual analogy between God and man is more evident in his description of anointing as participation in the anointing of Jesus. For him, anointing is a function of the Spirit because "to be anointed with the oil of gladness means nothing else but to be filled with the Holy Spirit."¹⁴⁷ Continuing his commentary on the anointing of Jesus, Origen says,

> The very fact, too, that it says, "God anointed thee, thy God with the oil of gladness above thy fellows," shows that that soul is anointed with the "oil of gladness," that is, with the word of God and wisdom, in one way, and his "fellows," that is, the holy prophets and apostles, in another. For the latter are said "to have run in the odor of his ointments" (Song 1:3), but that soul was the vase containing the anointing itself, of whose glowing effluence all the prophets and apostles became worthy *partakers*.¹⁴⁸

The anointing of Christ is uniquely constituted in the personal union of his two natures, while the anointing of the prophets is by participation in Christ. The analogous character of participation by anointing emerges as Christ-centered and Spirit-ual. To be "anointed" does not apply univocally to both Jesus and other men, but only analogously to the prophets and the apostles. We can see at play in participation, the healthy tension between the limitation of nature that cannot exceed itself, and the dynamism of its capacity for a life according to the Spirit of Christ. As the "vase containing the anointing itself," the humanity of Jesus is locus of growth in participation in the divine for others.

Thus, as we saw in Justin, there is also in Origen, a recapitulation of pneumatic and ecclesial (through the prophets and apostles) participation in the one anointing of Christ; a kind of primacy of Christ's

---

145. By virtue of the pre-eminence of union between the humanity and divinity of Jesus, whereby "[his soul] received the Son of God wholly into itself, [this soul] should itself be called, along with that flesh which it has taken, the Son of God" (Origen, *De Principiis* 2.6.3 [SC 252:316]).

146. Origen, *De Principiis* 2.6.3 (SC 252:314).

147. Origen, *De Principiis* 2.6.4 (SC 252:316, 318); cf. Ps 45:7 (8).

148. Origen, *De Principiis* 2.6.6 (SC 252:320, 322) (my emphasis).

anointing. The centrality of sacrifice, essential to the ecclesial dimension of participation, is more explicit in Origen. For Origen, ecclesial participation in the anointing of Christ is a partaking in his priestly sacrifice:

> And since the same Christ [anointed one] is called Priest as well as Bridegroom—Priest indeed, because He is *Mediator of God and men* and all creation, on whose behalf, moreover, He was made *the propitiation,* in that *He offered Himself as a sacrifice* for the sin of the world; but Bridegroom because He is united to the *Church not having spot, or wrinkle, or any such thing*.[149]

For him, the "flower of chosen myrrh," stipulated in Exodus 30:22 as essential ingredient of the oil of priestly anointing of the Levitical priesthood, foreshadows the priestly sacrifice of Christ "in which body *myrrh* signifies the death He underwent, alike as Priest for the people and as Bridegroom for the Bride."[150] However, he also insists that the *chosen myrrh* extends the sacrificial signification of Christ's anointing to those chosen (the Bride) to partake in the likeness of his death: "But the fact that what was written was not simply 'myrrh,' but 'flower of myrrh,' and 'chosen myrrh' too, foreshadowed not his death alone, but also that he was to be *the Firstborn from the dead*, and that those who had been *planted together in the likeness of his death* should not only be called, but chosen too."[151] Origen's indication of the sacrificial dimension of anointing is helpful for understanding the centrality of the paschal character of ecclesial participation in patristic Christological hermeneutic.

Origen helps us to discover the critical role of freewill and sacrificial anointing as constituents of the spiritual character of participation. We can speak analogously of spiritual participation in the Body of Christ on account of the paschal nature of such analogy, and freewill assures the diversity of such participation proportionate to the measure of one's capacity to love and follow Christ, the true Wisdom.

---

149. Origen, *Canticum Canticorum* 1.3.3 (SC 375:208). "From the garments of the Word of God, therefore, which denote the teaching of wisdom, myrrh proceeds, a symbol surely of the death He underwent for humankind" (2.10.5).

150. Origen, *Canticum Canticorum* 1.3.5 (SC 375:210).

151. Origen, *Canticum Canticorum* 1.3.5 (SC 375:210).

Conclusion

For the Fathers and ancient ecclesiastical writers, image grounds participation and participation expresses both the ontological and the pneumatic movements of Christian anthropology. Justin Martyr and Origen use the notion of the "seeds of the *logos*" (*semina Verbi*) to convey the ontological dimension of how various philosophical cultures "participate" in Christ the Word. Justin emphasizes the primacy of the *logos spermatikos* (the Seminal Word) in the philosophical participation of reason to Reason. Commenting on the use of *semina Verbi* among the Fathers, Ratzinger says, "The Word-made-man did not simply enter a world that knew nothing whatsoever about him. He sent his radiance ahead of himself into the world and thus awakened the yearning humanity.... In this connection the Church Fathers have spoken of the 'seeds of the Word,' which they sought and found in the pre-Christian world."[152]

With regard to the pneumatic dimension of participation, we have seen how the ancient authors use the concepts of likeness, anointing, companionship, and Christian sacrifice to describe the spiritual and the ecclesial elements of the analogy of participation. Irenaeus preserves the corporeal element of participation. The biblical and Stoic roots of anointing help Justin and Origen to articulate this pneumatic character of participation. The patristic insistence on the spiritual movement of participation points to Christ and his Church as offering the unifying vision of analogy. Participation then confirms and complements the analogy of image by indicating a living, historical, and spiritual image.

God-Talk

In this section, we are concerned with the patristic understanding of the relationship between human words about God and divine revelation with human words. Kizewski begins his consideration of this relationship from the so-called patristic negative theology, whereby the Fathers established a clear distinction between the limitations of human words on account of

---

152. Benedict XVI/Ratzinger, *On the Way*, 72. "Das menschgewordene Wort ist ja nicht in eine Welt hineingetreten, die schlechterdings nichts davon wusste. Es has seine Strahlen vorausgesandt in die Welt hinein, und es hat so die Sehnsucht der Menschheit geweckt. Es ist das Licht, das jeden Menschen erleuchtet, der in die Welt knommt (John 1:9). Die Väter haben in diesem Zusammenhang von den 'Samenkörnern des Wortes' gesprochen, die sie in der vorchristlichen Welt gesucht und gefunden haben" (Benedict XVI/Ratzinger, *Beiträge zur Christologie*, 1002).

our nature and the transcendence of God.[153] The distinction serves as a positive problem, which prepares the grounds for discussing the need for analogy in "God-Talk."[154] For Kizewski, "Locating negative theology in the context of speaking about God enables us to offer a tempered account of that negative theology and notice what is actually being said about God."[155] The apophatic approach, which emphasizes what we cannot say about God, offers a necessary distinction for a proper understanding of what we can say by analogy.[156] Within this necessary distinction, we examine how each of the following patristic thinkers identifies the place of Christ in their reflections on the analogical relationship between human words and divine revelation.

Irenaeus

Irenaeus's argument against his Gnostic adversaries alludes to their lack of the analogical sense of biblical talk about God. He accuses them of ignoring the biblical emphasis on the great dissimilarity between the divine and human nature: "But if they had known the Scriptures, and been taught by the truth, they would have known, beyond doubt, that God is not as men are; and that his thoughts are not like the thoughts of men."[157] He thus indicates how they ignored the *rule* of knowledge through biblical and faith analogies.

Limitations of Human Word and Divine Transcendence

Irenaeus expresses the vastness of the dissimilarity between God and man in terms of man as "composite in nature" and God as "a simple, uncompounded being."[158] For him, God remains "unknown to all," "unutterable," or "inexpressible" to human speech:

---

153. See Kizewski, "God-Talk," 218–19.

154. In the General Introduction of this study, we briefly explained how Kizewski derived the expression "God-Talk" from Gregory of Nyssa's "baby-talk."

155. Kizewski, "God-Talk," 220.

156. Kizewski, "God-Talk," 218: "When we want to emphasize what we cannot say, then we are emphasizing the disparity between God and creatures. When we want to emphasize what we can say, we are in the vicinity of analogy."

157. Irenaeus, *Adversus Haereses* 2.13.3 (SC 264:279).

158. Irenaeus, *Adversus Haereses* 2.13.4 (SC 294:116).

[God] is above all earthly names and therefore inexpressible. He may well and correctly be called a Mind that comprehends all things; but his Mind is not like the mind of men. He may most correctly be called Light, but he is nothing like our light. And so, with regard to all other particulars, the Father of all is in no way similar to mankind's littleness. We speak of him in such terms because of His love; but it is understood that he is above them by virtue of his greatness.[159]

This chasm between inexpressibleness of the divine reality and human words creates the space for the necessity of analogy for a positive human utterance about God. Kizewski rightly observes that the word "inexpressible," though an utterance of our limited nature, is "itself a word applied to God."[160] The limitation of human nature does not amount to its incapacity for God. For Irenaeus, the inadequacy of human mind for conceiving the reality of divine utterance, does not render it completely unable to communicate something true about God's Word. The one who declares "that [the] divine Nous (Thought) is God's Logos (Word), will still indeed have only an inadequate conception of the Father of all, but will entertain far more becoming than do those who transfer the generation of the word to which men gave utterance."[161] The limitation in analogy of word consists in the discursive nature of human thought, in which thought (nous) precedes speech (logos), which is incongruent with divine simplicity. However, precisely because of the simplicity of divine Truth, one can analogously say that "the divine Nous is his Logos." For Irenaeus, the reason for the human capacity for speech about God is the priority of God's love itself: "We speak of him in such terms because of love; but it is understood that he is above them by virtue of his greatness."[162]

Analogy of Scriptures and Priority of the Word

We have mentioned that God's love is the rationale behind Irenaeus's argument for the capacity of human word for speech about God. We now examine what this divine love consists in. For him, God utters his love both via the gift of creation and the gift of his self-revelation. In his

---

159. Irenaeus, *Adversus Haereses* 2.13.4 (SC 294:116).
160. Kizewski, "God-Talk," 219.
161. Irenaeus, *Adversus Haereses* 2.13.8 (SC 294:124).
162. Irenaeus, *Adversus Haereses* 2.13.4 (SC 294:116).

exegesis of the words of Christ in Matt 9:27,[163] he affirms that in and through the Word, the Father utters his love both in a created and revealed way: "since God cannot be declared [by anyone else], the Word does himself declare Him to us."[164] With regard to God's love through the gift of creation, Irenaeus says that "by means of the creation itself, the Word reveals God the Creator . . . and by the means of the formation of man [does he declare] the Artificer who formed him."[165] Regarding the gift of revelation, he says, "by the law and the prophets did the Word preach both himself and the Father alike . . . and through the Word himself who had been made visible and palpable, was the Father shown forth."[166] In the end, to learn and speak well about God, we need grace, which comes through his Word, since knowledge of God comes from his speech.[167] By the gift of creation, the Word declares God as Creator. Through the preaching of the prophets fulfilled in Incarnation, the Word uses human words to speak well about God. Therefore, for Irenaeus, the Word is the center of the analogy between God's Word and man's word.

Origen

Regarding Origen, Kizewski also recognizes that the limitation of human knowledge is the context in which Origen considers God-Talk: "When Origen considers what we know by reason, he locates it precisely in the context of talking about God."[168] At first, Origen suggests that human words cannot be applied to God:

> We must know, therefore, that the Paraclete is the Holy Spirit, who teaches truths greater than can be uttered by the voice, truths which are, if I may so say, "unspeakable," and which "it is not lawful for a man to speak," that is, which cannot be indicated in human language. For the phrase "not lawful" was spoken, we believe, by Paul as the equivalent of "not possible."[169]

---

163. No one knows the Son except the Father, and no one knows the Father except the Son and anyone to whom the Son wishes to reveal him (cf. Luke 10:22). All Biblical citations are from the Saint Joseph Edition of the New American Bible, Revised.

164. Irenaeus, *Adversus Haereses* 4.6.3 (SC 100:442).

165. Irenaeus, *Adversus Haereses* 4.6.6 (SC 100:448).

166. Irenaeus, *Adversus Haereses* 4.6.6 (SC 100:448).

167. See Osborn, *Irenaeus of Lyons*, 150.

168. Kizewski, "God-Talk," 167.

169. Origen, *De Principiis* 2.7.4 (SC 252:332).

PATRISTIC CONSENSUS ON ANALOGY 55

Divine truths, which are "unspeakable" convey God's transcendence relative to human speech. However, Origen also acknowledges that "although one is not able to speak worthily of God the Father, still it is possible to gain some notion of him from our experience of the visible creation and from the instinctive thoughts of the human mind."[170] From his emphasis on the unspeakableness of the mysteries of divine truth, we learn about the greater dissimilarity between what we say about God and the real truth of his mystery. But from his assertion of the applicability human words to God, he indicates the necessity of analogy for the comprehension of how words apply to God. We have already seen this in our investigation of Origen's use of participation. For him, by virtue of reason, "participation in God the Father extends to all, both righteous and sinners" and "Christ is 'in the heart' of all men, in virtue of his being the word or reason, a participation in which men are rational."[171]

Significant to our study is Origen's reason for the analogy present between the incorporeal "God" and our corporeal "talk." For him, it is God's "providence" and his desire for our knowledge of his will that gives reason to God-Talk: "As we profess . . . nothing happens without his providence. In accordance with this profession, therefore, that God is the provider and manager of all things . . . makes known what he wishes or what is advantageous for men."[172] For him, the silence of God, which would be more consistent with his transcendent nature is never separate from his providence:

> For if, for example, we should say that God is silent, which is believed to be appropriate to his nature, how will anything be supposed to be made by him through silence? But now, therefore it is said that he has spoken, that men, since they know that the will of the one becomes known to another by this means, might acknowledge that those words which are delivered to them by the prophets are disclosures of God's will.[173]

Hence, in his providence, God talks "by dispositions that are common and known, so that men can understand."[174] His talk is on account of

---

170. Origen, *De Principiis* 1.3.1 (SC 252:144).
171. Origen, *De Principiis* 1.3.6 (SC 252:154).
172. Origen, *Homiliae in Genesim* 3.2 (SC 7bis:116).
173. Origen, *Homiliae in Genesim* 2.2 (SC 7bis:116).
174. Origen, *Homiliae in Genesim* 2.2.3 (SC 7bis:118).

his desire for us to understand the transcendent mysteries in accordance with the limits human intelligence.

Descending and Ascending God-Talk

Origen finds within Scripture, both the descending and ascending movements of God-Talk. With regard to the descending analogy, which we have just indicated, he says, "But in this manner God is said to have spoken to man: he either inspires the heart of each of the saints or causes the sound of voice to reach his ears."[175] Regarding the ascending capacity of human words to address God, he says, "So also [God] makes known that what each one says or does is known to him [when] the Scripture says that he 'has heard.'"[176] Scripture testifies that God hears what we say with words. When God confirms that he has heard what we say, he affirms the capacity of human words for self-transcendence, and stretching towards him. He also indicates elsewhere that Scripture confirms the ascending capacity of human nature for knowledge and speech about God:

> Although one is not able to speak worthily of God the Father, still it is possible to gain some notion of him from our experience of the visible creation and from the instinctive thoughts of the human mind; and moreover, it is possible for such knowledge to be confirmed from the Holy Scriptures.[177]

The knowledge of God via "our experience of visible creation" and "the instinctive thoughts of human mind" corresponds with our earlier discussion on Origen's metaphysical notion of participation of man in Being. As Kizewski says, "Though he is aware of the limitation of words, Origen never doubts their ability to bear meaning, [and] he extends this conviction to God-Talk in both senses of the phrase."[178] What is significant for our work is that Origen finds within the bible, both the descending and the ascending senses of God-Talk. It is an indication of *analogia entis* within *analogia fidei*.

In his reflections on naming God and creatures, we also find Origen's identification of ontological analogy *within* the biblical or spiritual "God-Talk." His "natural" analogy of participation, which is fundamentally a

---

175. Origen, *Homiliae in Genesim* 2.2.3 (SC 7bis:118).
176. Origen, *Homiliae in Genesim* 2.2.3 (SC 7bis:118).
177. Origen, *De Principiis* 1.3.1 (SC 252:144).
178. Kizewski, "God-Talk," 225.

participation in Christ the primordial Wisdom,[179] also corresponds with his understanding of how Scripture applies names to both God and creatures. He says, "If then there are any other things called good in the Scriptures, such as an angel, or man, or a slave, or a treasure, or a good heart, or a good tree, all these are so called by an inexact use of the word, since the goodness contained in them is accidental and not essential."[180] In the Bible, names are assigned to things according to their nature. When Scriptures apply the same name such as "goodness," and "wisdom" to creatures, it is only by virtue of their participation in divine Goodness and Wisdom,

> For in [creatures] Goodness does not reside essentially, as it does in God and his Christ and in the Holy Spirit. For only in this Trinity, which is the source of all things, does goodness reside essentially. Others possess it as an accident, liable to be lost, and only then do they live in blessedness, when they participate in holiness and wisdom and in the divine nature itself.[181]

Origen underscores not only the "accident-[al]" participation, which he says is "liable to be lost" by sin, but also the spiritual participation through the descending gift of divine nature in Christ. As Kizewski says, "In Origen, participation accounts for how things are said of creatures less precisely, inexactly, secondarily, and accidentally. In Origen, participation accounts for how things are said of creatures analogically."[182] When Scripture applies earthly or temporal words to God, they take on a spiritual and analogical meaning. Such biblical application of names to God and creatures is neither merely conventional nor arbitrary, but corresponds to the nature of the thing to which the name is addressed.

---

179. See Origen, *De Principiis* 1.3.8 (SC 252:162): "God the Father bestows on all the gift of existence; and a participation in Christ, in virtue of his being the word or reason, makes them rational."

180. Origen, *De Principiis* 1.2.13 (SC 252:142).

181. Origen, *De Principiis* 1.6.2 (SC 252:198). Origen is commenting on the eschatological consummation of all things (1 Cor 15:25–27) through the restoration of their blessedness and original goodness in Christ, which was lost by sin.

182. Kizewski, "God-Talk," 247.

Priority of Christ in Analogy of Scripture

In defense of the inspired character of the words of the prophets and the Law, Origen points to the analogical value of their poor and humble state as vessels of "concealing" the divine mystery: "The weakness of our understanding cannot discover the deep and hidden thoughts in every sentence; for the treasure of divine wisdom is *concealed* in vessels of poor and humble words."[183] On account of the limitation of human words, they serve as concealing vessels when God choses to communicate his truth through them. We can then locate the analogy of biblical words at the space where the poverty of words allow the exceeding greatness of divine thoughts to shine forth: "The greatness of the divine power may shine the more, when no taint of human eloquence is mingled with the truth of the doctrines."[184] The humble form of the biblical words validates them as appropriate vessels for the descending truth of God's Word.

For Origen, the "revelation" or un-concealment of the divine content of the prophetic words, is the work of Christ and his words. He says that "it was after the advent of Jesus that the inspiration of the prophetic words and the spiritual nature of Moses' law came to light. For before the advent of Christ it was not at all possible to bring forward clear proofs of the divine inspiration of the old scriptures."[185] Origen locates analogy of Scripture in Christ as the place of correspondence between the concealing and revelatory words of Scripture. The correspondence consists in the fact that "the words spoken in prophecy [were] about him" and "the words which announce his sojourning here and his teaching were spoken with all power and authority."[186] Faith in Christ becomes the illuminative key constituting the awareness of such analogy present in Scriptures as God's talk about himself. The hermeneutic principle operative in Origen's Christological hermeneutic is what he describes as "reading Scripture with Scripture": "If someone can, at leisure, bring together Scripture with Scripture, and compare divine Scripture, and fit together 'spiritual things with spiritual,' we are not unmindful that he will discover in this passage many secrets of profound and hidden mystery."[187]

---

183. Origen, *De Principiis* 4.1.7 (SC 268:398).
184. Origen, *De Principiis* 4.1.7 (SC 268:398).
185. Origen, *De Principiis* 4.1.6 (SC 268:397).
186. Origen, *De Principiis* 4.1.6 (SC 268:280).
187. Origen, *Homiliae in Genesim* 2.6 (SC 7bis:112).

In conclusion, the biblical focus of Origen's analogy of God-Talk highlits the ascending and descending movements of analogy in Christ. He presents the simplicity of biblical words as the standard bearer for the significance of humility in speaking well about and to God.

Clement of Alexandria

Like Irenaeus and Origen, Clement acknowledges the difficulty with speech about God, "for the God of the universe, who is above all speech, all conception, all thought, can never be committed to writing, being inexpressible even by his own power."[188] For him, Moses testifies to this difficulty, when he says "'Show thyself to me' (Exod 33:18)—intimating most clearly that God is not capable of being . . . expressed in speech";[189] and "when the Scripture says, 'Moses entered into the thick darkness where God was,' this shows that . . . God is invisible and beyond expression by words."[190] Clement not only expresses the difficulty of speaking about God but he also explains what the difficulty is. He says, "For how can that be expressed which is neither genus, nor difference, nor species, nor individual, nor event, nor that to which an event happens."[191] The difficulty with speaking about God consists in the inability of containing the inexpressible in the human categories of speech.

Clement uses the notion of *naming* things to demonstrate how we can still say something well about God. Philosophically, we cannot name God "properly" because "predicates are expressed either from what belongs to things themselves, or from their mutual relation."[192] Reason alone cannot name God according to his divine nature. But "on account of his greatness," we can rank him as "the All" and we can use terms "indicative of [his] power" as the All-powerful (omnipotent).[193] Kizewski rightly noted that Clement confirms this distinction elsewhere by speaking of the "difference between *declaring God*, and *declaring about God*."[194] For Clement, faith is significant in naming God as a descend-

---

188. Clement of Alexandria, *Strom.* 5.10 (PG 9:100A).
189. Clement of Alexandria, *Strom.* 5.11 (PG 9:109B).
190. Clement of Alexandria, *Strom.* 5.12 (PG 9:116B).
191. Clement of Alexandria, *Strom.* 5.12 (PG 9:121A).
192. Clement of Alexandria, *Strom.* 5.12 (PG 9:121B).
193. Clement of Alexandria, *Strom.* 5.12 (PG 9:124A).
194. Clement of Alexandria, *Strom.* 6.17 (SC 446:362); Kizewski, "God-Talk," 237.

ing illumination of our mind. Commenting on Paul's explanation of the Athenian altar "To the Unknown God," Clement says, "It remains that we understand, then, the Unknown, by divine grace, and by the word alone that proceeds from him."[195] We need divine grace through faith in Christ for the perfection of our human philosophical attempts to name the Unknown. The analogy of naming God, whereby we can philosophically speak *about* him in a partial way or more perfectly by faith, consists in the similarity and dissimilarity between philosophy and faith, which we earlier explained under the first patristic category, as neither a univocal not a strictly equivocal analogy.

We conclude with Clement's synthesis of both philosophical and theological God-Talk in the "grace of the son." He says,

> Everything then which falls under a name, is originated, whether they will or not. Whether, then the Father Himself draws to Himself everyone who has led a pure life, and has reached the conception of the blessed and incorruptible nature; or whether our freewill, by reaching the knowledge of the good, leaps and bounds over the barriers, as the gymnasts say; yet it is not without eminent grace the soul is winged, and soars, and is raised above the higher spheres, laying aside all that is heavy, and surrendering itself to its kindred element. . . "No one," says the Lord, "hath known the Father but the Son, and he to whom the Son reveal him" (Matt 11:27).[196]

Naming things "originates" from the "eminent grace" of the Son in two ways: either by the gift of created order or the gift of faith. Naming God, whether the Father reveals it himself to the blessed through faith, or the soul, through the exercise of natural freewill, "reaches the knowledge of the good," they originate from the Son, through whom the Father created all things and perfects them.

Gregory of Nyssa

According to Kizewski, "Gregory's own account of 'God-Talk' represents one of the clearest examples of analogy in the patristic patrimony."[197] He helps us to see the many ways in which Gregory articulates the apophatic

---

195. Clement of Alexandria, *Strom.* 5.12 (PG 9:124A).
196. Clement of Alexandria, *Strom.* 5.13 (PG 9:124B).
197. Kizewski, "God-Talk," 225.

grounds for God-Talk. Like Clement, Gregory interprets Moses' entry into the dark cloud, as a biblical example of the apophatic character of human knowledge and expression of God. He says, "the one who is going to associate intimately with God must be beyond all that is visible and believing that the divine is *there* where the understanding does not reach."[198] Like Clement, Gregory affirms reason's capacity to know "that God is," but not to know "what [God] is or how he exists."[199] Nevertheless, knowing what cannot be known is itself a kind of knowledge. Similarly, expressing with words that something is inexpressible is nonetheless, a disclosure of that thing with words. Gregory notes that we speak of God "insofar as it is possible to speak of him, given the poverty of our nature, which keeps the workings of the mind, undisclosed, unless they are brought into the open by voice and word."[200]

Kizewski highlights in great details, two significant ways in which Gregory articulates how Scripture uses analogy in God-Talk: first, we cannot speak about the "essence" of God, but we can apprehend things about him by analogy; second, Scriptures indicate both the descending and ascending movement of words in God-Talk.

Analogical Meaning of Biblical Words

According to Gregory, "if anyone should ask for some interpretation, and description, and explanation of the divine essence, we are not going to deny that in this kind of wisdom we are unlearned."[201] However, "whatever names we have learned to clarify the way we apprehend God, all such have something in common with and analogous to the kind of names which indicate the individuality of a particular man."[202] Gregory considers our knowledge and speech about God as analogous to how our acquaintance with the "characteristics" of a person does not equate to our knowledge of his "inward nature": "Those who describe the unknown person by some recognizable characteristics . . . do not describe the

---

198. Gregory of Nyssa, *De vita Moysis* 1.46 (SC 1:84).
199. Gregory of Nyssa, *Contra Eunomium* 2.97 (SC 551:168).
200. Gregory of Nyssa, *Contra Eunomium* 2.161 (SC 551:208).
201. Gregory of Nyssa, *Contra Eunomium* 3.5 (PG 45:601B).
202. Gregory of Nyssa, *Contra Eunomium* 2.104 (SC 551:172): "Εἰ γάρ τι πρὸς δήλωσιν τῆς θείας κατανοήσεως μεμαθήκαμεν ὄνομα, πάντα ταῦτα κοινωνίαν ἔχει καὶ ἀναλογίαν πρὸς τὰ τοιαῦτα τῶν ὀνομάτοω, ἃ τοῦ τινὸς ἀνθρώπου τὴν ἰδιότητα δείκνυσιν."

inward nature of the one described, but some characteristics known about him."²⁰³ Similarly, this is how the Scriptures help us by use of analogy to become well acquainted with the Person of God, whom we never knew before, without claiming to know his nature. For instance, "all the words found in Holy Scriptures to indicate God's glory describe some feature of God, each providing particular emphasis"²⁰⁴ without meddling with his essence. According to Kizewski, "the fault of Eunomius's words, including his Arianism, is that there is nothing said unequivocally concerning the being of God. Things are said not unequivocally. Gregory then can be taken to mean . . . a kind of less-than-strict equivocity, namely, one that is analogical."²⁰⁵

Descending and Ascending Movement of Words in Scripture

Like Origen, Gregory indicates how the descent and ascent of inspired words of Scripture, whereby the divine transcendent mystery assumes human concepts in words, is a function of the providential dispensation of the Holy Spirit. For him, Scripture draws upon the analogy of "generation," to speak in different ways of the mystery of God's creation of the world and the eternal generation of the Son. To underscore the spiritual character of this analogy, he says,

> And now that we have distinguished the various modes of generation, it will be time to remark how the benevolent dispensation of the Holy Spirit (τοῦ ἁγίου πνεύματος οἰκονομία), in delivering to us the divine mysteries, imparts that instruction which transcends reason by such methods as we can receive. For the inspired teachings adopts, in order to set forth the unspeakable power of God, all the forms of generation that human intelligence recognizes, yet without including the corporeal senses attaching to the words.²⁰⁶

The "benevolent dispensation of the Holy Spirit," gives a new intelligibility to the human concept of "generation" when applied in an analogous way to the eternal generation of the Son. The Holy Spirit, who enables human concepts to communicate divine truths, renders the analogous

203. Gregory of Nyssa, *Contra Eunomium* 2.105 (SC 551:172).
204. Gregory of Nyssa, *Contra Eunomium* 2.105 (SC 551:172).
205. Kizewski, "God-Talk," 252.
206. Gregory of Nyssa, *Contra Eunomium* 2.9 (PG 45:505D, 508A).

character of such a concept to be spiritual. Gregory highlights the analogical meaning of the term generation, which can convey both the mode of God's creation of the world, and communicate the eternal generation of the Son from the Father. In both cases, there is a condescension of divine meaning to human concepts, "For when it speaks of the creative power, it gives to such an energy the name of generation, because its expression must stoop to our low capacity."[207] The descending movement consists in the "stooping to our low capacity" of the divine transcendent mystery of creating the world. About the condescension of "transcendent existence of the Only-begotten" to the name "Son," Gregory says,

> Again when it interprets to us the unspeakable and transcendent existence of the Only-Begotten from the Father, as the poverty of human intellect is incapable of receiving doctrines which surpass all power of speech and thought, there too it borrows our language and terms him "Son"—a name which our usage assigns to those who are born of matter and nature.[208]

When Scripture uses words like "creation" or "generation," they are descending analogies whereby God descends to the level of human words to express his creative power and the mystery of his existence. Simultaneously, the lowering of divine mystery to human words, in turn, elevates the words by moving them from their temporal and metaphorical meaning to a new analogical meaning: "when using the term Son, it rejects both all here below,—I mean affections and dispositions and the co-operation of time, and the necessity of place,—and, above all, matter, without all which natural generation here below does not take place."[209] The elevation of the word "son" from its "material and temporal" meaning of generating a son, to "Son" as "community of nature alone"[210] is a movement from material to its *conceptual meaning*. Conceptual meaning of temporal terms can "reasonably be transferred to the expression of divine conceptions."[211]

---

207. Gregory of Nyssa, *Contra Eunomium* 2.9.2 (PG 45:508A): "διὰ τὸ δεῖς πρὸς τὸ ταπεινὸν τῆς ἡμετέρας δυνάμεως καταβῆναι τὸν λόγον."

208. Gregory of Nyssa, *Contra Eunomium* 2.9.2 (PG 45:508B).

209. Gregory of Nyssa, *Contra Eunomium* 2.9.2 (PG 45:508C).

210. Gregory of Nyssa, *Contra Eunomium* 2.9.2 (PG 45:508C).

211. Gregory of Nyssa, *Contra Eunomium* 2.9.4 (PG 45:510B).

Primacy of Christ's Talk

Eunomius once claimed that all biblical words are provided by God directly in a univocal way, and considers the use of philosophical concepts for speaking about God to be illegitimate because they are not in Scriptures.[212] Gregory offers his objections in two ways: by argument from self-contradiction and argument from the primacy of Christ's words.

First, Eunomius accused Gregory and Basil of equivocal or analogical application of their own conceptual words to God. Gregory quotes Eunomius's accusation, "To put forward equivocity based on analogy, he [Eunomius] says, as the basis of human conceptualization, is the work of a mind which has discarded the valid, correct meaning and considers the words of the Lord to have an invalid meaning and a sort of debased usage."[213] Gregory objects to his claim as self-defeating because Eunomius himself speaks of God with the conceptual term "unbegottenness," which Gregory says, is not used by the Scriptures. He asks,

> But are you able to find any reference in any of the ancient writers to the word "unbegottenness," or to its being used as the name of the actual being of God, "or rather that the Unbegotten is itself the Being." . . . Eunomius attacks the conceptual account, while himself using conceptual words to argue that one should not say anything conceptually.[214]

With Eunomius's self-contradiction so evident, Kizewski concludes that, for Gregory, "the argument that some philosophically inspired enlightening term is illegitimate [in exegesis] because it is not in Scriptures, is not a valid one."[215]

Second, Gregory also argued from what indicates the primacy of Christ's words. He argues that if Christ uses conceptual words to speak about himself, so must we because he affirms the use of human mind in his own humanity. He says, "How then are our words refuted if it is said that Christ uses these titles himself? The question was not about who used the titles; our purpose was rather to consider what the titles mean, whether they denote the nature, or whether they are applied conceptually

---

212. See Kizewski, "God-Talk," 253–54.
213. Gregory of Nyssa, *Contra Eunomium* 2.306 (SC 551:308).
214. Gregory of Nyssa, *Contra Eunomium* 2.310 (SC 551:308–10).
215. Kizewski, "God-Talk," 254.

on the basis of action."²¹⁶ As Kizewski rightly said, "That Christ applies words conceptually, or analogically, to himself gives us confidence that we can do the same."²¹⁷ For Gregory, while God remains the *cause* of all things, including that of naming things, however, the *power* to name things is inherently a function of human nature:

> So therefore the cause of our giving names to God, who is by his nature what he is, is by general consent attributable to God himself; but the power of giving names of one sort and another to all the things that come into our minds, lies in our nature, and whether one chooses to call it conceptual thought or something else, we shall not dissent.²¹⁸

We have already explained how Scripture applies the name "Son" as a divine concept. However, the mind's capacity to apply conceptual comparisons to God does not mean that conceptual thought is the source of a divine name. The application of the concept "Son" to the divine simply confirms that conceptual use of words, which inherently pertains to the power of created reason is indispensable for the minds articulation of its perceptions, either from reason or infused by faith. A conceptual perception cannot claim knowledge of the essence of what it perceives, but can articulate its intention by analogy between naming things and naming God.

By deferring to Christ's analogical talk about himself for his defense of philosophical conception, Gregory recapitulates our discoveries on patristic primacy of Christ. He affirms Christ as the grounds for the analogy between philosophy and theology, image and participation, human and divine words. His words confirm in a primary way, the use of analogy between God and creatures for clarifying the meaning of truth through conceptual comparisons.

Conclusion

The patristic notions of *semina Verbi*, *spolia Aegyptiaca* and *Verbum abbreviatum*, which Ratzinger references, introduce the collective referential continuity between the ancient authors and Joseph Ratzinger. Between Origen's "seeds of wisdom" and Justin Martyr's "Seed of the Word,"

216. Gregory of Nyssa, *Contra Eunomium* 2.354 (SC 551:336).
217. Kizewski, "God-Talk," 255.
218. Gregory of Nyssa, *Contra Eunomium* 2.396 (SC 551:364).

an identification of the pre-Christian seeds of the Word emerged in our study of participation by analogy of reason. The seeds of the Word signify the ontic dimension of how various philosophical cultures participate in Christ the Word; hence, analogy of being. Ratzinger rightly concludes, "The Church Fathers found the seeds of the Word, not in the religions of the world, but rather in philosophy, that is, in the process of critical reason."[219]

The ecumenical significance of *spolia Aegyptiaca*, which consists in its indication of *analogia entis* within *analogia scripturae* offers an insight into our investigation of the patristic roots of the use of analogy in Ratzinger's primacy of Christ. We also discovered under our study of Origen's and Gregory of Nyssa's God-Talk, another evidence of *analogia entis* within *analogia fidei*. The two ancient authors find in Scriptures a Christocentric movement of both descending and ascending analogy. What they indicated is not different from how Ratzinger describes *analogia entis* within *analogia fidei* in his commentary on the universalism of Balthasar: "The religions of Canaan, of Babylonia and of Egypt, the political and cultural influence of the ancient near East: all of these are truly present in the human word with which God speaks."[220]

Irenaeus's and Tyconuis's thoughts on image and recapitulation are most representative of how the ancient authors use the notion of image to demonstrate the primacy of the Incarnation. Ratzinger's reference to the patristic patrimony on the analogy of "image," which conveys the primacy of Christ in God's intention to create will play a significant role in our study of Ratzinger's notion of image in chapter 4. With regard to the concept of participation, the pneumatic character of participation is predominantly evident in our study. The patristic use of analogy is comprehensive in the way they understand participation as presupposing and perfecting the ontological similarity between God and creature. Using the biblical and Stoic concept of anointing, Justin and Origen demonstrates the particularly pneumatic character of participation in a Christocentric way. While Origen and Justin Martyr use the term participation to signify what will later be called analogies of being and of faith, Irenaeus, who uses *likeness* in a similar way includes the corporeal dimension in man's

---

219. Benedict XVI/Ratzinger, *On the Way*, 72; *Beiträge zur Christologie*, 1007.

220. Benedict XVI/Ratzinger, *Beiträge zur Christologie*, 1056: "Die Religionen Kanaans, Babylons, Ägyptens, der politisch und kulturelle Einfluss des Vorderen Orients: all das ist in dem Menschenwort, in dem Gott redet, wirklich vorhanden" (my translation).

orientation toward "becoming like God." Both participation and likeness highlights the dynamic orientation of the soul toward perfection. This orientation of the soul explained by Granados to be characteristic of Stoic pneumatic cosmology sheds light into Justin Martyr's pneumatic notion of participation. Thus, the spiritual character of the patristic use of "participation" and "becoming like God" as analogical terms, bear a dynamic and comprehensive meaning.

Chapter 2

The Fathers whom Ratzinger Quotes

IN EXAMINING THE INDIVIDUAL Fathers and the ancient ecclesiastical authors whom Ratzinger quotes explicitly, we present the "specific referential continuity" of the patristic patrimony in Ratzinger's theology. While Ratzinger quotes a broad range of ancient authors on different topics, our concern is with those to whom he directs his readers on how the use of analogy confirms Christ's primacy.

Truth in Faith, Philosophy, and Politics

Justin Martyr, Origen, and Augustine are the three main ancient authors whom Ratzinger quotes on the analogy of faith and reason.

Justin Martyr: Primacy of Logos

Ratzinger finds in Justin the "mark" of "the ancient Church's forceful option for philosophy, for reason, rather than for the religion of the pagans."[1] Justin's primary concern is the question of truth. In his first *Apologia,* he argues for the priority of reason over mythical religions. He says, "Reason dictates that those who are truly pious and philosophical should honor and love only the truth, declining to follow the opinions of the ancients, if they are worthless."[2] "Love" for "the truth" guided by reason is the measure of true philosophy and religious opinions. He did not see in the pagan myths a consistency with the truth as it is the case

---

1. Benedict XVI/Ratzinger, *Church Fathers,* 19.
2. Justin Martyr, *Apologia* 1.2.2 (SC 507:128).

with Greek philosophy. Justin saw in the pagan myths absence of "the form of God"[3] who "formed all things out of unformed matter" and is himself not made.[4] The truth of God cannot be formed by human hands since the pagans make images of gods with material things.

Justin Martyr presents the similarity between faith and reason in three principal ways: (1) the significance of reason in speaking well of God; (2) the absence of contradiction in the wisdom of Christ; (3) Christianity is the true philosophy.

First, in Justin's consideration of the significance of reason in "speaking well" of God, while God remains unknowable and thus unnamable, created reason is still capable of intuiting from God's good deeds, names of God: "But these words Father, and God, and Creator, and Lord and Master, are not names, but appellations derived from His good deeds ... the intuition implanted in human nature of an inexpressible reality."[5] On the one hand, this intuition of natural wisdom about supernatural realities is within the limits of its capacity for expressing an inexpressible reality by means of human words. On the other hand, Justin affirms the fundamental principle of reason, as grounds for the capacity of reason for "speaking well" of the truth, but only in a way proportional to its participation in the Divine Logos. He says, "For each one of them—[philosophers, poets and historians], seeing, through participation of the seminal Divine Word, what was related to it, spoke very well."[6] The things not well spoken of the truth are indicative of the limits of reason without the aid of revelation.

Second, Justin's argument for the philosophical principle of non-contradiction in the wisdom of Christ, hinges primarily upon the significance of typology for the true meaning of Scriptures. He first considers illegitimate any investigation of the coherence of Christian wisdom through the heretical teachings of the Marcionites, Valentinians, Basilians and Saturnilians. For him, such false teachings "profess not [Christ's] doctrines."[7] Crucial to his rejection of these heresies is their lack of any robust sense of the unity of Scriptures. Commenting on the unity of Scriptures in his *Dialogue with Trypho*, he says to him:

---

3. Justin Martyr, *Apologia* 1.9.1 (SC 507:146–47).
4. Justin Martyr, *Apologia* 1.10.2 (SC 507:151).
5. Justin Martyr, *Apologia* 2.6.2 (SC 507:332) [*First Apology; Second Apology*].
6. Justin Martyr, *Apologia* 2.13.3 (SC 507:362).
7. Justin Martyr, *Dialogus cum Tryphone* 35 (PG 6:551).

> But you are sadly mistaken if you did so in the hope of embarrassing me into admitting that some passages of Scripture contradict others, for I would not be so bold as to assert, or even imagine, such a thing. If such a passage were quoted, and apparently contradicted another (since I am positive that no passage contradicts another), I would rather openly confess that I do not know the meaning of the passage, and I shall do my utmost to have my opinion shared by those who imagine that the Scriptures are sometimes contradictory.[8]

Arguing from typology, Justin shows methodically how the figure of Christ is continuously present in a veiled form throughout the Old Testament, and how he unifies them. He sees Christ as the fulfillment of the prophets, for "what the prophets said or did they often expressed in parables and types, thus hiding the truth they held."[9] The Patriarchs do not belong only to the Hebrews, but to all Christians who are children of Abraham by faith and the gems of the promise. For Justin, the words of Christ bear the fullness of understanding clouded in the passages of the Old Testament. Justin's Christocentric explanation of the absence of contradiction in Scripture underscores the coherence of a philosophical principle with the hermeneutic of faith.

Finally, for Justin, philosophical inquiry, which is supposed to be for "a clear understanding of the truth,"[10] finds its goal in Christ. As already indicated, for the Martyr, the primacy of "the Logos of whom all mankind partakes"[11] is the principle of fundamental similarity between faith and reason. He calls "Christians," all "those who lived by reason" and were persecuted for it, such as Socrates and Heraclitus: "Those who lived by reason are Christians, even though they have been considered atheists."[12] He sees Christianity as the true philosophy. For him, the Christian God is the same as the God of reason, by whom the philosophers lived their lives in a partial way. Yet, he insists that Greek philosophers did not benefit from a supernatural revelation as the Hebrew prophets, since contemplation of the truth by unaided human reason is incapable of achieving on its own the content of revealed truth. According to Joseph Carola, Justin

---

8. Justin Martyr, *Dialogus cum Tryphone* 65 (PTS 47:182).

9. Justin Martyr, *Dialogus cum Tryphone* 90 (PG 6:690).

10. Justin Martyr, *Dialogus cum Tryphone* 3 (PTS 47:75) [*First Apology; Second Apology*].

11. Justin Martyr, *Apologia* 1.46.2 (SC 507:250).

12. Justin Martyr, *Apologia* 1.46.3 (SC 507:250).

accounts for the "elements of divine or supernatural revelation present in Greek thought" by relying on "a notion that afterwards becomes standard among the Church Fathers: the Greeks practiced plagiarism."[13] The Martyr says: "To let you know that Plato plagiarized from our teachers—the prophets—when he affirmed that God changed shapeless matter and created the world, listen to the authentic words of Moses, who was mentioned above as the first of the Prophets and older than the writers of Greece."[14]

Justin's assertion of the essential difference between Greek philosophy and the faith of the prophets indicates their inner unity as that of analogy. It is the light of Christian faith that fully reveals this analogy between philosophy and revealed truth as dependent on the primordial Logos, who is Christ. Neither philosophy alone nor the Hebrew faith was able to do so in its complete form. Benedict XVI finds in Justin's Christocentric harmony between faith and reason, the similarity between the God of philosophers and the God of faith:

> For Justin if the Old Testament leaned toward Christ, just as the symbol is a guide to the reality represented, then Greek philosophy also aspired to Christ and the Gospel, just as the part strives to be united with the whole. . . . The Old Testament and Greek philosophy, are like two paths that lead to Christ and the *Logos*.[15]

Origen: Faith and Politics

In his debate with the Hellenist Celsus, Origen uses the analogy of faith and reason to argue that Christ is the original and common unity of all nations. Celsus accused Christians of defying the authority of national identity over religious and political laws.[16] He claims that the origin of nation states is divine, and considers Israel a nation among nations. On the contrary, Origen considers the origin of national identity to be a

---

13. Carola, "Non-Christians in Patristic Theology," 36.
14. Justin Martyr, *Apologia* 1.59 (SC 507:282).
15. Benedict XVI/Ratzinger, *Church Fathers*, 19.
16. Origen, *Contra Celsum* 5.33 (PG 11:1229C); Benedict XVI/Ratzinger, *Unity of Nations*, 35–36. For Celsus, Christians defied the law of their nation (Jewish nation) given by God for the governance of religious and political laws, "I would like to ask them where they came from and who the author of their fatherland's laws is. They cannot produce him. They are from there [i.e., Judaism] and they have their teacher and leader from nowhere else. They are fallen-away Jews."

departure from the original unity of all peoples prior to the Tower of Babel, and sees Israel as the custodian of original unity all of nations. In doing so, he exonerates the Christian faith from subjugation to what Celsus claims to be their national identity. Celsus considered Christians as "fallen-away Jews" and he reduced Christian identity to a rebellion against Jewish national identity.[17] In his *Unity of Nations*, Ratzinger offers a detailed analysis of Origen's philosophy of nations in a way that it highlights the priority of Christ in faith and reason.

Priority of Faith over National Identity

According to Origen, national cultures owe their existence to the two constitutive elements of a nation: *language* and *land*. With regard to language, he makes the distinction between the divine language and native languages. The "divine language" is the original unifying language of all peoples, symbolized by the original language of the east: "All the people upon the earth are to be regarded as having one divine language, and so long as they lived harmoniously together were preserved in the use of this divine language, and they remained without moving from the east so long as they were imbued with the sentiments . . . of the reflection of the eternal light."[18] Divine language is a spiritual concept that connotes fidelity to the "reflection of eternal light." On the other hand, "native languages," also understood spiritually, indicate departure from the reflection of the eternal light: "But when they departed from the east, and began to entertain sentiments alien to those of the east . . . they were conducted by those angels, who imprinted on each his native language, to the different parts of the earth."[19] Acquisition of a native language indicates a departure from the east to a "land" devoid of the support of eternal light: "But when they departed from the east . . . they found a place in the land of Shinar (which, when interpreted, means 'gnashing of the teeth,' by way of indicating symbolically that they have lost the means of their support) and in it took up their abode."[20] Thus, departure from the unity of divine language, symbolized by a departure from the east, explains the two constitutive elements of national identity: native language and land.

---

17. Origen, *Contra Celsum* 5.33 (PG 11:1229C).
18. Origen, *Contra Celsum* 5.30 (PG 11:1225C).
19. Origen, *Contra Celsum* 5.30 (PG 11:1227A).
20. Origen, *Contra Celsum* 5.30 (PG 11:1225D).

Origen's spiritual hermeneutic of national identity presents a negative origin of nations and their political laws. National identity involves a departure from governance of the divine to the governance of the "princes of the world" (*archons*), who serve as angels of the peoples.[21] These rulers or princes correspond to powers of disorder and disunity of humanity. For Origen, Israel does not share the burden of a national identity because it retained the "original language" and divine governance by remaining "the portion of the Lord" and stayed in the east:

> Those who preserved their original language continued, by reason of their not having migrated from the east, in possession of the east, and of their eastern language. And let him notice, that these alone became the portion of the Lord, and His people who were called Jacob, and Israel the cord of His inheritance; and these alone were governed by a ruler who did not receive those who were placed under him for the purpose of punishment, as was the case with others.[22]

Origen considers Israel the "portion of the Lord," not a nation among other nations. According to Ratzinger, "Origen realized from the outset that the problem of national identity had nothing to do with Israel; it was never a nation in any real sense . . . but instead had remained what all others could and should have been—namely, humanity in direct relationship with God."[23] Faith is what offers this direct relationship with God and is the original divine language. The faith of Israel understood as the preserver of the divine language common and original to all humanity, is prior to the multiplication of nations. By relieving Israel of the burden of national identity, Origen lays the foundation for clarifying the relationship between the Christian faith and the national identity of many nations.

For Origen, Christ is the fulfillment of the faith of Israel, which maintained the original divine language. He presents Jesus as the righteous ruler of the primordial unity of the human family: "Jesus, [is] the one possessed of the greatest power, who has rescued us 'from the present

---

21. Origen, *De Principiis* 3.3.1 (PG 11:314B). The angels represented by the "princes of this world" and the powers of disorder, are bad angels. They are distinct from the good angels represented by Moses and the prophets, apostles and teachers, whose labors lead peoples to the one inheritance of Jesus Christ. See Origen, *Commentary* 13.46.

22. Origen, *Contra Celsum* 5.31 (PG 11:1228B).

23. Benedict XVI/Ratzinger, *Unity of Nations*, 39–40.

evil world,' and 'from the princes of the world that come to naught.'"[24] The salvific work of Jesus consists in liberating people from the "prison of national identity into the unity of God and into the unity of a common humanity."[25] For example, when state law is contrary to the Law of God's Word, Origen argues that Christians have no problem choosing the Law of Christ because it is more divine. For instance, if a public duty inhibits Christians from their service to Christ, "it is not for the purpose of escaping public duties that Christians decline public offices, but that they may reserve themselves for a more divine and more necessary service in the Church of God—for the salvation of men."[26] The Christian rejection of the absolute rule of state law is not based on their rejection of the divine plan for the governance of the cosmos, but is based on the claim that the Son of God has come to call peoples out of the disorder and power mongering of the nations to the original unity and peace among peoples.[27]

Origen's identification of Christ as "the divine and original language" of all peoples, demonstrates the analogical nature of how peoples of many nations are united in God. Christ is the primordial center of this unity. With Christ as the center, Origen's close association of "divine language" with "original language" confirms that what is most "original" about national languages and identities is relative to the divine original intention for the unity of peoples. The ascent of national languages to the divine language is by analogy, and Christ is the bearer of the primordial language intended by God for all people. Origen suggests that Christian identity, which is at the service of the human ascent to what is original and divinely oriented, takes primacy over national identity.

---

24. Origen, *Contra Celsum* 5.32 (PG 11:1229B).

25. See Origen, *Contra Celsum* 8.75 (PG 11:1629B); Benedict XVI/Ratzinger, *Unity of Nations*, 46. For Ratzinger, Origen considers the Christian mission of leading humanity to their original unity to be an eschatological mission to the extent that it involves the end of the absolute rule of state law and the beginning of a new fatherland based on God's Word: "We recognize in each state the existence of another national organization (σύστημα πατρίδος, the primitive churches), founded by the Word of God.... And those who rule over us well are under the constraining influence of the great King, whom we believe to be the Son of God, God the Word."

26. Origen, *Contra Celsum* 8.75 (PG 11:1629C).

27. See Origen, *Contra Celsum* 5.37 (PG 11:1237).

Primacy of Reason in Politics

In his exegesis of 1 Corinthians 2:6 Origen demonstrates a positive view of national identity by identifying the presence of some "philosophical wisdom" within the political "wisdom of the rulers of this world." According to Origen, Paul had described three kinds of wisdom: "He describes one as a 'wisdom of this world,' one as a 'wisdom of the rulers of this world,' and another as 'God's wisdom.'"[28] The "wisdom of this world" deals with the knowledge of human arts and sciences devoid of philosophical or theological meaning in and of themselves.[29] Instances of human wisdom are "the arts of poetry, grammar, rhetoric, geometry, and music, to which we should probably add the art of medicine."[30] For Origen, the "wisdom of the rulers of this world" is a reference to the vestiges of philosophy operative in the governance of particular nations.

> As for the wisdom of the "rulers of this world," we understand this to be what they call the secret and hidden philosophy of the Egyptians and the astrology of the Chaldeans and Indians, who profess a knowledge of high things, and further the manifold and diverse opinions of the Greeks concerning the divine nature.[31]

For Origen, Scriptures recognize a certain philosophical wisdom present in the opinions of the particular rulers of this world such as the "Queen of the South" who came from the ends of the earth to hear Solomon (Matt 7:42), the "Prince of the kingdom of the Persians and of the Greeks" (Dan 10:13, 20), and the "Prince of Tyre" (Ezra 28).[32] However, Origen also addresses how Scripture confirms that these philosophies are liable to error without the guidance of Christian faith. The error of the rulers of nations consists in substituting their particular opinions for the whole truth. These rulers contrived against Christ, not out of their rejection of wisdom, but because they thought that Christ came to destroy the doctrines governing all nations.[33] Origen maintains the positive Pauline

---

28. Origen, *De Principiis* 3.3.1 (PG 11:313C); Benedict XVI/Ratzinger, *Unity of Nations*, 53.

29. Origen, *De Principiis* 3.3.2 (PG 11:314–15).

30. Origen, *De Principiis* 3.3.2 (PG 11:315A).

31. Origen, *De Principiis* 3.3.2 (PG 11:315A).

32. Cf. Origen, *De Principiis* 3.3.1–2 (PG 11:315B).

33. Origen, *De Principiis* 3.3.2–3 (PG 11:315B): "When these, therefore, and other similar princes of this world, each having his own individual wisdom and formulating

approach that if the rulers of the world had known Christ to be the true wisdom, they would not have crucified him (1 Cor 2:6–8). The political philosophies of particular nations have a preparatory role on account of their "relative innocence" prior to the Incarnation.[34]

Origen's positive view of the role of reason in politics is more evident in his giving faith and reason priority over state laws. He considers the law of nature to be the law of God, which takes priority over the law of the cities:

> As there are, then, generally two laws presented to us, the one being the law of nature, of which God would be the legislator, and the other being the written law of cities, it is a proper thing, when the written law is not opposed to that of God, for the citizens not to abandon it under pretext of foreign customs; but when the law of nature, that is, the law of God, commands what is opposed to the written code, observe whether reason will not tell us to bid a long farewell to the written code, and to the desires of its legislators, and to give ourselves up to the legislator God, and to choose a life agreeable to His Word.[35]

Politics is at its best when it is in harmony with the law of reason, which is the law gifted by God to created nature. Origen insists that the Christian God is the same as the God of the law of nature. When the law of the state is in conflict with the law of reason, Christian faith and philosophy share the same task of giving reason priority over state law.[36] If a philosopher acquiesces to a national superstitious custom when it is contrary to reason, "he would be a ridiculous philosopher, acting very unphilosophically."[37] Ratzinger comments that for Origen, "faith in Christ" discloses for the first time, the "true meaning" of the primal law of nature because Christ

---

his own doctrines and peculiar opinions, saw our Lord and Savior promising and proclaiming that he had come into the world for the purpose of destroying all doctrines ... they immediately laid snares for him, not knowing who was concealed within him." With regard to their confusion of "the truth" with a philosophical wisdom, Origen says, "the rulers of this world think their wisdom to be true and are therefore anxious to teach others what in their opinion is the truth." Christian faith is not built on any philosophical ideology but on the truth itself, who is Christ.

34. Benedict XVI/Ratzinger, *Unity of Nations*, 55.

35. Origen, *Contra Celsum* 5.37 (PG 11:1237B).

36. Origen, *Contra Celsum* 5.35 (PG 11:1236A).

37. Origen, *Contra Celsum* 5.35 (PG 11:1236B); cf. Benedict XVI/Ratzinger, *Unity of Nations*, 61–62.

is the Word through whom the logic of nature came to be.[38] Christian faith discloses that the "original unity" of all nations literally refers to the "original reason" of creation.

In Origen's political philosophy, faith and philosophy find a common ground in "reason," which is the primary analogy between God and creatures. As Origen explained, to the extent that the Christian God has been present in a preliminary way in Greek philosophy, He is not a "new" God: "For the Son of God, 'the First-born of all creation,' although he seemed recently to have become incarnate is not by any means on that account new."[39] When Christians act in the same way as philosophers by rejecting unreasonable political laws, they act according to the law of the same God of the cosmos. The analogy of reason, where faith and philosophy converge, points to Christ as the fullness of reason.

Augustine's Theory of Illumination

The primary analogy Augustine uses to articulate the epistemological relationship of faith and reason is the analogy of "light." In his theory of knowledge, he speaks of two distinct but interrelated illuminations of the mind: the light of reason and the light of faith. Augustine grounds his analogy of light on the "priority of the truth." The unity of truth is contained in the one divine illumination, and creation partakes in this one truth by the light of reason and the light of faith.

The Analogy of Light and the Priority of Christ

According to Justin Kizewski "in place of 'analogy,' Augustine often employs 'similitude.'"[40] Augustine considers the use of similitude a significant pedagogical tool because it makes more readily perceptible, things that are difficult for the mind to discover. He says, "For the present, however, no one doubts that things are perceived more readily through similitudes and that what is sought with difficulty is discovered with more pleasure."[41] The "similitude of light" is one of the primary analogies by which he sought to facilitate the mind's discovery of the priority of truth

---

38. Benedict XVI/Ratzinger, *Unity of Nations*, 60–61.
39. Origen, *Contra Celsum* 5.37 (PG 11;1237D, 1240A).
40. Kizewski, "God-Talk," 280.
41. Augustine, *Doctr. chr.* 2.5.8 (PL 34:39).

as the primacy of Christ. Commenting on the *similitudine* between the rational and divine illumination, he says, "So, for those things taught in the sciences, which everyone acknowledges without a shadow of doubt that they are true, one must also believe that they cannot be known unless they are illuminated by something else corresponding to the sun."[42] Just as the light of the sun is prior to human physical vision, so also the intellectual light is prior to the created intellect itself. Augustine's comparison of the external origin common to both the physical and intellectual light, underscores that the intellectual light originates from God, not from created reason itself. In other words, to the extent that "[Christ] is to the soul what the sun is to the eye,"[43] there is a priority of Christ to all human cognition. Augustine's explanation of the analogy present in the relationship between the epistemic illumination and Christ also corresponds with the three properties of being also known as the "transcendentals": truth, goodness, and beauty.

The Priority of Truth in the Light of Reason

For Augustine, truth and light are analogous terms relative to creatures. He sees in the perpetual character of the principles of reason, evidence of the priority of truth before understanding. Augustine says, "The truth of valid inference was not instituted by men; rather it was observed by men and set down that they might learn or teach it. For it is perpetually instituted by God in the reasonable order of things."[44] He indicates that the perpetual character of the principles of logic is analogous to the

---

42. Augustine, *Solil.* 1.8.15 (PL 32:877) ["Soliloquies"]: "Nunc accipe, quantum praesens tempus exposcit, ex illa *similitudine* sensibilium etiam de Deo aliquid nunc me docente. Intellegibilis nempe Deus est, intellegibilia etiam illa disciplinarum spectamina; tamen plurimum differunt. Nam et terra visibilis, et lux; sed terra, nisi luce illustrata, videri non potest. Ergo et illa quae in disciplinis traduntur, quae quisquis intellegit, verissima esse nulla dubitatione concedit, credendum est ea non posse intellegi, nisi ab alio quasi suo sole illustrentur." Augustine explains the similitude as follows: "Ergo quomodo in hoc sole tria quaedam licet animadvertere; quod est, quod fulget, quod illuminat: ita in illo secretissimo Deo quem vis intellegere, tria quaedam sunt; quod est, quod intellegitur, et quod caetera facit intellegi"; "Therefore, just as one notices three things about the sun, that it exists, it shines, it illumines, so also in knowing the hidden God, you must observe three things; that He exists, He is known and He causes other things to be known."

43. Nash, *Light of the Mind*, 92.

44. Augustine, *Doctr. chr.* 2.32.50 (PL 34:58) [*On Christian Doctrine*].

eternal nature of the divine truth. The truth content of the principles of logic reflects the divine truth because truth of created realities originates from God: "Reality is knowable because it was created by God after the pattern of the divine ideas."[45]

Augustine also considers the objectivity of mathematics as an indicator of how reason reflects the perpetual order of divine forms. He says, "The law and truth of numbers is present to all who reason. . . . Their truth presents itself equally to all who can grasp it. . . . When a man makes a mistake about it, he does not change it, the truth does not fail but remains entirely true, while he is in error in proportion to his failure to see it."[46] The objectivity of the truth of numbers makes it comprehensible to all rational beings in an unalterable way, thus accounting for the "oneness of truth." The mind's recognition of the objectivity of the logic and mathematics is a function of an "inner light": "By what idea or image do we see so sure a truth so confidently throughout innumerable instances, unless we do it by an inner light, unknown to the bodily senses."[47] This "inner light," which enables reason to perceive the objectivity of truth is the light of reason. Teaching and learning presupposes the presence of the light of reason, by which we possess knowledge of *a priori* (independent of experience) truths. He says,

> Concerning the universals of which we can have knowledge, we do not listen to anyone speaking and making sounds outside ourselves. We listen to Truth which presides over our minds within us, though of course we may be bidden to listen to someone using words. Our real Teacher is he who is said to dwell in the inner man, namely Christ, that is, the unchangeable power and eternal wisdom of God.[48]

The "real Teacher" who dwells in the inner man as the inner light of truth, is Christ. By this inner light, reason recognizes the object of its desire as something prior to it—the Truth. Augustine asks, "What does the soul desire more than truth?"[49] In response, he says, "I [Christ] give each what

---

45. Nash, *Light of the Mind*, 77.
46. Augustine, *Lib. arb.* 2.8.20 (PL 32:1251).
47. Augustine, *Lib. arb.* 2.8.23 (PL 32:1253).
48. Augustine, *Mag.* 11.38 (PL 32:1216) [LCC 6].
49. Augustine, *Tract. Ev. Io.* 26.5, 6 (PL 35:1609) ["Homilies on the Gospel of St. John"]. "Quid enim fortius desiderat anima quam veritatem? Quo avidas fauces habere debet, unde optare ut sanum sit intus palatum vera iudicandi, nisi ut manducet et bibat sapientiam, iustitiam, veritatem, aeternitatem?"

he loves, I give each the object of his hope."[50] For him, Christ, who is the indwelling of the truth in the light of reason, is the object of the soul's desire.

THE PRIMACY OF GOODNESS IN MORAL ILLUMINATION

In Augustine's writings, the light of reason pertains not only to logic and mathematical principles but also to moral ethics; a more practical dimension of reason. Like the principles of logic and mathematics, "the principles of ethics also are universal and are known by the reason."[51] While explaining the priority of *Logos* in the notion of conscience, Ratzinger directs his readers to Augustine's indication of how goodness precedes moral judgment.[52] Augustine says, "We could never judge that one thing is better than another if a basic notion of the good (*notio ipsius boni*) had not already been impressed in us."[53] It is from our primordial sense of goodness that we derive the wisdom to exercise good moral judgment. According to Ratzinger, what Basil understands as the "spark of divine love," Augustine expresses in terms of an impressed "notion of the good."[54]

For Augustine, to the extent that man's ontological sense of goodness corresponds to his natural desire for happiness, he is not in error. He says, "Therefore, in so far as all men seek a happy life, they are not in error.... No one is happy without the supreme good, which is distinguished and grasped in that truth which we call wisdom."[55] The moral error is a question of volition, not of the nature of truth because the choice of "a way of life" contrary to the object of goodness, is what leads to error:

---

50. Augustine, *Tract. Ev. Io.* 26.6 (PL 35:1609): "Reddo illi quod amat, reddo quod sperat."

51. Nash, *Light of the Mind*, 81.

52. Benedict XVI/Ratzinger, "Conscience and Truth," 535.

53. Augustine, *Trin.* 8.3 (4) (PL 42:949): "Neque enim in his omnibus bonis, vel quae commemoravi, vel quae alia cernuntur sive cogitantur, diceremus aliud alio melius cum vere iudicamus, nisi esset nobis impressa notio ipsius boni, secundum quod et probaremus aliquid, et aliud alii praeponeremus."

54. Benedict XVI/Ratzinger, "Conscience and Truth," 534–35. In the development of his theory of two levels of conscience, Ratzinger finds in both Augustine and Basil, a sense of the presence of the Logos, in the ontological capacity of man for moral reason. Basil speaks of the practical dimension the analogy of reason as "the spark of divine love," a natural capacity for observing the divine commandments (Basil, *Regulae fusius tractatae*, Resp. 2.1 [PG 31:908]).

55. Augustine, *Lib. arb.* 2.8.26 (PL 32:1254).

> In so far, however, as anyone does not keep to the way of life which leads to happiness, even though he confesses and professes that he wishes only for happiness, to that extent he is in error. For error comes about when we follow an aim which does not lead us where we wish to go. The more a man errs in this way of life, the less wise he is, for to this extent he departs from the truth, in which the supreme good is sought and grasped.[56]

Moral error is cultivated on the level of the *habitus* of life, for the more a man errs in this way of life, the less wise he is, for to this extent he departs from the truth. On the other hand, the more a man lives by a moral code, the more he remembers the truth of goodness. The practice and discipline of moral life is an exercise of remembering of the truth of goodness in the present.[57]

Primacy of the Form of Beauty in Aesthetic Illumination

Augustine considers the human capacity for perceiving physical beauty to be a function of the light of reason. The truth of aesthetic judgement consists in the epistemic illumination of the synthetic presence of order, number, unity and form.[58] He says,

> All things which are beautiful to the senses, whether they are produced by nature or are worked out by the arts, have a spatial or temporal beauty, as, for example, the body and its movements. But the equality and unity which are known only by the mind, and according to which the mind judges of corporeal beauty by the intermediary of the senses, are not extended in the space or unstable in time.[59]

For Augustine, beauty is not only perceived by the senses, but also judged by the mind. The judgement of beauty abstracts from perceived beauty, the presence of unchanging truths—such as equality and unity—as the

---

56. Augustine, *Lib. arb.* 2.8.26 (PL 32:1254).
57. Nash, *Light of the Mind*, 83–84.
58. See Chapman, *Saint Augustine's Philosophy of Beauty*, 12.
59. Augustine, *Ver. rel.* 30.56 (PL 34:146): "Et cum omnia quae sensibiliter pulchra sunt, sive natura edita, sive artibus elaborata, locis et temporibus sint pulchra, ut corpus et corporis motus; illa aequalitas et unitas menti tantummodo cognita, secundum quam de corporea pulchritudine sensu internuntio iudicatur, nec loco tumida est, nec instabilis tempore."

form of beauty. Artistic works and the beauty of creation point the mind to unchanging truth. They provide analogies for spiritual truths, as the sun's illumination of physical things provides analogy for an idea of the divine illumination of the mind.[60] The unchanging form of beauty is prior to the experience of beautiful things. Augustine considers the experience of the beauty of the earth, the sea, the sky and all created realities as reflections of the beautiful, which is prior to created beauty: "Question the beauty of the earth, question the beauty of the sea, question the beauty of the air distending and diffusing itself, question the beauty of the sky... question all these realities. All respond: 'See, we are beautiful.' Their beauty is a profession [*confessio*]."[61] For him, reason is capable of abstracting the beautiful from the beauty of passible things, and reach for the Creator reflected by the beauty of the universe.[62] In one of his papal audiences, Benedict XVI quotes this passage from Augustine in defense of the capacity of reason for perceiving the evidence of the existence of the Creator through the beauty of creation.[63]

Light of Reason as "Recollection"

Both Ronald Nash and Ratzinger closely associate Augustine's analogy of light with his theory of recollection. Nash argues that for Augustine, the illumination by which created reason recognizes universal principles of logic, math and ethics—eternal forms—comes neither through experience nor through Platonic reminiscence nor through teaching, but through "divine illumination."[64] The experience of the senses does not

---

60. Augustine, *Solil.* 1.8.15 (PL 32:877); cf. Harrison, *Beauty and Revelation*, 19.

61. Augustine, *Serm* 241.2 (PL 38:1134): "Interroga pulchritudinem terrae, interroga pulchritudinem maris, interroga pulchritudinem dilatati et diffusi aeris, interroga pulchritudinem coeli, interroga ordinem siderum, interroga solem fulgore suo diem clarificantem, interroga lunam splendore subsequentis noctis tenebras temperantem, interroga animalia quae moventur in aquis, quae morantur in terris, quae volitant in aere; latentes animas, perspicua corpora; visibilia regenda, invisibiles regentes: interroga ista, Respondent tibi omnia: Ecce vide, pulchra sumus. Pulchritudo eorum, confessio eorum."

62. Augustine, *Serm* 241.2 (PL 38:1134): "Ista pulchra mutabilia quis fecit, nisi incommutabilis pulcher? In ipso denique homine, ut possent intellegere et cognoscere Deum universi mundi creatorem."

63. Benedict XVI/Ratzinger, *Transforming Power of Faith*, 33.

64. Nash, *Light of the Mind*, 91: "But if man cannot come to know the eternal forms through sense experience, through Platonic reminiscence, or through teaching, how

account for the light of reason because it reports only actions that fluctuate, not principles that are perpetual and one. According to Augustine, "Whatever is the object of a bodily sense is proved to be many and not one, because it is a bodily thing and so has countless parts."[65] Augustine's use of recollection to speak of how reason attains knowledge is different from the Platonic recollection. Unlike the Platonic recollection, Augustine's "theory of recollection is not a remembering of the past" knowledge prior to birth.[66] In his *Retractationes*, he says,

> For it is a more credible reason that those who are ignorant of them [the discipline of the arts], when properly questioned, are able to reply correctly concerning certain disciplines because they have present in them, the capacity by the light of eternal reason (*lumen rationis aeternae*) to perceive those unchangeable truths. This is not because they knew these things at some time or another, and have forgotten them, as it seemed to Plato or men like him.[67]

In Book XIV of *De Trinitate*, Augustine describes recollection as a kind of "*awareness* of anything that is in the mind even while it is not being thought about."[68] He underscores once again the non-Platonic character of his understanding of recollection: "Nor was it the image of a thing that had been seen outside, caught in a certain fashion and stacked away in the memory, which thought discovered when it turned to it, and from which the inner gaze was informed in recollection."[69] Nash concludes that Augustine speaks of recollection as "a remembering of the *present*," which is essentially the same as "the continuous presence

---

can we know them? Augustine's answer is divine illumination." See pages 82–91 for a detailed argument.

65. Augustine, *Lib. arb.* 2.8.22 (PL 32:1252).

66. Nash, *Light of the Mind*, 83; cf. Plato, *Phaedo* 72D–76A; *Meno* 85C–86D.

67. Augustine, *Retract.* 1.4.4 (PL 32:590B) [*Retractations*]: "Credibilius est enim propterea vera respondere de quibusdam disciplinis etiam imperitos earum, quando bene interrogantur, quia praesens est eis, quantum id capere possunt, lumen rationis aeternae, ubi haec immutabilia vera conspiciunt, non quia ea noverant aliquando et obliti sunt, quod Platoni vel talibus visum est."

68. Augustine, *Trin.* 14.6.9 (PL 42:1042) [*Trinity*]: "Quaerendum est quonam modo ad cogitationem pertineat intellectus; *notitia* vero cuiusque rei, quae inest menti, etiam quando non de ipsa cogitatur, ad solam dicatur memoriam pertinere."

69. Augustine, *Trin.* 14.8.11 (PL 42:1044): "Nec imaginem rei quae foris visa est, quodam modo raptam et in memoria reconditam cogitatio cum ad eam converteretur, invenit, et inde formatus est recordantis obtutus."

of God's light with us." Augustine's theory of recollection confirms the priority of the *inner light*, whom he identifies as Christ.

While Ratzinger acknowledges the Platonic roots of Augustine's theory of recollection, he also highlights the Christian difference that Augustine brings to it. For Ratzinger, Augustine's notion of the light of Christ in the interiority of man is a significant shift from a neo-Platonic cosmic view to a more personal view of the analogy. He observes a change of emphasis in the thought of Augustine against the traditional forms of the neo-Platonic ideas: "In place of the cosmic view of Neoplatonism [Augustine] treads the path of a radical concentration on the 'interiority of man'; an interpretation of the world as it were from the personal interiority of the human spirit."[70] Ratzinger also quotes Augustine's *Confessiones* and *De vera religione* to demonstrate how Augustine's metaphysics of light touches his personal life.[71]

The Limits of Reason

In Augustine's epistemology, reason without the help of faith is incapable of attaining the fullness of the truth. Augustine says, "The truth is not obtained by itself with reasoning but it is what those who use reason seek. . . . It confesses that what the truth is, is not you, for it does not seek itself; you, on the other hand, have not attained it by passing from one place to another, but by seeking it with the disposition of your mind."[72] The function of reason is not create the truth because the priority of truth before its discovery by reason testifies to the uncreated nature of truth. Augustine continues in his reflection, "These things are not made by the process of reasoning, but discovered. Therefore they abide in themselves before they are discovered, and once they are discovered, they renew us."[73] Truth

---

70. Benedict XVI/Ratzinger, *Offenbarungsverständnis*, 306 (my translation).

71. Benedict XVI/Ratzinger, *Transforming Power of Faith*, 34: "St. Augustine was to write a famous sentence in which he says that God is more intimate to me than I am to myself. Hence he formulates the invitation, *do not go outside yourself, return to yourself: the truth is higher than my highest and more inward than my innermost self. Reach, therefore to where the light of reason is lit*" (cf. Augustine, Ver. rel. 39.72 [PL 34:154]).

72. Augustine, Ver. rel. 39.72 (CCSL 32:234).

73. Augustine, Ver. rel. 39.73 (CCSL 32:235). In October 16, 2008, in his address to the participants in a Congress held on the occasion of the tenth anniversary of the publication of Pope John Paul II's encyclical *Fides et Ratio*, Benedict XVI makes reference to this quote from Augustine in addressing the proper achievement of reason within its limitations.

is first and foremost a gift, and reason becomes increasingly analogous to the truth in the process of discovering it. While reason is capable of arriving at certain truths such as the immortality of the soul, however, only a few people with great talent, sufficient leisure and laborious training have been able to arrive at such a truth.[74]

For Augustine, the use of reason without the aid of authority is prone to error. His comments on the philosophical presuppositions undergirding the religious status of the Roman polis demonstrate how the errors of Platonic and Stoic philosophies raise questions about the truth content of Rome's claim of a religious power.[75] On the one hand, Augustine considers the opinion of the ancient Roman scholar, Varro, to be errant because of its Stoic concept of God.[76] He comments,

> The same most acute and learned author also says that those alone seem to him to have perceived what God is who have believed Him to be the soul of the world, governing it by design and reason. And by this, it appears that [Varro] did not attain to the truth—for the true God is not a soul, but the maker and author of the soul.[77]

What Augustine rejects is the Stoic idea behind Varro's notion of God as the "soul of the world." For him, Varro's error consists in his reduction of the immutable God to a mutable soul: "The true God is that immutable nature which made the soul itself."[78] Augustine challenges the Stoic confusion of the created and uncreated order as an abolition of the transcendent. The religious status of the governing power of Rome derives

---

74. Augustine says, "Humanis quippe argumentationibus haec invenire conantes, vix pauci magno praediti ingenio, abundantes otio, doctrinisque subtilissimis eruditi, ad indagandam solius animae immortalitatem pervenire potuerunt" (With regard to those who have endeavored to discover these things from human reasons, scarcely a few have been able to arrive at the investigation of the immortality of the soul alone, and they were men endowed with great talent, and had sufficient leisure, and were trained in the most subtle learning) (Augustine, *Trin.* 13.9.12 [PL 42:1023]).

75. According to Ratzinger, Augustine's theology of the political "were developed over and against the two most important political philosophies of his time, Stoicism and Platonism" (Benedict XVI/Ratzinger, *Unity of Nations*, 82).

76. Stoic monism "meant the mingling of God and the world and thus the abolition of transcendence," in such a way that it "allowed for the whole world to be viewed as saturated with divinity" (Benedict XVI/Ratzinger, *Unity of Nations*, 82–83).

77. Augustine, *Civ.* 4.31 (PL 41:138) [*City of God*]; cf. Benedict XVI/Ratzinger, *Unity of Nations*, 82–23n13.

78. Augustine, *Civ.* 4.31 (PL 41:138).

an errant concept of the state from the Stoics. The identification of Rome as the earthly concentration of the divine power reflects the Stoic philosophical presuppositions behind Roman politics.

On the other hand, in contrast to the Stoic abolition of the transcendent, Augustine recognizes also the Platonic radical exaggeration of the transcendent. He comments,

> That opinion, which the same Platonist avers that Plato uttered, is not true, that no god holds intercourse with men. . . . He affirms, indeed, that the supreme God, the Creator of all things, whom we call the true God, is spoken of by Plato as the only God whom the poverty of human speech fails even passably to describe.[79]

The error of Platonism is its "radical exaggeration of transcendence: God has nothing to do with the world."[80] Recognizing the limits of Platonic and Stoic philosophies, Augustine confirms the partial nature of their truth content: "There is no doctrine so false but contains some truth."[81]

Priority of Christ in Faith and Reason

Augustine appeals to the distinction between faith and reason as a parallel to the distinction between authority and truth. He comments, "Let us not doubt with unbelief about things to be believed, and let us affirm without rashness about things to be understood; in the former case, authority is to be upheld; in the latter, the truth is to be sought."[82] The function of reason is to understand the truth and that of faith is to uphold the authority of things to be believed.

On the one hand, reason needs the authority of faith to achieve the truth it desires without error. Augustine wrote, "No good may be known perfectly unless one loves perfectly."[83] Faith enables reason to love the good perfectly and thus capable of knowing the good perfectly. Reason

---

79. Augustine, *Civ.* 9.16 (PL 41:269): "Non enim verum est, quod idem Platonicu ait dixisse Platonem, *Nullus deus miscetur homini.*"

80. Benedict XVI/Ratzinger, *Unity of Nations*, 83.

81. Augustine, *Quaest. Ev.* 2.40 (PL 35:1354): "Nulla porro falsa doctrina est quae non aliqua vera intermisceat."

82. Augustine, *Trin.* 9.1.1 (PL 42:961).

83. Augustine, *Div. quaest.* 35.2 (PL 40:24): "Quidquid autem mente habetur, noscendo habetur; nullumque bonum perfecte noscitur, quod non perfecte amatur."

cannot be judged by reason but "must be tried by a higher court . . . the Supreme Tribunal of Divine Revelation."[84] He says, "But we being sustained by Divine authority in the history of our religion, have no doubt that whatever is opposed to it is most false, whatever may be the case regarding other things in secular books, which, whether true or false, yield nothing of moment to our living rightly and happily."[85] The authority of divine revelation stems from Christ who is the center of the analogy between the Old Testament and the New Testament. In *De utilitate credenda*, Augustine makes explicit reference to "analogy" when "it is shown that the two testaments, the Old and the New, are not opposed to each other."[86] In *De Genesi contra Manichaeos*, he shows how Christ is the primordial center of the "analogy" of the unity of Scripture. He says, "For, when the Jews asked him who he was, our Lord Jesus Christ answered, *The beginning; that is why I am speaking to you*" (Cf. John 8:25).[87] The New Testament reveals Christ as the original "beginning" of the Old Testament.

On the other hand, faith needs reason for understanding what is believed. In his commentary on Mark 9:23 (*Lord I do believe, help my unbelief*), Augustine presents his two famous formulas that explains the interdependence of faith and reason for knowledge of the truth: "I understand, the better to believe, I believe in order to understand."[88] Benedict XVI quotes this coherent synthesis of Augustine, as an expression of how the harmony of faith and reason show above all that God is not remote or far from our reason or our life.[89]

With regard to faith and philosophy, Augustine presents divine revelation in Christ as the fundamental criterion for evaluating the political results of the Stoic and Platonic philosophers; "the philosophers against

---

84. Vega, *Saint Augustine*, 89.

85. Augustine, *Civ.* 18.40 (PL 41:600).

86. Augustine, *Util. cred.* 3.5 (PL 42:68): "Secundum *analogiam*, cum demonstratur non sibi adversari duo Testamenta Vetus et Novum." Kizewski comments, "Analogy, when Augustine uses it explicity, is that 'by which the harmony of the two testaments is clearly seen.'"

87. Augustine, *Gen. Man.* 1.3 (PL 34:176) [*On Genesis*]: "Dominus enim noster Iesus Christus, cum eum Iudaei interrogassent quis esset, respondit: *Principium, quia et loquor vobis*."

88. Augustine, *Serm.* 43.9 (PL 38:258): "Ergo intellege ut credas, crede ut intellegas."

89. Benedict XVI/Ratzinger, *Church Fathers*, 180–81.

whose slanders we are defining the city of God—that is, his Church."[90] The Church as the *City of God* will remain a universal city within the earthly cities. Faith in Christ is the completion of what is lacking in the Stoic idea of the City of God on earth and the platonic transcendence of God. Faith purifies philosophy for the service of the truth about God, humanity and their relationship. For Augustine therefore, Christian faith completes what is lacking in the Platonic and Stoic worldly-*polis* on three fronts: (1) In place of the platonic dogma that between God and man there is no contact, Christianity introduces the reality of the Incarnation that God became man; (2) in place of the stoic reduction of divinity to creatures, Christianity maintains the metaphysical distinction between God and creatures; (3) in place of the intermediary beings, Christ, God's only Son, is Lord of the universe, through who God rules the world without mediation, and only him is truly divine and human, not the rulers of peoples.

Conclusion

In Justin Martyr's, Origen's, and Augustine's reflections on the matters of faith, philosophy, and politics the primacy of reason serves as the point of synthesis. Justin Martyr, the priority of reason shapes his argument for the primacy of Christ. Origen shows how Christ embodies the analogy of reason in both a primordial and eschatological way. In the primordial sense, he reveals the divine intent for the unity of humanity as demonstrated in the biblical unity of language prior to the Tower of Babel. Eschatologically, Christ fulfils the long expected unity of nations in his own person, deeds, and words, by illuminating what was hidden in the Old Testament and completing what was lacking in Greek philosophy. For Augustine, it is the analogy of light that contributes to our understanding of the priority of Christ in our knowledge of the truth. He saw in the discipline of arts, science, philosophy, and politics, indications of universal truths that point to Christ as the Light. His theory of illumination demonstrates the uncreated nature of truth and the primacy Christ in knowledge of the truth.

---

90. Augustine, *Civ.* 13.16 (PL 41:387).

The Original Man and the Priority of Love

Gregory of Nyssa and Augustine are the Fathers that Ratzinger quotes in his discussion of image analogy. With regard to Gregory, Ratzinger highlights how his distinction between the unity of our nature in Adam and in Christ makes a difference in the way we speak of human nature relative to its reflection of God's image.[91]

Priority of the Universal Nature of Man

In Gregory's theory, Adam represents the numerical and sinful nature of man while Christ bears the perfect and universal human nature. Gregory uses the numerical distinction between male and female to argue for the priority of Christ relative to Adam. God "saw . . . what would be, [and] He devised for His image the distinction of male and female, which has no reference to the Divine Archetype, but, as we have said, is an approximation to the less rational nature."[92] For him, in Christ the divine archetype, there is no distinction between male and female because Christ as the original Image is prior to creation of Adam and Eve. He sees a certain conceptual gap between God's declaring of what he intends for his image and the actual creation of Adam. When God declared his intention for creating man in his image, "accordingly, the Image of God, which we behold in the universal humanity, had its consummation then [even though] Adam had not been created yet."[93] Christ, who is the "Image of God" is the original image in God's intention for creating man. When we

---

91. Ratzinger shares Lubac's insights on Gregory of Nyssa's notion of human nature in an explicit way. See Benedict XVI/Ratzinger, *Unity of Nations*, 26. According to Lubac, "The doctrine of Gregory of Nyssa, we know, makes a distinction between the first individuals of our kind, coming forth 'as by degrees' from their causes, in their time, 'by a natural and necessary genesis' in the fashion of all other living creatures, and Man, made according to the image, the object of a direct creation out of time, who is in each one of us and who makes us to be entirely one that we ought not to speak of man in the plural any more than we speak of three Gods" (Lubac, *Catholicism*, 29).

92. Gregory of Nyssa, *De Hominis Opificio* 16.14 (PG 44:135B).

93. Gregory of Nyssa, *De Hominis Opificio* 22.3 (PG 44:204D): Gregory makes this distinction between the real universal nature and the numerical one in the context of his discussion of the Resurrection of Christ. Gregory's resurrection realism is also more evident in his *De Anima et Resurrectione*. In his *Resurrection Realism*, Patrick J. Fletcher investigated Ratzinger's resurrection realism based on the Augustinian influence. However, we suggest that Ratzinger also quotes Gregory of Nyssa as he indicates a realism based on the priority of Christ in the understanding of human nature.

think of the universal human nature, we think not of Adam but of Christ since Christ is the universal Image for the creation of Adam. Gregory is referring to Christ as the archetypal image of God who bears the universal nature of man: "Man, then, was made in the image of God; that is, the universal nature, the thing like God; not part of the whole, but all the fullness of the nature together."[94]

The Redeemed Nature of Man

Gregory integrates into God's intention for a perfect image, a divine foreknowledge of the "bias towards evil" inherent in created nature.[95] This bias toward evil is on account of the human "state of independence and freedom . . . the tendency of the motion of man's will."[96] But as the bearer of the fullness of human nature and the original Image of God, Christ does not partake in human sin. As the bearer of the original image prior to the fall, Christ is rather the universal remedy of our sinful nature. Thus, the ontological unity of humanity that pertains to Christ as the universal Image or the real Man, is constituted both in a cosmic and soteriological way. In the Incarnation, what happens in the humanity of Christ "the Man," happens in the nature of all men. With the Incarnation, human nature is redeemed from sin and renewed from the beginning.

Christ the Perfect Image and Man the Image

In reference to Augustine's Exposition of Psalm 94, Ratzinger highlights Augustine's insistence on the meaning of "image" as a reference to God the origin of man. Ratzinger comments, "[Human nature] is the living coin that bears the image of God and hence is to be given back to God, just as the coins that bear the emperor's likeness are to be given back to him."[97] "Giving back to God" the image that belongs to him demonstrates the intrinsic orientation of being toward Being and the meaning of image relative to man's love of God. However, at the end of Book VI and into

---

94. Gregory of Nyssa, *De Hominis Opificio* 22.4 (PG 44:204D).

95. Gregory of Nyssa, *De Hominis Opificio* 22.4 (PG 44:205A).

96. Gregory of Nyssa, *De Hominis Opificio* 16.14 (PG 44:135B).

97. Benedict XVI/Ratzinger, *Unity of Nations*, 27; cf. Augustine, *Enarrat. Ps.* 94.2 (PL 37:1218).

Book VII of *De Trinitate*, Augustine speak of the Son as the perfect Image of the Father:

> For if any image answers perfectly to that of which it is image, then it is made equal to it, not the object to its own image. He gave the name form to the Image, I believe on account of the beauty, which arises from this perfect harmony, this primal equality, this primal similarity, but which corresponds in everything to that of which it is the image. This Image possesses the primal and supreme life.[98]

Augustine uses the qualities of "perfect harmony, primal equality, primal similarity" to highlight the unique way in which one applies the notion of image to Christ. Comparing man's similitude to that of Christ, he says, "And with the example of this Image before us, let us also not depart from God. For we are likewise the image of God, not indeed an equal image, since it was made by the Father through the Son, not born of the Father as that is."[99] While Christ is an "equal image" of the Father, man is simply the image of God. What Augustine underscores is the primacy of "Image" and the corresponding analogy to man. What Christ has in primordial perfection, we partake by analogy.

Priority of Love

According to Kizewski, "Augustine refers to Christ as 'the similitude'" and he "relates the notion of similitude to the notion of image."[100] The foundation of Augustine's analogy of image[101] is from his Trinitarian exegesis of Genesis 1:26: "For man was not made to the image of the Father alone, or of the Son alone, or of the Holy Spirit alone, but to the image of the Trinity."[102] He speaks of the Trinity based on the image of it that he

98. Augustine, *Trin.* 6.10.11 (PL 42:931).
99. Augustine, *Trin.* 7.3.5 (PL 42:938).
100. Kizewski, "God-Talk," 282.
101. Kizewski observes that "Augustine's starting point for the search for an analogy in the image [is] Scripture" (Kizewski, "God-Talk," 303). According to Merriell, "Augustine lays the foundation for the search for the image of the Trinity by giving the Trinitarian exegesis of Gen 1:26" (Merriell, *To the Image of the Trinity*, 24).
102. Augustine, *Gn. litt. lib. imperf.* 16.61 (PL 34:241) ["On the Literal Interpretation of Genesis"]: "Ille autem sensus est potius in his divinis verbis eligendos, ut ideo non dictum intellegamus singulariter, sed pluraliter: *Faciamus hominem ad imaginem et similitudinem nostram*; quia non ad solius Patris, aut solius Filii, aut solius Spiritus sancti, sed ad ipsius Trinitatis imaginem factus est homo."

finds in the human interiority: "Thus, 'Let us make man to our image and likeness' (Gen 1:26) is correctly understood according to what is within man."[103] In other words, if man is created in the image of the Trinitarian God, we ought to recognize a Trinitarian trace [*vestigium*] in him.[104]

Donald Merriell notes that "there are several stages in Augustine's investigation of man as an image of the Trinity, yet the entire search unfolds from the analogy of love in Book VIII of *De Trinitate* and is explicitly aimed at the solution of the problem concerning the distinction of the Holy Spirit from the Son by means of the notion of love."[105] The orientation of *De Trinitate* toward the notion of love explains Augustine's later modification of his psychological explanation of *imago* from memory, understanding, and self-love to memory, understanding, and *love of God*.[106] For him, memory, understating, and self-love constitute a sort of potential image of God that is not the image in the full sense. Thus, Augustine shows how the Trinitarian image found in the human soul is of provisional importance relative to the full spiritual sense found in man's remembering, understanding and loving the God who created man in the divine image. Nevertheless, in so far as image represents an analogy between God and man, Augustine highlights the "great dissimilitude" present in the similitude: "And yet let him beware lest he so compare to its maker this image made by the Trinity as to believe it entirely like it; whatever be the likeness between the two, let him also discern the great dissimilitude."[107]

---

103. Augustine, *Gn. litt. lib. imperf.* 16.60 (PL 34:241): "Recte igitur secundum hoc quod interius et principale hominis est, id est secundum mentem, accipitur: Faciamus hominem ad imaginem et similitudinem nostram."

104. See Augustine, *Trin.* 6.10.12 (PL 42:932).

105. Merriell, *To the Image of the Trinity*, 25.

106. Augustine, *Trin.* 14.12.15 (PL 42:1048): "Haec igitur trinitas mentis non propterea Dei est imago, quia sui meminit mens, et intellegit ac diligit se: sed quia potest etiam meminisse, et intellegere, et amare a quo facta est. Quod cum facit, sapiens ipsa fit. Si autem non facit, etiam cum sui meminit, seque intellegit ac diligit, stulta est. Meminerit itaque Dei sui, ad cuius imaginem facta est, eumque intellegat atque diligat" (This trinity of the mind is not really the image of God because the mind remembers and understands and loves itself, but because it is also able to remember and understand and love him by whom it was made. And when it does this it becomes wise. If it does not do it, then even though it remembers and understands and loves itself, it is foolish. Let it then remember its God to whose image it was made, and understand and love him). See also Merriell, *To the Image of the Trinity*, 28.

107. Augustine, *Trin.* 15.20.39 (PL 42:1088).

The Intelligible Word as the Image of the Trinitarian Word

In his psychological presentation of the concept of image, Augustine finds an analogy between the divine creative Word and the interior intelligible word:

> If anyone then can understand how a word can be, not only before it is spoken aloud but even before the images of its sounds are turned over in thought—this is the word that belongs to no language, that is to none of what are called the languages of the nations, of which ours is Latin; if anyone, I say, can understand this, he can already see through this mirror and in this enigma some similitude of that Word of which it is said, *In the beginning was the Word, and the Word was with God and the Word was God* (John 1:1).[108]

The interior intelligible word is the bearer of the truth, "for when we utter something true, that is when we utter what we know, a word is necessarily born from the knowledge which we hold in the memory, a word which is absolutely the same kind of thing as the knowledge which it is born from."[109] How the human word operates in the human faculties of memory and intellect has a similitude to the relationship between the Father and his Word. Therefore, the psychological movement of the human intelligible word is similar to the Trinitarian *Logos*. In considering the human mind as image of God, Augustine places priority on the interior intelligible *logos*. In other words, it is the human intelligible word that is the image of the divine *Logos*.

Regarding the speech form of the analogy of word, Augustine speaks of the similitude between the incarnate Word and the human spoken word. He says,

> Thus in a certain fashion our word becomes a bodily sound by assuming that in which it is manifested to the senses of men, just as the Word of God became flesh by assuming that in which it too could be manifested to the senses of men. And just as our word becomes sound without being changed into sound, so the Word of God became flesh, but it is unthinkable that it should have been changed into flesh. It is by assuming it, not by being consumed into it, that both our word becomes sound and that Word becomes flesh.[110]

---

108. Augustine, *Trin.* 15.11.20 (PL 42:1072).
109. Augustine, *Trin.* 15.10.19 (PL 42:1072).
110. Augustine, *Trin.* 15.11.20 (PL 42:1072).

As the interior word exists before and independently of the voice, so also does the eternal Word subsist independently and prior to its assumption of our humanity. As the intelligible spoken word remains both in the mind of the speaker and the listener, so also does the divine Word remain in the Father at the Incarnation of the Son.[111] Augustine's reader must always be attentive to the greater dissimilarity present in his similitude of word. For Augustine, the analogy of word affirms the fittingness of God's creation and salvation of the world by his *Logos*. The "perfection of the image" depends on conformity of human word and deed to "instruction of the good master in Christian faith and divine doctrine."[112] In his study of Bonaventure's theology of history, Ratzinger highlights Bonaventure's development of the soteriological dimension of Augustine's analogy of word as speech.[113]

The influence of Gregory of Nyssa and Augustine on Ratzinger's theology of image intimates Ratzinger's ecumenical sensibility to the Eastern and Western ways of speaking about the analogy of image. Gregory expresses the ontological structure of image relative to the primordial second Adam, who bears the universal human nature. Augustine highlights divine love as fundamental to the patristic idea of man as "image of the primal Image." By considering the Trinitarian stamp on the human soul as ultimately a reflection of divine love, he prioritizes love as the source and actualization of the ontology of image. In what does Augustine's analogy of man's image of divine love consist? He articulates the analogy of man's image of divine love in terms of the great dissimilitude present in the similitude. Thus, he anticipates the Fourth Lateran Council, to which Ratzinger references in his discussions on the use of analogy. Augustine's analogy of word also introduces into our study of Ratzinger's theology the speech form of *logos*.

---

111. Ferri, *Gesù E La Verità*, 48. Ferri adds a third analogy not present in Augustine's *De Trinitate*. As the thought of speech is intelligible to the receiver without abandoning the speaker, so also does the incarnate Word remain with us after the Resurrection.

112. Augustine, *Trin.* 15.11.20 (PL 42:1072).

113. Benedict XVI/Ratzinger, *Offenbarungsverständnis*, 134. See chapter 3, under Bonaventure.

Pneumatic and Ecclesial Participation

While Ratzinger appeals to several ancient authors on participation, our concern is with those whose conversations on participation sheds light on the primacy of Christ. Origen, Gregory of Nyssa, Athanasius, Hilary of Poitiers, John Chrysostom, Augustine, and Maximus the Confessor fall within this category. Origen and Augustine play a significant role in the patristic foundations of Ratzinger's pneumatic primacy of Love. However, Ratzinger singles out Origen, as the principal ancient ecclesiastical writer to seize the opportunities offered by the profound philosophical intuition of the Stoic anthropology of the heart to achieve a new synthesis between the Greek philosophical inheritance and biblical faith.

Origen: *Participation in the Heart*

Origen says that "the names of the organs of sense are applied to the soul, so that we speak of seeing with the eyes of the heart, that is, of drawing some intellectual conclusion by means of the faculty of intelligence."[114] When understood as an epistemic process, "seeing with the eyes of the heart" suggests a transference of the intellectual function and the faculties of the soul to the heart. The term "heart" can either describe a corporeal organ or an intellectual faculty. Origen notes, "That heart is used for mind, that is, for the intellectual faculty, you will certainly find over and over again in all Scripture, both the New and the Old."[115] However, Origen is also aware that to speak of the heart as intellectual faculty is not a reduction of the heart to the intellect. In his close association of the heart with the Stoic concept of the ἡγεμονικόν (guiding spirit, ruling center), Origen uses the heart to describe the center of man and his ruling spirit:

> After this there is another testimony of the same Baptist about Christ, which further teaches that this preeminent substance extends to all the world in relation to the rational souls, when he says, "He who comes after me has stood in your midst whom you did not know, the strap of whose sandal I am not worthy to loose" (John 1:26–27). And considering the statement, "He whom you did not know has stood in your midst," can be understood in relation to the reason (λόγον) in each person because the heart is in the center of everybody (διὰ τὸ ἐν μέσῳ τοῦ

---

114. Origen, *De Principiis* 1.1.9 (SC 252:110).
115. Origen, *De Principiis* 1.1.9 (SC 252:110).

παντὸς εἶναι σώματος τὴν καρδίαν), and the ruling principle is in the heart (ἐν τῇ καρδίᾳ τὸ ἡγεμονικόν).[116]

The "heart" (καρδιά) as corporeal metaphor for the "guiding or ruling spirit" in man, is for Origen, the "innermost reason" (logos) of man, which analogically corresponds to the primordial Logos. Endre von Ivánka and Ratzinger confirm the Stoic roots of Origen's notion of the heart as the ruling or guiding principle (ἡγεμονικόν) of man's knowledge of the truth.[117] For the Stoics, the anthropological concept of "ἡγεμονικόν" is the pneumatic center of man, the "primal fire," which unifies both the passions and the intellectual parts. The Stoic identification of the center of man with the primal fire borders on anthropomorphism. However, Origen's Christian notion of ἡγεμονικόν bears an epistemology similar to one that anticipates Augustine's "inner light."[118] The inner reason dwells in the center of man in a way prior to his understanding. This inner pneumatic *logos* which precedes man's knowledge of God, is not only intellectual but also is existential. Elsewhere, Origen speaks of the epistemic meaning of "ἡγεμονικόν" as "τὸ διανοητικῶν," the intellectual center of man.[119] Ivánka confirms that Origen's pneumatic concept of "central reason," which he refers to as Christ, is the personal *Logos*, which John the Baptist speaks of as being "in unserer Mitte" (in our center).[120] The notion of Christ as the ground or center of our soul then points to his primacy,

---

116. Origen, *Johannescommentar* 2.215 (GCS IV, 94:18) [*Commentary on the Gospel*, 152–53].

117. See Ivánka, *Plato Christianus*, 324–27: "Erst da konnte stoiche ἡγεμονικόν zu einem "Seelengrunde" im Sinne der mittelalterlichen Mystiker werden. Diese Verbindung des stoichen Schemas mit der platonishcen Grundhaltung—zugleich mit der Verchristlichung beider Motive—hat erst Origenes vollzogen." Ivánka describes the anthropology of stoic "hegemonikon" as one that concentrates the spiritual powers of the soul at the heart as the highest point of the soul—"Seelenspitze or apex mentis," thereby shifting focus from the platonic conceptual partitioning of the soul to its deeper and existential sense. In place of the platonic hierarchy of intellect, will and sensibility, they speak of the "Seelenfunke" (the primal spark) in the soul. See also Benedict XVI/Ratzinger, *Behold*, 66–67.

118. Origen's comment is part of his discussion on the "six witnesses of John the Baptist" about Christ in John 1:6, which began with testifying that Christ is the Light, and ends with Christ is the Lamb. Thus, the central motif is how Christ is precedes our knowledge of the truth in an interior way.

119. Origen, *Johannescommentar* XIV–XVII (GCS IV, 497:20): "Ὑπονοεῖταί τινιν ἐν τῷ μεσωτάτῳ ἡμῶν εἶναι τὸ διανοητικῶν, ὃ τινες ἡγεμονικὸν καλοῦσιν." See Ivánka, *Plato Christianus*, 325.

120. See Ivànka, *Plato Christianus*, 325.

since in this pneumatic *Logos*, the ontological and the pneumatic meets as one organic unit. The metaphor of the heart, which conveys a more spiritual image of the primordial indwelling of the *Logos* is more comprehensive than the image of the mind.

Thus, in Origen, the heart serves as a metaphor for the analogy of pneumatic participation. By identifying the heart as the center of man's knowledge of God, Origen conveys that we do not know God only with the intellect but with our whole being, expressed in a unified way through the heart. A Christian heart is not related to Christ in a univocal way, but by analogy of spiritual participation. Origen's commentary on John 1:26 is crucial to Ratzinger's argument for a synthetic notion of participation in the *Logos*, by analogy of correspondence. After paraphrasing Origen, Ratzinger concludes, "It is the Logos which enables us to be logical, to *correspond* to the Logos; he is the image of God after which we were created."[121]

Analogy of "Resemblance" in Origen's Primacy of Love

Origen demonstrates how the ontological and spiritual participation stems from the priority of love. Ontologically, all human beings possess "seeds of love": "When the maker of the universe created you, He sowed in your hearts the seeds of love."[122] However, the "seed" of love and "Love" itself are not bound together on the same plane. As the higher term, Love takes primacy over the seeds because, the seed cannot arrive at its actuality in itself, but beyond itself.[123] Therefore, it is fitting that the "Paraclete, the Spirit of truth . . . goes around seeking for any souls he may find that are worthy and receptive, to whom he might reveal the greatness of this love, which is from God."[124] It is by faith that the Holy Spirit enlightens the receptive heart with the fullness of divine Charity. An unreceptive heart, which still possesses the seed of love is asleep: "So now is love asleep in you."[125] Benedict XVI says, "[Origen] was convinced that the best way to

---

121. Benedict XVI/Ratzinger, *Behold*, 69.

122. Origen, *Canticum Canticorum*, Hom. 2.9 (PG 13:55).

123. See Przywara, *Analogia Entis*, 174–75. Przywara uses the Aristotelian *enthelechy* (inner telos) to speak of the distance relative to the analogical dynamism between creature and God, the metaphysical and the theological, the lower term and the higher term. In this distinction, the higher term takes primacy over the lower term.

124. Origen, *Canticum Canticorum*, Prol. (PG 13:73A).

125. Origen, *Canticum Canticorum*, Hom. 2.9 (PG 13:55).

become acquainted with God is through love and . . . the highest degree of knowledge of God stems from love."[126] In Origen's priority of love, the epistemic is bound up in the mystical.

Origen describes the ascending movement of spiritual participation with the analogy of *resemblance* of or *becoming like* the divine *agape*. Indicating the analogy of "likeness" he says, "And because God is Charity, and the Son likewise, who is of God, is Charity, he requires in us something *like* himself; so that through this charity which is in Christ Jesus, we may be allied to God who is Charity."[127] Elsewhere, he describes spiritual participation as "resemblance": "This present tribulation is not described as momentary and light for everyone, but only for Paul and those who *resemble* him in having the perfect 'charity of God in Christ Jesus poured out in their hearts by the Holy Spirit' (Rom 5:5)."[128] Lubac clarifies that Origen does not speak merely of the Platonic resemblance to God, which is about contemplating the divine forms, rather "it is another resemblance and another assimilation that Origen proposes to the Christian . . . summed up in one word: charity."[129]

However, it is Origen's description of the descending movement of participation that conveys its paschal character of the analogy of resemblance. Origen describes divine love as a "passionate Fire." He says, "I do not think one could be blamed if one called God Passionate Love (*Amorem*), just as John calls him Charity (*Caritatem*)."[130] "So you must take whatever Scripture says about charity as if it had been said with

---

126. Benedict XVI/Ratzinger, *Church Fathers*, 38–39.

127. Origen, *Canticum Canticorum*, Prol. (PG 13:69C): "Et quia Deus caritas est, et Filius qui ex Deo est, caritas est, sui *simile* aliquid requirit in nobis: ut per hanc caritatem quae est in Christo Jesu, qui est caritas, velut cognate quadam per caritatis nomen affinitate sociemur" (my emphasis).

128. Origen, *Canticum Canticorum*, Prol. (PG 13:72B): "Non enim omnibus, sed Paulo, et his qui ei *similes* sunt, praesens haec et momentanea ac levis dicitur tribulation."

129. Lubac, *History and Spirit*, 277.

130. Origen, *Canticum Canticorum*, Prol. (PG 13:70D). In numbers nine and ten of Benedict XVI's encyclical *Deus Caritas Est*, one finds echoes of Origen's reference to divine Charity as passionate Love. Benedict claims that God's love, which can be called *eros* is also *agape*: "God's *eros* for man is also totally *agape*. . . . God is the absolute and ultimate source of all being; but this universal principle of creation—the *Logos*, primordial reason—is at the same time a lover with all the passion of a true love. *Eros* is thus supremely ennobled, yet at the same time it is so purified as to become one with *agape*" (Benedict XVI/Ratzinger, *Deus Caritas Est* 13–15).

reference to passionate love, taking no notice of the difference of terms."[131] In reference to this quotation, Ratzinger comments that "it was Origen who gave the normative definition of the way in which the theme of the suffering God is to be interpreted."[132] Origen categorically emphasizes the paradox that "The Father himself is not impassible."[133] Commenting on the philosophical implication of Origen's paradox of the passiblility of the impassible God, Lubac says, "The revelation of Love overturns all that the world had conceived of the divinity."[134] Origen also touches on the Christological import of his theology of suffering when he says, "The Savior ... was subject to our passions before suffering the Cross, before he had even deigned to assume our flesh: for if he had not first been subject to them, he would not have come to *participate* in our human life."[135] In other words, in the heart (*Logos*) of Jesus, the Father's love descends as a suffering heart, and the heart of man ascends by *becoming like* or resembling the divine suffering love. While the Christological synthesis of the descending and the ascending movements of love points to the Cross, Origen suggests that it is also prior to it. Thus, the God of Christian resemblance is not an impassible Greek God, but a passionate or suffering God. Origen's analogy of resemblance to God is bound to the paschal synthesis of the primacy of divine love, whereby, in Christ, God's descending participation in human suffering has primacy over the ascending participation in divine love.

In the previous chapter, we saw how Origen holds that the cosmic priesthood of Christ the Anointed One is fundamental to our ecclesial

---

131. Origen, *Canticum Canticorum*, Prol. (PG 13:70A-B): "Sic ergo quacunque de charitate scripta sunt, quasi de amore dicta suscipe, nihil de nominibus curans. Eadem namque in utroque virtus ostenditur."

132. Benedict XVI/Ratzinger, *Behold*, 58.

133. Origen, *Homiliae in Ezechielem* 6.6 (PG 13:715A) [*Homilies 1-14 on Ezekiel*]: "Ipse Pater non est impassibilis."

134. Lubac, *History and Spirit*, 277.

135. Origen, *Homiliae in Ezechielem* 6.6 (PG 13:714D): "Descendit in terras miserans humanum genus, passiones perpessus est nostras antequam crucem pateretur et carnem nostram dignaretur assumere." Ratzinger considers Origen's theology of the suffering God as significant shift from the classic restriction of Christ's passion to his humanity: "Origen who grasped most profoundly the idea of the suffering God and made bold to say that it could not be restricted to the suffering humanity of Jesus but also affected the Christian picture of God. He indicates that the notion of a suffering God is fundamental to the Christian analogy of *resemblance* of God in so far as it clarifies the kind of God that Christ calls us to participate in" (Benedict XVI/Ratzinger, *Behold*, 58).

ascent to God. Benedict XVI says, "At the peak of this ascent of perfection, Origen places martyrdom."¹³⁶ In his *Homily in Leviticus,* Origen says, "If I renounce all my possessions, take up my cross, and follow Christ, I offer my holocaust on the altar of God; and if I give up my body to be burned with love and achieve the glory martyrdom, I offer my holocaust on the altar of God."¹³⁷ For Origen, sacrifice of holocaust in the form of martyrdom further explains the constitutive elements of resemblance to God and the nature of Christian love.

Gregory of Nyssa: God's Back

Gregory speaks of ontological participation in terms of participation in all goodness. God "made human nature participant in all good."¹³⁸ Man as the image of God is participation in the archetypal goodness: "If the Deity is the fullness of good, and [man] is His image, then the image finds its resemblance to the Archetype in being filled with all good."¹³⁹ For Gregory, the mind (*nous*) as the anthropological center of man's image of God has two dimensions: the static or complete ontological dimension and the dynamic or graced one. When "the mind is adorned by [divine] similitude,"¹⁴⁰ it becomes a living image, bearing the likeness of divine nature, as an added gift of "Godlike" grace to the image. Gregory describes this dynamic image as "a living image (*imago quasi viva*) that participates in the archetype by dignity and by name."¹⁴¹ Our becoming like God is by analogy of participation in Christ who is the archetype.

In the nature-grace schema, Gregory emphasizes that it is necessary for the "inferior nature" to follow (ἀκολουθία) the "superior nature": "But when there is any interruption of this beneficent connection, or when, on the contrary, the superior comes to follow the inferior, then is displayed the misshapen character of matter, when it is isolated from nature."¹⁴² Grace is necessary for the cohesive and integral functioning of

---

136. Benedict XVI/Ratzinger, *Church Fathers*, 41.

137. Origen, *Homiliae in Leviticum* 9.9 (PG 12:521D).

138. Gregory of Nyssa, *De Hominis Opificio* 16.10 (PG 44:184B).

139. Gregory of Nyssa, *De Hominis Opificio* 16.10 (PG 44:184B).

140. Gregory of Nyssa, *De Hominis Opificio* 12.9 (PG 44:161C).

141. Gregory of Nyssa, *De Hominis Opificio* 4.2 (PG 44:135C) [Louth, *Genesis 1-11*].

142. Gregory of Nyssa, *De Hominis Opificio* 12.10 (PG 44:161D). For Gregory, "following God" also has an epistemic dimension, whereby as the spiritual way we come to

nature. For him, when nature refuses to follow grace, it loses its function of providing form and order to its corporeal part, since "in itself matter is a thing without form or structure."[143] The "beauty of nature with which it is adorned through the mind"[144] consists in the mind's capacity to hold in harmony with the goodness of the archetypal image, our corporeal parts. The withdrawal of the mind from following Christ "is the genesis of evil, arising through the withdrawal of that which is beautiful and good."[145] Here the concept of ἀκολουθία affirms participation as a concept that applies strictly to the correspondence of the lesser to the superior; thus an analogy. Gregory expresses the ascending movement of spiritual participation as ἀκολουθία.

Gregory's ἀκολουθία is not only a psychological participation of the mind in God, but is a biblical concept expressing the mode of spiritual progress or ascent. According to Paulos Gregorios, Gregory's ἀκολουθία is characteristic of the Stoic thought, which links ontology, epistemology and ethics.[146] In his *De Vita Moysis*, he explains how "seeing the back" of or "following" Christ is how we know and see the face of God:

> But when the Lord [Christ] who spoke to Moses came to fulfill his own law, he likewise gave a clear explanation to his disciples, laying bare the meaning of what had previously not "if any man will go before me." And to the one asking about eternal life he proposes the same thing, for he says *come, follow me* [ἀκολούθει μοι] (Mark 10:21). Now, he who follows sees the back.[147]

In his commentary on Exodus 33, Gregory recognizes how Christ uses "following him" to describe to both his disciples and the rich young man the true meaning of participation in eternal life. For him, biblical ἀκολουθία preserves the tension between the souls longing for self-transcendence and the soul's incapacity to see God face-to-face. Participation

---

know God. He explains this in his *Contra Eunomius*, where he uses the Biblical image of Moses' seeing of God's back, as image of this analogy of participating in divine likeness by way of *following* him. Ratzinger twice quotes, Gregory's epistemic analogy of participation by following.

143. Gregory of Nyssa, *De Hominis Opificio* 12.10 (PG 44:161C).
144. Gregory of Nyssa, *De Hominis Opificio* 12.10 (PG 44:161C).
145. Gregory of Nyssa, *De Hominis Opificio* 12.11 (PG 44:164A).
146. See Gregorios, *Cosmic Man*, 52: "This linking ontology, epistemology and ethics, characteristic of Stoic thought as well as of Gregory's thinking, was a central notion in Christian patristic thought."
147. Gregory of Nyssa, *De vita Moysis* 2.251 (SC 1bis:278).

is grounded in the truth of God's inaccessibility and in man's desire for him,[148] in the tension between the soul's desire for beholding God's face, and the ontological gap between God and creature. According Gregory, "This truly is the vision of God: never to be satisfied in the desire to see him... Thus, no limit would interrupt growth in the ascent to God, since no limit to the Good can be found nor the increasing of desire for the Good brought to an end because it is satisfied."[149] Gregory's biblical ακολουθία expresses the proper analogy of creature's participation in the Good. He also indicates Christ's primacy as the "rock" of the ascending movement of ακολουθία: "If someone, as the Psalmist says, should pull his feet up from the mud of the pit and plant them upon the rock (the rock is Christ who is absolute virtue), then the more steadfast and unmovable he becomes in the Good the faster he completes the course."[150] For Gregory, "Moses' entrance into the rock" prefigures Christ as the locus of following God, "since Christ is understood by Paul as the rock, [and] all hope of good things is believed to be in Christ, in whom we have learned all the treasures of good things to be. He who finds any good finds it in Christ who contains all good."[151] Following Christ is the proper way of participating in the Good; because in him, the fullness of Goodness is revealed to us. Gregory's explanation of participation as following God or seeing his back is one of Ratzinger's favorite patristic depiction of true discipleship.[152]

Athanasian *Assumptio Hominis*

In his anti-Arian exegesis, Athanasius demonstrates the significance of the use of analogy for the defense of Christ's divinity. He highlights the analogical character of man's participation in Christ by prioritizing the condescending movement of the Word's *assumptio hominis*. He clarifies

---

148. Gregory of Nyssa, *De vita Moysis* 2.230 (SC 1bis:264): "[Man] asks to attain as if he had never partaken, beseeching God to appear to him, not according to his capacity to partake, but according to God's true being."

149. Gregory of Nyssa, *De vita Moysis* 2.239 (SC 1bis:270).

150. Gregory of Nyssa, *De vita Moysis* 2.244 (SC 1bis:274).

151. Gregory of Nyssa, *De vita Moysis* 2.248 (SC 1bis:276).

152. See Benedict XVI/Ratzinger, *On the Way*, 26–27: "Personally, I always find particularly moving the commentary on this passage (Exod 33) that Gregory of Nyssa gives. Being able to see God only from the back." See also Benedict XVI/Ratzinger, *Transforming Power of Faith*, 80.

that "The [Lord's] being in creation does not mean that he shares its nature; on the contrary, all created things partake of his power (δυνάμεως μετέχει)."[153] The Word's *assumptio hominis* is not a participation on the part of Christ, but a condescension to our humanity for the purpose of our participation in him. In the katabatic movement of the Incarnation, the uniqueness of Christ's relation to the Father as the "Only-begotten" constitutes the uniqueness of his relation to us as "First-born" of many brethren:

> If he is also called First-born (πρωτότοκος) of the creation, still this is not as if he were levelled to the creatures, and only first of them in point of time (πρῶτος αὐτῶν κατὰ χρόνον) [for how should that be, since He is "Only-begotten"?], but it is because of the Word's condescension (συγκατάβασιν τοῦ Λόγου) to the creatures, according to which, he has become the "Brother" of many.[154]

Relative to us his brethren, the name of Christ as First-born is analogical because on account of his condescension, we are his brethren anabatically, i.e., by ascent into his divinity. For Athanasius, Christ's *assumptio hominis* does not only manifest the true man, it also raises man into the immortality of the divine: "He, indeed, assumed humanity that we might become God."[155] Our ascending response to Christ's condescension is what constitutes participation.

Athanasius goes on to explain in an ecclesial way, how we become like God. Central to his ecclesial participation is the synthesis of sacrifice, temple (worship), and immortality in the body (σῶμα) of Christ. He says, "[Christ] next offered up his sacrifice also on behalf of all, in order firstly to make men free of their old transgressions, and further to show himself more powerful even than death, displaying his own body (σῶμα) incorruptible, as first-fruit (ἀπαρχή) of the resurrection of all."[156] The body of the crucified and risen Christ is the locus of participating in immortality through worship. As the first-fruit of the resurrection, Christ's body is for us in a unique way, the temple of worship and locus of participation in God. We become God's temple by analogy to Christ's body, "for because of our relationship to his body (σῶμα) we too have become God's temple

---

153. Athanasius, *De Incarnatione* 43 (PG 25:173A) [*Selected Works and Letters*].
154. Athanasius, *Or. ad. Ar.* 2.62 (PG 26:277C).
155. Athanasius, *De Incarnatione* 54 (PG 25:192B).
156. Athanasius, *De Incarnatione* 20 (PG 25:132A).

(ναος Θεοῦ), and in consequence are made God's sons, so that even in us the Lord is now worshipped."¹⁵⁷ Athanasius's ἀπαρχή indicates ecclesial participation as an analogy by highlighting Christ's primal relationship to his temple, clarifying that he is not merely the eldest among many brethren.¹⁵⁸ According to Ratzinger, in Athanasius, "the connection between the 'historical' body of Christ and the 'ecclesial' one, would be intended in the sense that the human historical body of Christ is the vicarious representation that prefigures precisely the ἀπαρχή of 'the body of the Church.'"¹⁵⁹ Our theologian finds in Athanasius, an anticipation of Chrysostom's and Augustine's ecclesial primacy of Christ.

Ecclesial and Eucharistic Communication of Unity

Like Athanasius, Hilary of Poitiers identifies the assumed humanity (body) of Christ as the locus of participation. He speaks of the "body" of Christ as the means by which he "unites" the flesh (nature) of us all: "He took on himself the nature of us all; ... he took on himself the nature of all flesh and through it became true life; he has in himself the root of every vine shoot. ... Through the relationship with his flesh, access to Christ is open to all, on the condition that they divest themselves of their former self (Cf. Eph 4:22), nailing it to the Cross (Cf. Col 2:14)."¹⁶⁰

In his comments on the sacramental way of Christ's habitation in us, Hilary indicates the primacy of Christ as foundation of such participation.¹⁶¹ First, he finds a metaphysical ground for participation operative

---

157. Athanasius, *De. inc. et co. Ar.* 14 (PG 26:1008B).

158. Athanasius, *De. inc. et co. Ar.* 12 (PG 26:1004): "ὅπερ σῶμα ἀπαρχή ἐστι τῆς ἐκκλησίας. Ἀπαρχή γάο φησιν ὁ Χριστός." In spite of the fact that the authenticity of this work is disputable, Ratzinger acknowledges and quotes it as one that offers a good synthesis of the Athanasian thought, even if the words were not his own. See Benedict XVI/Ratzinger, *Popolo e Casa di Dio*, 288n33.

159. Benedict XVI/Ratzinger, *Popolo e Casa di Dio*, 207.

160. Hilary of Poitiers, *Tractatus super Psalmos* 54.9; 51.16; 91.9 (PL 9:352, 317, 499) [Benedict XVI/Ratzinger, *Church Fathers*, 116].

161. Benedict XVI/Ratzinger, "Volk und Haus Gottes," 278 (my translation): "Auch er betont einerseits scharf entschieden die *Hineinnahme* des ganzen Menschengeschlechtes in Christus, aber ezeigt zugleich auf, wie diese unsere Hineinnahme in Christus sich entfaltet und wirksam wird in der Hineinnahme Christi in uns. Und zwar gescheit dieses Gegenwärtigenwerden Christ zu uns in einer doppelten Weise: (a) In der christlichen Liebe zum Nächsten . . . (b) unser Einssein im Eucharistie-Sakrament" (On one hand, he [Hilary] also sharply and decisively highlights the

in Christian love for neighbor: "Christ assumed the body of us all and by reason of this unity of the body, was made neighbor to each of us."[162] He characterizes the meaning of the "body of Christ" as "the community of those who love on account of their radical unity in Christ."[163] Ratzinger comments that Hilary's notion of the body of Christ as "community of love" is not physiological or ethical unity of love, but "a love founded on an *original* unity of 'being' in Christ."[164] In other words, there is a primal and metaphysical fundament grounding such unity, which is rooted in a universal assumption of "being human" in Christ. The priority placed on "original unity" of our humanity as the common ground for ecclesial charity, indicates Christ's assumed body as the original humanity of us all. Thus, in Hilary, the unifying primordial role of Christ explains the metaphysical grounds of the ecclesial unity of *caritas* in Christ.

Secondly, Hilary (anticipating Augustine's *De Trinitate*) introduces a sacramental notion of participation as "*communicandae unitatis*" (a communication of unity) analogous to the Trinitarian unity between the Father and the Son. He says,

> Now, how it is that we are in him through the sacrament of the flesh and blood bestowed upon us, he himself testifies, saying, "In a little while the world will not see me. . . . I am in the Father and you are in me and I in you" (John 14:19-20). If he wished to indicate a mere unity of will, why did he set forth a kind of gradation and sequence in the *communication of the unity*, unless it were that since he was in the Father through the divine nature, and we on the contrary in him through his birth in the body, he would have us believe that he is in us through the mystery of the sacraments.[165]

---

assumptio of all mankind in Christ, while he points out at the same time how this our assumption into Christ develops and becomes operative in the inhabitation of Christ in us. And this being present of Christ in us occurs in two ways: [a] in the Christian love of neighbor . . . [b] our "unity" in the sacrament of the Eucharist).

162. Hilary of Poitiers, *Commentarium in Matthaeum* 19.5 (PL 9:1025) (my translation): "Christus, qui omnium nostrum corpus assumpsit et unicuique nostrum assumpti corporis ratione factus est proximus."

163. Benedict XVI/Ratzinger, *Popolo e Casa di Dio*, 208.

164. Benedict XVI/Ratzinger, *Popolo e Casa di Dio*, 208.

165. Hilary of Poitiers, *De Trin.* 8.15 (PL 10:247). In reference to this paragraph, Ratzinger identifies the following as the decisive phrase, "Si voluntatis tantum unitatem intelligi vellet, cur gradum quemdam atque ordinem *communicandae unitatis* exposuit, nisi, ut cum ille in patre per naturam divinatis esset, nos contra in eo per corporalem eius nativitatem et ille rursum in nobis per sacramentorum inesse

Shortly thereafter, Hilary notes that the sacrament of participation in the body of Christ, which he described as the means of communicating the unity between Christ and the Father, is an "analogy of comparison" for the purpose of our understanding. He says, "For all comparison is chosen to shape our understanding, so that we may grasp the subject of which we treat by help of *analogy* set before us. This is the cause of our life that we have Christ dwelling within our flesh, and we shall live through him in the same manner as he lives through the Father."[166] As Christ's life subsists in the Son's union with the Father, so also does our sacramental life constituted by the indwelling of Christ in our humanity. The mystery of sacramental unity with Christ is for Hilary, a real analogy because it is founded on the ontological unity that we all share in Christ's humanity. As the unity of the Father and the Son are not merely union of will, so also what is sacramentally communicated to us is not merely a unity of will with Christ, but a real primordial unity, which in turn unites us with his divinity: "If indeed Christ has assumed to himself the flesh of our body, . . . and we indeed receive in a mystery the flesh of his body, how can a unity of will be maintained, seeing that the special property of nature received through the sacrament is the sacrament of perfect unity."[167] With Hilary, primacy of Christ unfolds in a sacramental way as the center of communicating perfect unity in Christ, such that it enacts a unity among us in accord with our original unity with the Trinity.

In John Chrysostom, the full Eucharistic implication of the Athanasian participation by "*assumptio hominis*" and Hilary's sacramental "*communicandae unitatis*" becomes more apparent. While Hilary's sacramental unity highlights an analogy to the Trinitarian unity, Chrysostom's notion of Eucharistic participation emphasizes a comparison to Christ's union with his body. Commenting on I Corinthians 10:16, he says, "For as that body (i.e., the body of the historical Christ) is united to Christ, so also we are united to him by this bread."[168] There is a shift from an inter-

---

mysterium crederetur ac sic perfecta per mediatorem unitas doceretur, cum nobis in se manentibus ipse maneret in patre et in patre manens maneret in nobis et ita ad unitatem patris proficeremus, cum qui in eo naturaliter secundum nativitatem inest, nos quoque in eo naturaliter inessemus ipso in nobis naturatiler permenente." Ratzinger translates "communicandae unitatis" as "participazione all'unita" (Benedict XVI/Ratzinger, *Popolo e Casa di Dio*, 208).

166. Hilary of Poitiers, *De Trin.* 8.16 (PL 10:248).
167. Hilary of Poitiers, *De Trin.* 8.13 (PL 10:246).
168. John Chrysostom, *In 1 Cor. homiliae* 24.4 (PG 61:200).

personal (Trinitarian analogy) unity to an incorporational (Eucharistic analogy) unity. Ratzinger notes this shift as evident in the intermediary and "causal" role placed on the Eucharistic bread between the historical body of Christ and the community incorporated into Christ: "We are united to him (Christ of history) by his bread."[169] To speak of "the bread" is to speak of both the historical and the ecclesial "body" of Christ. On account of Chrysostom's sense of the causality of the "the body" by "the bread," we can speak of the primacy of the "Eucharistic bread" as a substitute for the primacy of the assumed body of Christ.

What grounds the reality of the sacramental analogy between the Eucharist and the historical body of Christ remains the Greek tradition of *assumptio hominis*. He indicates the profundity of such unity when he insists that Eucharistic participation is not merely "a sharing with" but a union at the very level of being; i.e., a communion in Christ, *"The bread we break, is it not a communion* (κοινωνία, *communicatio* in Vulgate) *in the Body of Christ* (1 Cor 10:16)? Why did he [Paul] not speak of participation? Because he intended to express something more and point out how close was the union. We communicate not only by participating or partaking, but also by being united."[170] Chrysostom's robust theology of the Eucharist, indicates how ecclesial implication of the Greek tradition of the primacy of Christ's *assumed* body consists in the Eucharistic *assumption* of the Christian community into the one body of Christ. The Eucharist then takes primacy of causality in Chrysostom's understanding of the Pauline analogy of ecclesial "κοινωνία."

Augustine: Primacy of the Heart of Christ

According to Kizewski, "Augustine singles out the participation in God's grace [and] wants to consider first what the mind is when abstracted

169. Benedict XVI/Ratzinger, "Volk und Haus Gottes," 281. Here is Ratzinger's observation regarding Chrysostom's commentary on the 1 Cor 10:16: "Hier ist eine Doppelebene der Christusleibschaft ausgesagt: Der Leib des historischen Christus und daneben die Gemeinschaft der Christen als christusgeeinter Leib. Zwischen beiden steht vermittelnd das eucharistische Brot, desessen Aufgabe es ist, unsere Einung mit Christus zum Leibe Christi herbeizuführen" (Here is expressed two levels of Christ's corporeality: the historical body of Christ [τὸ σῶμα ἐκεῖνο] and next to it, the community of Christians as a body united in Christ [οὕτω καὶ ἡμεῖς αὐτῷ ... ἐνούμεθα]. Between the two lies as intermediary, the Eucharistic bread [διὰ τοῦ ἄρτου τούτου] whose task consists in causing our unification with Christ to form the body of Christ).

170. John Chrysostom, *In 1 Cor. homiliae* 24.4 (PG 61:200).

from participation."¹⁷¹ Augustine says, "But we must first consider the mind in itself before it is a partaker of God, and before His image is to be found in it."¹⁷² We saw earlier, how Augustine closely associates "image" with the "mind." The mind considered as nature remains an image. However, Augustine does not only abstract participation from image, but he also grounds the former in the latter,

> For we have said that, even though it has become impaired and disfigured by the loss of its participation in God, it remains nonetheless an image of God. For it is His image by the very fact that it is capable of Him, and can be a partaker of him; and it cannot be so great a good except that it is His image.¹⁷³

Participation in God's grace is possible only because the image bears nature's capacity for God. By abstracting participation from image, Augustine distinguishes participation as a spiritual concept. While in Justin, Origen and Gregory of Nyssa, participation is either ontological or spiritual, in Augustine, participation takes on a distinctly spiritual meaning, without losing its ontological anchor. The significance of this distinction becomes clearer in Ratzinger's use of the same analogy.

Alluding to Eucharistic communion, he highlights "transformation" as the effect of participation: "You will not change me into yourself, as you change food into your flesh, but you will be transformed into me."¹⁷⁴ While the descent of the Word is not a change in Him, his assumed humanity changes its participants into his likeness. Hence, relative to the descending movement of the Word's *assumptio hominis*, the transformational element of the participation underscores the "greater dissimilarity" of the analogy.

Ratzinger's presentation of Augustine's pneumatic ecclesiology of communion is centered on Augustine's understanding of the Holy Spirit as both love (*caritas*) and gift (*donum*).¹⁷⁵ Augustine uses his

---

171. Kizewski, "God-Talk," 300.

172. Augustine, *Trin.* 14.8.11 (CCSL 50A:436): "Sed prius mens in se ipsa consideranda est antequam sit particeps Dei, et in ea reperienda est imago eius."

173. Augustine, *Trin.* 14.8.11 (CCSL 50A:436): "Diximus enim eam etsi amissa Dei participatione obsoletam atque deformem, Dei tamen imaginem permanere. Eo quippe ipso imago eius est, quo eius capax est, eiusque particeps esse potest; quod tam magnum bonum, nisi per hoc quod imago eius est, non potest."

174. Augustine, *Conf.* 7.10.16 (PL 32:742): "Cresce et manducabis me. Nec tu me in te mutabis sicut cibum carnis tuae, sed tu mutaberis in me."

175. Benedict XVI/Ratzinger, *Pilgrim Fellowship of Faith*, 38–59.

pneumatic *caritas* and *donum* to explain how participation takes place in the historical and ecclesial body of Christ. The analogical trajectory of his pneumatic body of Christ, interprets the Pauline *koinonia* in a unitive and Trinitarian way. We now consider how the primacy of Christ is the key to the comprehensive character of Augustine's ecclesial analogy of participation.

Primacy of "Caritas" in Ecclesial Communion

In chapter 15 of Augustine's *De Trinitate* and his *Tractatus* 26 and 37 on John's Gospel, one finds in Augustine's pneumatic exegesis on *caritas*, a synthesis of Hilary's Trinitarian analogy of *communicatio unitatis* and Chrysostom's Eucharistic incorporation analogy. Augustine capitalizes on the unifying identity of the Holy Spirit as *caritas* between the Father and the Son,[176] for his analogous explanation of the communion of the Body of Christ. Like Hilary, he affirms that through faith in Christ, the Trinitarian unity of *caritas* is communicated into our lives as *gift* of God, since "the love which is from God and is God is distinctly the Holy Spirit; through him the charity of God is poured out in our hearts (Rom 5:5). This is the reason why it is most apposite that the Holy Spirit, while being God, should also be called the gift of God."[177] God's *donum* of *caritas* communicates to us as divine communion, makes us become *communio* in God with neighbor. This communication of divine unity takes place via the communion of the Eucharistic bread, which in turn makes us one house of God: "For they who eat such bread do not strive with one another; for we being many are one bread, one body. And by this bread, God makes people of one sort to dwell in a house."[178] Thus, like Chrysostom, Augustine employs the Eucharistic incorporation analogy to explain the ecclesial reality of the Spirit-ual communication of the Trinitarian *caritas*.

---

176. Augustine, *Trin.* 15.19.37 (CCSL 50:513): "Et si caritas qua Pater diligit Filium, et Patrem diligit Filius, ineffabiliter communionem demonstrat amborum; quid convenientius quam ut ille dicatur caritas proprie, qui Spiritus est communis ambobus?" (If the *caritas* by which the Father loves the Son and the Son loves the Father inexpressibly shows forth the communion of them both, what more suitable that he who is the common Spirit of them both should be distinctly called *caritas*?).

177. Augustine, *Trin.* 15.18.32 (CCSL 50:508): "Dilectio igitur quae ex Deo est et Deus est, proprie Spiritus Sanctus est, per quem diffunditur in cordibus nostris Dei caritas, per quam nos tota inhabitet Trinitas. Quocirca rectissime Spiritus Sanctus, cum sit Deus, vocatur etiam Donum Dei."

178. Augustine, *Tract. Ev. Io.* 26.14 (PL 35:1613).

Alluding to Eucharistic communion, he highlights "transformation" as the effect of communion: "You will not change me into yourself, as you change food into your flesh, but you will be transformed into me."[179] The transformation consists in becoming united as one body of Christ by the outpouring of the gift of *caritas*: "The Church is the body of Christ, in this body you are a member. . . . For the unity of the members is of one mind by charity; and that unity speaks as one man then spoke. Consequently, we too receive the Holy Spirit if we love the Church, if we are joined together by charity."[180]

The ontology of Augustine's analogy of ecclesial communion between Christ and mankind remains consistent with the *assumptio hominis* of the Greek fathers, which identifies the humanity of the Word as the locus of participation: "But that you might participate in Being-Itself, he first of all became a participant in what you are; the Word was made flesh (John 1:14) so that flesh might participate in the Word."[181] In the ecclesial communion, the descent of the Word does not constitute a change in Him, but a change in its participants into his likeness. The descent of "Being-Itself" takes priority of movement as the enabler of our participation. Augustine's explanation of the similarity and dissimilarity between Christ and mankind is soteriological. As the Mediator, Christ is fully human without sharing in our sin. Employing the Pauline expression *similitudine carnis peccati*,[182] Augustine explains the dissimilarity, i.e., "although truly human Christ has been born only in the *likeness* of sinful flesh."[183]

---

179. Augustine, *Conf.* 7.10.16 (PL 32:742): "Cresce et manducabis me. Nec tu me in te mutabis sicut cibum carnis tuae, sed tu mutaberis in me."

180. Augustine, *Tract. Ev. Io.* 32.7-8 (PL 35:1645): "Ecclesia est corpus Christi, in hoc corpore membrum es . . . cum ergo membrum sis eius corporis quod loquitur omnibus linguis, crede te loqui omnibus linguis. Unitas enim membrorum caritate concordat; et ipsa unitas loquitur quomodo tunc unus homo loquebatur. Accipimus ergo et nos Spiritum sanctum, si amamus Ecclesiam, si caritate compaginamur, si catholico nomine et fide gaudemus." Cf. Augustine, *Enarrat. Ps.* 29.2.1 (CCSL 38:174): " Inter illam Trinitatem et hominum infirmitatem et iniquitatem, mediator factus est homo, non iniquus, sed tamen infirmus; ut ex eo quod non iniquus, iungeret te Deo."

181. Augustine, *Enarrat. Ps.* 121.5 (CCSL 40:1805).

182. Augustine, *Tract. Ev. Io.* 41.5 (PL 53:1695): "Venit enim in carne, hoc est in similitudine carnis peccati, non tamen in carne peccati, non habens ullum omnino peccatum: et ideo factus est verum sacrificium pro peccato, quia nullum habebat ipse peccatum."

183. Carola, *Augustine of Hippo*, 161.

In effect, with his thoughts on ecclesial communion, Augustine synthesizes his patristic predecessors. What is particular to Augustine is how he comprehensively develops an ecclesiological emphasis on the primacy of Christ's gift of his Spirit as *caritas*. In his polemic against the Donatists, Augustine further explains in practical terms how the gift of *caritas* shapes ecclesial communion. He makes the distinction between an efficacious and valid participation, which corresponds with *communio sanctorum* (*res*) and *communio sacramentorum* respectively.[184] For Augustine the Spirit communicates unity to the Church in the form of "*caritas*" through the "universal society of saints": "The presentation of the little ones to receive the spiritual grace is the act not so much of those by whose hands they are borne up as of the universal society of saints ... by whose holy and perfectly united *caritas* they are assisted in receiving the communion of the Holy Spirit."[185] Those who have broken unity with the Catholic communion, i.e., the heretics, do not participate in the *communio sanctorum*, by whose prayers, the Spirit, symbolized by the dove, communicates efficaciously the sacraments of divine *caritas*: "Nor will the prayers of the saints, in other words, the groaning of the one dove, be able to help one who is set in heresy or schism."[186]

Augustine claims that although the Donatists administer a valid baptism, they lack efficacious sacraments because they are outside of the *caritas* of Catholic *communio* communicated through the prayers of the saints: "For if the sacrament of Christian baptism, being always one and

---

184. According to Ratzinger, Augustine indicates *communio Sanctorum* when he speaks of "the true baptismal maternity [of the church] as the affairs of the saints, of those who as *communio sanctorum* are the Church in the proper sense" (Denn die Zeugung im stellvertretenden Glauben, die eigentliche Taufmutterschaft, ist Sache der Heiligen in der Kirche, derer, die als *communio sanctorum* im eigentlichen Begriff die Kirche sind) (Benedict XVI/Ratzinger, *Volk und Haus Gottes*, 215 [142]). We see this in his *Ep.* 98, where is designates to *unity of caritas in the saints,* the salvific power of baptism.

185. Augustine, *Ep.* 98.5 (PL 33:362) [*Confessions and Letters*, 408]: "Offeruntur quippe parvuli ad percipiendam spiritalem gratiam, non tam ab eis quorum gestantur manibus (quamvis et ab ipsis, si et ipsi boni fideles sunt), quam ab universa societate sanctorum atque fidelium. Ab omnibus namque offerri recte intelleguntur, quibus placet quod offeruntur, et quorum sancta atque individua caritate ad communicationem sancti Spiritus adiuvantur. Tota hoc ergo mater Ecclesia, quae in sanctis est, facit, quia tota omnes, tota singulos parit."

186. Augustine, *De bapt.* 3.17.22 (PL 43:149–50) [*Writings against the Manicheans and the Donatists*]. "Nec in haeresi aut schismate constitutum sanctorum orationes, id est, illius unicae columbae gemitus poterunt adiuvare."

the same, is of value even when administered by heretics, and suffices to seal his consecration to God, however does not suffice to secure to the baptized, participation in eternal life."[187] Bearing "the seal of consecration to God" and lack of sufficiency for "securing participation in eternal life" distinguishes validity from efficacy of a sacrament. Therefore, while acknowledging the visible ecclesial communion as an indispensable expression of the interior and spiritual communion, however, the reality (*res*) of participation takes on an exclusively Spirit-ual and interior character; thus a primacy of *caritas*. Augustine's primacy of ecclesial *caritas* consists in a priority of the Spirit-ual reality of communion over the visible sacramental communion.

To further highlight the analogical nature of ecclesial participation, following Tyconius's notion of a mid Church,[188] the anti-Donatist Augustine maintains that as long as we are still pilgrims on earth, the visible body of Christ the Church consist of both saints and sinners—*corpus permixtum*.[189] Participation in the sacramental body of Christ, though necessary, does not suffice for salvation. Rather, the analogy of *corpus* prioritizes participation in the interior reality of the body over that of the exterior. Thus the primacy of *caritas* is the logic behind the necessity of the ongoing purification of the visible body of Christ, because it explains transformation as ascending movement from a corporeal vision of unity to a spiritual unity of love in Christ.

In light of Augustine's analogy of the mind as image of the Trinity, his ecclesial primacy of *caritas* concretely explains how the Trinitarian analogy of image (memory, intellect, and will) finds its realization in ecclesial participation (*communion*), whereby through the gift of divine charity, the mind always remembers, understands, and loves God his creator.[190] The gift of divine charity is fundamental to the realization of the inner reason for creation. But as we shall see later, Augustine's

---

187. Augustine, *Ep.* 98.5 (PL 33:362): "Nam si christiani baptismi sacramentum, quando unum atque idipsum est, etiam apud haereticos valet et sufficit ad consecrationem, quamvis ad vitae aeternae *participationem* non sufficiat."

188. According to Joseph Carola, "Tyconius significantly influenced Augustine's reading of the Pauline corpus and had a profound effect upon his theological development" (Carola, *Augustine of Hippo*, 172).

189. See Benedict XVI/Ratzinger, "Volk und Haus Gottes," 210 (138): "Wir begegnen ihm, wenn Augustin die Kirche in dieser Zeitlichkeit im Anschluss an Tyconius als corpus permixtum bezeichnet" (We encounter this when Augustine, adhering to Tyconius, describes this temporal Church as *corpus permixtum*).

190. See Augustine, *Trin.* 14.12.15 (CCSL 50:443).

communion analogy does not only involve the mind, but the totality of the person expressed by the unifying metaphor of the heart.

Participation in the Heart

According to Ratzinger, "The view that the heart is the locus of the saving encounter with the Logos has a very firm basis . . . in Augustine's exhortation in connection with the Psalms."[191] We have already established that for Augustine, the Spirit as the *gift* of participation in Christ's body, dwells in our heart (Cf. Rom 5:5). In his commentary on Psalm 119, he confirms that the heart is the center of spiritual ascent: "Now listen to the Psalm. Let us present to ourselves a man who will ascend. Where will he ascend? In his heart."[192] Why the heart? Because the psalmist presents the heart as both the center of tears of passion and of love. For Augustine, the psalmist speaks of the heart of "one man" who suffers and cries because it possesses here on earth, the gift of divine love:

> Who among us cries from the ends of the earth? Neither I, nor you, nor he, but the Church. It is the entire inheritance of Christ that cries toward God from the ends of the earth. . . . All the saints form only one man in Christ (*omnes sancti unus homo in Christo*), since holy unity is in Christ. And this one man exclaims: "From the ends of the earth I have cried out to you, when my heart was in anguish."[193]

The analogy of ecclesial communion becomes evident in Augustine's theology of the heart, whereby through the communion of the saints, the cry and anguish of Christ's heart unifies that of all people who partake in his gift of self-giving love. Augustine's notion of ascent of the heart is about the heart of those who partake in the communion of the saints, where the descending gift of *caritas* finds a corresponding ascent of communion with God and neighbor. The suffering "heart of *unus homo*" is an analogy for both the suffering heart of Christ and that of his mystical body, the Church. The "one man" is really and universally the primordial man, Christ. Based on the primacy of the suffering heart of this one man, Augustine is able to speak of the crying heart of the Church, as analogous

---

191. Benedict XVI/Ratzinger, *Behold*, 68.
192. Augustine, *Enarrat. Ps.* 119.2.75 (CCSL 40:1779): "Iam ergo Psalmum audite. Ecce ante oculos nostros ponamus ascensurum hominem: ubi ascensurum? *In corde.*"
193. Augustine, *Enarrat. Ps.* 119.7 (CCSL 40:1783).

to that of Christ by way of the unity of *communio sanctorum*. We must add that in this context where Augustine discusses the heart of ecclesial ascent, he does not explicitly give any further exposition of the connection between the theology of the Cross and pneumatic ecclesiology, as Ratzinger will do later.

However, according to Carola, "the climactic moment of Saint Paul's conversion depicted in the Acts 9:4 figures prominently in Augustine's demonstration of the indivisible unity which the members of Christ's body enjoy with their head."[194] Augustine explains this indivisible communion as the unity of the Head and Body in the one *Totus Christus*.[195] The bond of charity, which is the gift of the Spirit, is what links the *corpus* to the *caput* such that when Christians suffered persecution in the hands of Saul, Christ was suffering. As Carola says, "a *communication idiomatum* is operative within the *Totus Christus*."[196] On account of the unity of the person of Christ, we can speak analogically of the suffering Son of God when his body suffers with him in the bond of charity. In the bond of charity, the priority of the suffering heart of the *Totus Christus* is the grounds for the merit of the suffering heart of the saints who participate in the one communion. Therefore, Augustine's ecclesial participation involves living in an eschatological hope whereby what began in Christ's suffering is being brought to fulfillment in the suffering of his mystical body. As Ratzinger says, "His [Augustine's] city of God . . . is a sacramental-eschatological entity, which lives in this world as a sign of the coming world."[197]

In the context of his commentary on Psalm 119, Augustine focuses on the disunity and sins of the pilgrim Church as cause for tears in the heart of the Church. As *corpus permixtum*, the Church consists of both the spiritual children of the promise (prefigured in Isaac) and the carnal children of Ishmael. He says,

---

194. Carola, *Augustine of Hippo*, 172.

195. Augustine, *Enarrat. Ps.* 30.2.3 (CCSL 38:192): "Hoc autem corpus nisi connexione caritatis adhaereret capiti suo, ut unus fieret ex capite et corpore, non de coelo quemdam persecutorem corripiens diceret: *Saule, Saule, quid me persequeris?* quando eum iam in coelo sedentem nullus homo tangebat, quomodo eum Saulus in terra saeviens adversus Christianos aliquo modo iniuria percellebat? Non ait: Quid sanctos meos, quid servos meos? Sed, *quid me persequeris,* hoc est, quid membra mea?."

196. Carola, *Augustine of Hippo*, 173.

197. Benedict XVI/Ratzinger, *Unity of Nations*, 113.

All those in the Church today who only know how to ask God for the temporal happiness belong to Ishmael. . . . Against these the Psalmist, when ascending, prayed and was given hot coals which lay waste and the sharp arrows of the Mighty One for his defense. He still lives in the midst of them until the whole floor be winnowed, and therefore said: "I have dwelt under the tents of Kedar." For the tents of Ishmael are called those of Kedar. . . . Those who belong to Isaac live amidst those who belong to Ishmael. These wish to ascend, those wish to topple them. . . . The spiritual man suffers persecution from the carnal man.[198]

For Augustine, the spiritual ascent of the heart is never between the individual and God, but involves the witness (martyrdom) that accompanies communal ascent with the whole body of Christ. While the sins of the false brethren (schismatics and lapse Catholics) inflicts anguish in the heart of the communion, nevertheless, perseverance in the gift of *caritas* demands living in eschatological hope with the true and false brethren. The "sharp arrow" that pierces the hearts of the saints indicates their tears of prayer and tolerance for the sake of unity: "The Catholic Church declares that unity must not be lost, the Church of God must not be divided. . . . If today it is impossible to separate the good from the wicked, it is necessary to tolerate this for a time . . . whoever humbly bears with the wicked for a time will come to eternal rest."[199]

Ratzinger notes that it is on account of his insistence on "*tolerare pro pace*" that Augustine explains how ecclesial concept of brotherhood encompasses both the false brothers and the true ones.[200] Preceding Augustine's concept of brotherhood is that of Athanasius. The analogy of brotherhood recognizes Christ as the primordial center of unity among many brethren.[201] In his humanity, Christ is the first born of many breth-

---

198. Augustine, *Enarrat. Ps.* 119.7 (CCSL 40:1784).

199. Augustine, *Enarrat. Ps.* 119.8.30 (CCSL 40:1786).

200. Benedict XVI/Ratzinger, "Studien zur Theologie der Kirchenväter," 628: "Wobei er [Augustinus] hinzufügt, dass es in der Kirche su allen Zeiten falsche Brüder gibt, mit denen der Christ um das Gut des "Friedens" willen auszukommen suchen muss, das heißt, um die Einheit der Kirche aufrechtzuerhalten. Dieser Gedanke der Toleranz im Inneren der Kirche (tolerare pro pace) al eine wesentliche Bedingung der christlichen Existenz ist eines der Grundthemen in der Diskussion des Augustinus mit den Donatisten."

201. See also Benedict XVI/Ratzinger, "Studien zur Theologie der Kirchenväter," 623: "Athanasius treibt die Reflexion über diesen Punkt (Brüderlichkeit) noch weiter, wenn er daran geht, den von der Schrift auf Christus angewandten Begriff πρωτότοκος (Kol 1,15) auszulegen, den die Arianer missbrauchten, um zu beweisen, dass Chrisus

ren in two senses: as the grounds in which many are born again in water and Spirit, and then, through his resurrection as the first born from the dead. Thus he is not merely our older brother, but is the primordial brother in whom we partake true sonship in relation to the Father.

"Sacramentum" and "Exemplum"

Augustine employs the concept of *sacramentum* and *exemplum* to further articulate how soteriology is by analogy of participation. For him, the death and resurrection of Jesus is not merely an example to emulate but also a mystery to partake. His deeds have an interior re-orientating effect in the very being of man. Thus, the unity of his deeds are fundamentally an exterior sign of an interior change in our souls—*sacramentum* and an example for our bodily death. He says,

> So then, the one death of our savior was our salvation from our two deaths, and his one resurrection bestowed two resurrections on us, since in either instance, that is both in death and in resurrection, his body served as the sacrament of our inner man and as the model of our outer man, by a kind of curative accord or symmetry.[202]

The dissimilarity is on account of the integrity of his humanity and the disunity of our sinful humanity. Our salvation demands the primacy of the gift of the unified humanity of Christ and our spiritual participation in it. In communion with Christ's one humanity, we encounter an analogous unity through sacramental healing of the soul and exterior expression of the same death in the body. The primacy of the paschal gift points to the example as a mystery to be lived and an example to be emulated. Ratzinger notes that in Augustine's commentary on the Sermon on the Mount, he speaks of the "purification of the heart" as the fundamental task of a Christian because the one gift of Christ's purifying mercy, makes us interiorly full of love and exteriorly full of loving deeds.[203] Thus, Augustine's soteriology offers a paschal synthesis, which confirms both the ontological and historical dimensions of the primacy of Christ.

Geschöpf ist (*Ar.* 2.62 [PG 26:277c])."

202. Augustine, *Trin.* 4.3.6 (CCSL 50:166–67).
203. See Benedict XVI/Ratzinger, *Jesus of Nazareth*, 2:62.

The Volitional Analogy of Maximus the Confessor

Kizewski helps us to see that in Maximus, "creatures participate in God 'analogously' or 'proportionately.'"[204] Maximus says, "For by virtue of the fact that all things have their being from God, they participate in God [analogously (ἀναλόγως)], whether by intellect, by reason, by sensation, by vital motion, or by some essential faculty or habitual fitness."[205] Kizewski observes that "Maximus finds three levels of participation in creatures: the level of being, the level of well-being, and the level of eternal being."[206] Maximus says, "A nature endowed with reason and understanding participates in the holy God by its very being, by its aptitude for well-being (that is, for goodness and wisdom), and by the free gift of eternal being."[207] The participation in being and eternal being pertains to the essence of man while participation in well-being, whereby man shares in the attributes of God's goodness and wisdom, pertains to his volitive faculty: "To the essence he gives being and eternal being, and to the volitive faculty he gives goodness and wisdom in order that what he is by essence the creature might become by participation."[208]

In other words, while the origin and the goal of man are identical forms of ontological participation, the historical ascending movement of creation towards its goal of union with God is a volitional process. As the origin and the goal of man speaks to the difference between what participates and what is participated in, man's love of goodness and wisdom for his well-being speaks to the inner power of created being towards its goal. For Maximus, recapitulation explains how God is the synthetic grounds for the three levels of participation:

> We also believe that this same One is manifested and multiplied in all the things that have their origin in Him, in a manner appropriate to the being of each [κατὰ τὴν ἑκάστου ἀναλογίαν ἀγαθοπρεπῶς], as befits His goodness. And He recapitulates all things in Himself, for it is owing to Him that all things exist and remain in existence, and it is from Him that all things came to

---

204. Kizewski, "God-Talk," 214.
205. Maximus the Confessor, *Ambigua* 7 (PG 91:1080) [*On the Difficulties*].
206. Kizewski, "God-Talk," 213.
207. Maximus the Confessor, *Capita theologiae et oeconomiae* 3.24 (PG 90:1024).
208. Maximus the Confessor, *Capita de charitate* 3.25 (PG 90:1024).

be in certain way, and for a certain reason, and (whether they are stationary or in motion) participate in God.[209]

He indicates the historical dimension of recapitulation with eschatological primacy of Christ. With the Incarnation, creation already shares by faith in the end of the ages, "since our Lord Jesus Christ is the beginning, middle, and the end of all ages, past future, [it would be fair to say that] the *end of the ages*—specifically that end which will actually come about by grace for the deification of those who are worthy—*has come upon us* in the potency through faith."[210] Thus, participation, which plays an important role in Maximus's explanation of how creation and realization of man in God takes place, takes a synthetic form in the primacy of Christ. While we already grant a participation in God by faith, we still need to investigate the contribution of Maximus to the comprehensive Christian vision of participation.

Descending Analogy of Assimilation

With the notion of assimilation, Maximus explains how human beings participate in God by grace. On the cosmic level, the perfection of participation is for him "divinization," which consists in the "actively realized (καθ' ἐνργεια) identity of the participants with what they participate in":

> Now the fulfillment of [the believer's] longing is the rest of the loving heart in eternal motion around the beloved. But the rest of the loving heart in eternal motion around the beloved is eternal, immediate delight . . . participation in the supernatural blessings of God. And this is the forming of those who participate into the likeness of what they participate in; but such a likening consists in the actively realized (καθ' ἐνργεια) identity of the participants with what they participate in, which comes to its fullness with the likeness itself. And this identity . . . is divinization.[211]

For him, the transition from the natural motion of being to its fulfillment by grace of divinization is passive because it lies beyond the realm

---

209. Maximus the Confessor, *Ambigua* 7 (PG 91:1080).

210. Maximus the Confessor, *Ad Thalassium* 22 (CCSG 7:137) [*On the Cosmic Mystery*].

211. Maximus the Confessor, *Ad Thalassium*, 59 (PG 90:608-9A) [Balthasar, *Cosmic Liturgy*, 170-71].

of nature: "We experience divinization passively—we do not achieve it ourselves, because it lies beyond nature. For we have, within our nature, no power capable of receiving (δεκτικὴν δύναμιν) divinization."[212] He explains divinization with the analogy of "assimilation" or assumption (*Aufhebung*), a process that involves "no faculty, of any sort for being assimilated, because then it would no longer be grace but the revelation of an activity latent within the potentiality of nature."[213] If divinization is a passive ascent on the part of the participant in God, how does Maximus describe the descent of God into the nature of created material beings? For Maximus "God is beyond participation,"[214] and the descent of God's grace is no participation but an assimilation, since participation involves no change in God, only a change in the creature.

Maximus describes in his idea of divinization is a kind of "perfect analogy" between God and creature whereby, even in the most intimate degree of union, "the ideas of nature and grace [remain] ever unmingled with each other (οὐδαμῶς ἀλλήλοις συμφυρέτων).... Grace never does away with the passivity of nature."[215] The origin and goal of man is identical to the extent that the activity of both is only of the one who assimilates, God.

The Priority of Christ in Assimilation Analogy

In Maximus, divinization is the work of Christ. Christ, "unites created nature to uncreated nature in love—O miracle of God's tender kindness toward us!—and reveals that both, through the relationship of grace, are now but one single reality. The whole world now inheres (περιχωρήσας) as a totality in the whole of God, and becomes everything that God is except for the identity of his nature."[216] Extending the question of the mode of the descent of Christ to the question of the extent of his assimilation of our humanity, Balthasar comments on Maximus's position as follows:

---

212. Maximus the Confessor, *Ad Thalassium* 22 (CCSG 7:145, 28–31).
213. Maximus the Confessor, *Ad Thalassium* 22 (PG 90:321A).
214. Maximus the Confessor, *Capita de charitate* 3.22 (PG 90:1024).
215. Maximus the Confessor, *Ad Thalassium* 37 (PG 90:384C–385A; CCSG 7:249, 35–48); cf. Balthasar, *Cosmic Liturgy*, 149.
216. Maximus the Confessor, *Ambigua* PG 91:1308C; cf. Balthasar, *Cosmic Liturgy*, 274.

A different, question is how far that process goes, which Maximus calls the "assimilation" (οἰκείωσις) of even the dishonorable sufferings and corruption of fallen humanity by the divine physician; here it is once again essential to make it clear that the passive, unfree suffering of the soul of Christ, like that of his body, is rooted in the free and active core of the divine hypostasis, which also determines how it experiences these things.[217]

Maximus makes the distinction between the relational and natural assimilation (οἰκείωσις) of our humanity in Christ. While the incarnational descent of Christ is a natural assimilation, Christ's assimilation of human sin (becoming sin) for our sake is not ontological but based on relationship with us in the course of salvation history. He says,

> Our vulnerabilities (πάθη) have two aspects: that of punishment and that of guilt. The former is characteristic of our nature as such; the latter simply disfigures it. The former was freely and ontologically taken on by Christ along with his human existence; through this act, he gave strength to our nature as it is and freed it from the curse that lay on us. But he made the latter aspect his own in the course of salvation history, through his love for humanity, in that he took it up to destroy it, as fire consumes wax or the sun the mists of the earth, so that in its place he might bestow on us his own blessings.[218]

The mode (tropos) of Christ's absorption (*Aufhebung*) of our sin is for its destruction "as fire consumes wax," while his free descent into our human form by the Incarnation is a natural assimilation. In the relational dimension, assimilation becomes transformational *for us*.

According to Balthasar, while Christ appropriates our human will (θέλησις) and its operation (ἐνέργεια),[219] "Maximus refuses to attribute [γνώμη] '*gnome*' (deliberation) to the human nature of Christ [because] it is a sign of weakness that does not pertain to Christ."[220] It is in the context of his commentaries on the opposition of the two wills in the

---

217. Balthasar, *Cosmic Liturgy*, 255.

218. Maximus the Confessor, *Opuscula* (PG 91:237B) [Balthasar, *Cosmic Liturgy*, 267].

219. Maximus the Confessor, *Opuscula* 6 (PG 91:68A): "You have demonstrated that with the duality of his natures there are two wills (theleseis) and two operations (energeiai) respective to the two natures, and that he admits of no opposition between them."

220. Balthasar, *Cosmic Liturgy*, 269.

Mount of Olives that Maximus clarifies that the volitional synthesis between the two natures "depends on a *prior*, unconstrained, free act of the divine person, who steers the struggle from above and on the voluntary character of that person's 'ineffable self-immolation.'"[221] In his refusal to attribute γνώμη to the human will of Christ, Maximus indicates his primacy. As Maximus says,

> The Logos assumed our nature in its entirety and deified his human will in the assumption. It follows, then, that having become like us for our sake, he was calling on his God and Father in human manner when he said, *Let not what I will, but what you will prevail,* inasmuch as, being God by nature, he also in his humanity has, as his human volition, the fulfillment of the will of the Father.[222]

As the savior, Christ does not possess a hypostatic realization of nature the way we do because, while ours involves deliberation in the freewill, his humanity takes priority of perfection. Christ's human nature subsists in the one hypostasis of the person of the Son. Maximus argues that the negation *not what I will,* "is nevertheless not a dismissal of what is willed itself,"[223] i.e., our salvation. Our participation in the Sonship of Christ presupposes the priority of his humanity's volitional possession of subsistence in the person of the Son. What Christ assimilates volitionally into his *I*, we partake by faith in the *Yes* of Christ's human will. By refusing to

---

221. Balthasar, *Cosmic Liturgy,* 269; cf. Maximus the Confessor, *Opuscula* (PG 91:1048C).

222. Maximus the Confessor, *Opuscula* 6 (PG 91:68C). In his *Opuscule,* Maximus was responding to dilemma of the "emerging Monotheletism advanced in the *Psephos,* a document issued by Patriarch Sergius of Constantinople in June of 633. Sergius hoped to exploit Gregory Nazianzen's comments from *Orations* 30.12," which Maximus partly quotes in *Opuscula* 6 (*On the Cosmic Mystery,* 173–74n2). In a more Trinitarian and anti-Arian context, Nazianzen "took Jesus' word in John 6:38 ('for I have come down from heaven, not to do my own will, but the will of him who sent me') as definitive also for his prayer in Gethsemane. The subject of these statements is *not* the man Jesus, but the Son of God. . . . Sergius inferred from this the absence of a separate (contrary) *human* will in Christ as well (monotheletism). Now Maximus, interpreting both the Gethsamane prayer and Nazianzen's comments in a distinctly *Christological* register, and keen to recover the integrity and salvific importance of Christ's human will, [declares that] the subject of the prayer is precisely the man who is at once 'like us' in the possession of a natural human will *and* him 'whom we conceive in the role of Savior' insofar as his human will has already been assumed within the mode (tropos) of the hypostatic union" (*On the Cosmic Mystery,* 174n2).

223. Maximus the Confessor, *Opuscula* 6 (PG 91:68B).

attribute gnomic will to Christ, Maximus anticipates the Fourth Lateran Council's understanding of analogy. The absence of the γνώμη emphasizes the greater dissimilarity between our volition participation in God and the union of Christ's two wills. For us, volitional assimilation is by analogy of participation while for Christ, it is uniquely primordial and supremely perfect in his Sonship. Jesus' prayer on the Mount of Olives demonstrates how the analogical character of our participation in the incarnational assimilation affirms the primacy of Christ both in a cosmic and personal (historical) context.

Understanding Maximus's Christocentric analogy of volitional assimilation, is the key to understanding the core of Ratzinger's Christocentric analogy of volitional *aufnehme* (assimilation) and *umwandlung* (transformation).[224] In his commentary on the prayer of Jesus on the Mount of Olives, Ratzinger refers to Maximus as the patristic authority behind the volitional thesis of his spiritual Christology.[225]

For Maximus, what Christ has accomplished manifests in our ecclesial experience of "mystical participation" as a "realized participation" (μέθεξις κατ'ἐνεργείαν).[226] This participation occurs when we are able to have a "divine perception" through awareness of the intelligible content of the symbol of faith. Through the experience of faith, one may receive a knowledge prior to conception or natural thought process in such a way that what the thought longs to realize is realized through the mystical or spiritual participation in the redemptive work of Christ. He says,

> The direct experience of something puts an end to the concept that intends it; the perception of the same thing makes further reflection about it pointless. I call experience, however, fully realized knowledge itself, which becomes real when all conceiving has come to an end; but perception is the very participation in

---

224. Cf. Benedict XVI/Ratzinger, *Jesus von Nazareth,* 2:182–83.

225. Benedict XVI/Ratzinger, *Behold,* 40–41. While Maximus was trying to bring out the integrity of Christ's human will, Ratzinger seems to be emphasizing the personal nature of the volitional union. For Maximus, the subject of the prayer is the man Jesus, who possesses a human will like us, but a will already assumed in the hypostasis of the Son, Ratzinger will emphasize on the pre-eminent role of the human will of Christ already in the hypostasis of the Son, such that the subject of the prayer is the human will of the Son *assimilating* in a primal way, man's will to the Son's will. In both cases, there is no priority of mono-phyusis or mono-thelesis. We can say considering the context both theologians, they both complement each other the "similarity" and the "greater dissimilarity" analogy.

226. Balthasar, *Cosmic Liturgy,* 286.

the known object that is revealed to us only when all thinking has come to an end.[227]

Conceptual and non-experiential knowledge of God through created things "has as its overall purpose to awake in us a desire for mystical participation."[228] In other words, in the one spiritual participation, there is also a realization of the true goal of being.

Primacy of Christ in God-Talk

Ratzinger's reference to patristic God-Talk calls attention to its Christocentric unity of the descending and ascending movements of biblical words, Tradition, and prayer. We limit our study to his specific references to the works of Irenaeus of Lyon, Cyprian of Carthage, Gregory of Nyssa, and Augustine.

The Irenaean "Rule of Faith"

For Irenaeus, the inner principle of unity between Scripture and Tradition is the Spirit of God as the guarantor of truth. Thus the philosophical fundament of Irenaeus's "rule of faith" is primacy or oneness of the truth. The truth is prior to the linguistic and cultural vehicles by which it is transmitted in its integrity in the form of the Apostolic Tradition: "For, although the languages of the world are dissimilar, yet the import of the tradition is one and the same."[229] In his catechesis on the Church Fathers, Benedict XVI describes Irenaeus's analogy of Scripture and doctrine: "For Irenaeus, the 'rule of faith' coincided in practice with the *Apostles' Creed*, which gives us the key for interpreting the Gospel, for interpreting the Creed in light of the Gospel. The Creed, which is a sort of the Gospel synthesis, helps us understand what it means and how we should read the Gospel itself."[230] The Creed clarifies by way of synthesis what may be obscure in the Gospel. The analogy consists in the hermeneutic rule, whereby what is secondary clarifies what is primary. The words of doctrine clarify the words of Scripture on the grounds of the primacy of

---

227. Maximus the Confessor, *Ad Thalassium* 60 (PG 90:624A).
228. Maximus the Confessor, *Ad Thalassium* 60 (CCSG 22:77).
229. Irenaeus, *Adversus Haereses* 1.10.2 (SC 264:158).
230. Benedict XVI/Ratzinger, *Church Fathers*, 23.

truth, which the Spirit of Christ grants to the Church as a charism. For him, his Gnostic adversaries lack the analogical sense of the transmission of the truth through the tradition of the Church.[231] By departing from the rule of faith, the Gnostics relativize the truth and reduce it to "a fiction of [their] own invention."[232]

Irenaeus suggests the logic of the "rule of faith" to be comparable to the divine pedagogy. The divine pedagogy means the "pedagogy of the patience and attentiveness of God."[233] God "kept calling [his people] to what was primary by means of what was secondary, that is, through foreshadowings to the reality, through things of time to the things of eternity, through things of the flesh to the things of the spirit, through earthly things to heavenly things."[234] Comparable to the analogy of divine pedagogy is the pedagogy of the teaching tradition of faith. Benedict XVI rightly describes the "analogy of faith" as "the consistence of the individual truths of faith with one another and with the overall plan of the Revelation and the fullness of the divine economy contained in it."[235]

Cyprian: The Priority of Christ's Prayer

In his commentary on *The Lord's Prayer*, Cyprian offers a clear articulation of the primacy of the Word's words. Fundamental to his argument is the analogy of Scripture, for "God wished many things also to be said and heard through the prophets, His servants; but how much greater are the things which the Son speaks, which the Word of God, who was in the prophets, testifies with His own voice."[236] For him, prayer concerns conformity to the truth, and Our Lord's Prayer is "the form of praying in which *the true adorers would adore the Father in spirit and in truth* (cf.

---

231. Irenaeus, *Adversus Haereses* 3.2.1–2 (SC 211:26): "Ut digne secundum eos sit veritas aliquando quidem in Valentino, aliquando autem in Marcione, aliquando in Cerintho.... Unusquisque enim ipsorum omnimodo perversus semetipsum, regulam veritatis depravans, predicare non confunditur" (So that according to their idea, the truth properly resides at one time in Valentinus, at another in Marcion, at another in Cerinthus.... For every one of these men, being altogether of a pervese disposition, depraving the system of truth, is not ashamed to preach himself).

232. Irenaeus, *Adversus Haereses* 3.2.1–2 (SC 211:26): "Et hanc sapientiam unusquisque eorum esse dicit quam a semetipso adinuenerit, fictionem videlicet."

233. Kizewski, "God-Talk," 265.

234. Irenaeus, *Adversus Haereses* 4.14.3 (SC 100:548).

235. Benedict XVI/Ratzinger, *Address to the Pontifical Biblical Commission*, 2.

236. Cyprian of Carthage, *De dominica oratione* 2.1 (CSEL 3.1:267) [*Treatises*].

John 4:23)."[237] The words of the Son have a unique primacy in Truth in a way greatly dissimilar to the ascent of our words to the Truth. No "prayer to the Father can be more true than that which was sent forth from the Son, who is truth."[238]

Cyprian indicates how the condescension of God to human words is super-eminently present in the words of Jesus' prayer. He calls the prayer of Jesus "God's own words" that "ascends to His ears."[239] The prayer of Christ is the most pre-eminent convergence of the descending and ascending movement of human words drawn up most intimately into the divine mystery. We pray in Christ's primordial words by analogy of participation, whereby we receive and ascend to God's Word. In his first book on Jesus of Nazareth, Benedict XVI highlights Cyprian's comments on the prayer of Jesus as an indication of the priority of the truth contained in the words of Christ's prayer.[240] Benedict says, "The Our Father, then, like the Ten Commandments, begins by establishing the primacy of God, which then leads naturally to a consideration of the right way of being human."[241]

Cyprian speaks of the need for "restraint" and "modest" use of words when "standing in the sight of God."[242] As we shall see in Gregory of Nyssa, restraint, which indicates both limitation and the capacity of words relative to the divine transcendence is analogy. He says that prayer "should be commended to God in modesty because the hearer is not of the voice but of the heart."[243] With emphasis on the prayer of the heart, Cyprian anticipates Augustine's identification of the heart as the intimate locus of communion analogy. For Cyprian, praying in the words of Jesus unites us universally with the whole people, and together unites us to God. He says, "Before all things, the teacher of peace and master of unity

---

237. Cyprian of Carthage, *De dominica oratione* 2.2 (CSEL 3.1:267).

238. Cyprian of Carthage, *De dominica oratione* 2.2 (CSEL 3.1:267).

239. Cyprian of Carthage, *De dominica oratione* 2.3 (CSEL 3.1:268).

240. Benedict XVI/Ratzinger, *Jesus of Nazareth*, 1:131: "When we pray the Our Father, we are praying to God with words given by God, as Saint Cyprian says. And he adds that when we pray the Our Father, Jesus' promise regarding the true worshipers, those who adore the Father 'in spirit and in truth' (John 4:23), is fulfilled in us. Christ, who is the truth, has given us these words, and in them he gives us the Holy Spirit (*De dominica oration* 2; CSEL 3.1:267)."

241. Benedict XVI/Ratzinger, *Jesus of Nazareth*, 1:134.

242. Cyprian of Carthage, *De dominica oratione* 2.4 (CSEL 3.1:268).

243. Cyprian of Carthage, *De dominica oratione* 2.4 (CSEL 3.1:268).

did not wish prayer to be offered individually and privately as one would pray only when he prays."[244] Participation in the words of Jesus is intrinsically ecclesial and communal because it unifies all minds into one.

Finally, Cyprian clearly places priority on Christ's prayer as God's manifestation of how to speak to Him. He says, "Not by words alone, but also by deeds has God taught us to pray, Himself praying frequently and entreating and demonstrating what we ought to do by the testimony of his own example."[245] Anticipating Augustine's *sacramentum* and *exemplum*, he considers the unicity of Christ's "words" and "example" as the supreme revelation of the true mode of human speech to God. On account of the integrity of Christ's humanity that is devoid of sin, the mode of his prayer takes primacy relative to our participation in it: "If He who was without sin prayed, how much more ought sinners to pray, and if He prayed continually, watching through the whole night with uninterrupted petitions, how much more ought we to lie awake at night in continuing prayer!"[246] The prayer of the one "without sin" is in a pre-eminent way a supreme example to follow for us who seek freedom from sin. Thus the primacy of Christ's prayer not only confirms speech to God as analogy but also demonstrates the spiritual mode of such analogy as one involving both word and deed. Consequently, Cyprian notes that human speech to God must be both in word and example. He says, "Words without fruits cannot merit God's favor since they are fruitful in no deed.... For He who on the Day of Judgment is to render a reward for deeds and alms, today also is a kindly listener to a prayer which comes with works."[247]

Gregory of Nyssa: Restraint in God-Talk

We have already discussed in the previous chapter Gregory's analysis of how Scripture helps us to know the Person of God in a way analogous to how we know the characteristics of a person without claiming to know his very essence. His approach to biblical exegesis affirms "silence" or restraint when speaking about divine essence:

> Now if anyone should ask for some interpretation, and description, and explanation of the Divine essence, we are not going to

---

244. Cyprian of Carthage, *De dominica oratione* 2.8 (CSEL 3.1:271).
245. Cyprian of Carthage, *De dominica oratione* 2.29 (CSEL 3.1:288).
246. Cyprian of Carthage, *De dominica oratione* 2.29 (CSEL 3.1:288).
247. Cyprian of Carthage, *De dominica oratione* 2.32 (CSEL 3.1:290).

deny that in this kind of wisdom we are unlearned, acknowledging only so much as this, that it is not possible that that which is by nature infinite should be comprehended in any conception expressed by words. . . . For by what name can I describe the incomprehensible? By what speech can I declare the unspeakable? Accordingly, since the Deity is too excellent and lofty to be expressed in words, we have learnt to honor in *silence* what transcends speech and thought.[248]

Speaking properly of the "unspeakable" demands avoiding a reduction of what is ineffable to words. In human speech about God, *words* and *silence* are two sides of the same coin holding together in a spiritual way, the limitation of human words and the transcendence of the divine essence. Gregory calls this restraint of words a "cautious speech."[249] He observes that his interlocutor, Eunomius, lacks such a restraint. Restraint in God-Talk preserves the limitation of reason and guards against the lack of analogical imagination relative to the primacy of reason.

In Gregory of Nyssa's necessity of "cautious speech" about the ineffable mystery of God, Ratzinger finds one of the basis of his argument for the limitations of historical-critical method.[250] For Ratzinger, the Eunomian problem of blurring the ontological distinction between human speech and divine transcendence is a danger looming in the historical-critical method's attempt to completely explain biblical mystery in physiological terms.[251] The danger lies in the reduction of rationality to the logic of created things. Gregory's cautious speech rather affirms rationality as contingent of the transcendent Logos, who creatures can know only by ascending (ana-batic) movement to the Logos; hence by analogy. Gregory says, "By a certain analogy, one arrives at a knowledge of being [κατά τινα ἀναλογίαν εἰς γνῶσιν ἔρχεται τοῦ εἶναι]."[252] Treating

---

248. Gregory of Nyssa, *Contra Eunomium* 3.5 (PG 45:601B).
249. Gregory of Nyssa, *Contra Eunomium* 3.5 (PG 45:601C).
250. See Benedict XVI/Ratzinger, *New Song*, 64–65.
251. Benedict XVI/Ratzinger, *New Song*, 64: "In the fourth century, Gregory of Nyssa already dealt with these questions in a way that is still valid in his debate with the theological rationalist Eunomius. Eunomius had maintained that it was possible to form a completely satisfactory concept of God which really grasped and accurately described God's being. Gregory responded that Eunomius had tried "to encompass the unfathomable nature of God in the span of a child's hand."
252. Gregory of Nyssa, *Contra Eunomium* 12 (PG 45:916A). See also Balthasar, *Presence and Thought*, 93.

God's mystery as an object of natural science easily begets heresy.[253] Rather, knowledge of God lies in the middle ground "between knowledge and ignorance," words and silence.[254]

Augustine on "Words and Things"

In his distinction between "words" and the "things" they signify, Augustine suggests that while the sole purpose of words is to signify things, however "not everything is also a sign."[255] Just as there are certain things beyond signification, there are realities beyond words. Augustine affirms the patristic consensus that in His ineffableness, God is beyond words: "Nothing worthy may be spoken of Him [God]."[256] For Augustine, knowing the limitation of words is a precondition for using them adequately for speaking about God. A proper articulation of the mystery of God also requires "silence" in the face of things beyond words: "If that is ineffable which cannot be spoken, then that is not ineffable which can be called ineffable. This contradiction is to be passed over in silence rather than resolved verbally."[257] Between words and silence, Christianity finds the suitable space for saying things about God. "Although nothing worthy may be spoken of Him," yet God "has accepted the tribute of the human voice and wished us to take joy in praising Him with words."[258] Words when used suitably about God praises him.

For Augustine, words employed to speak about God undergo an ascent of meaning because they are taken out of the common human habitat as it were to a super-eminent suitability for God. Addressing how Scripture suitably applies words like "repent" to God, Augustine says,

> Just as you don't take this according to the common way of speaking, the way human beings normally repent, so too you should likewise understand that what is meant by "just" doesn't fit God's super-eminence, though scripture was indeed right to state this, so that the human spirit might be led gradually by all

---

253. Gregory of Nyssa, *In Cant.* 11(PG 44:1013C).

254. Balthasar, *Presence and Thought*, 93: "Knowledge through *epinoia*, therefore, holds the middle ground between knowing and ignorance."

255. Augustine, *Doctr. chr.* 1.2.2 (PL 34:19–20).

256. Augustine, *Doctr. chr.* 1.6.6 (PL 34:21).

257. Augustine, *Doctr. chr.* 1.6.6 (PL 34:21).

258. Augustine, *Doctr. chr.* 1.6.6 (PL 34:21).

sorts of words to that which cannot be said at all. Yes, you call God just, but you must understand something beyond justice which you are in the habit of attributing to human beings.[259]

By the ascending movement of words in God-Talk, Scripture suitably applies words analogously to "God's super-eminence." By analogy, one is able to apply to God the words that indicate change or ignorance such as *repent*. Augustine is describing what constitutes the meaning of biblical words. For him, the elevation of common use of words by the descent of divine mystery shows what happens in the analogy of Scriptures. He explains the unity of the Old and New Testament as an analogy: "It is a matter of analogy, when the conformity of the Old and New Testaments is shown."[260] The "conformity" involves an ascent of the meaning of the words of the Old Testament to the fullness of meaning in Christ. The fullness of the revelation of divine mystery in Christ elevates the words of the Old Testament to the habitat of the Incarnate Word.

Naming God

Scripture uses names to talk about God. In harmony with Irenaeus, Origen and Gregory of Nyssa, Augustine highlight's the primacy of the Word while indicating how the limitations of human words and divine transcendence create the space for the analogy of God-Talk. To establish the limits of words in expressing "Being-Itself," he says,

> What is Being-Itself? How express it if not as Being-Itself? Understand Being-Itself, my brothers, if you can. For in using any word I do not express the Being-itself. Let us yet try by some expressions approaching it to lead our feeble minds to think upon the Being itself (*Idipsum*).... What is Being-Itself save That Which Is?... And what is That Which Is if not the One who said to Moses in sending him: "I am Who am" (Exod 3:14)?[261]

In spite of our limitations, Augustine remains confident that the human mind and words are capable of understanding and speaking about God on the grounds of the analogy of participation. In his commentary on Psalm 121, central to his analysis of God's revelation of his name are his comments on the descending and the ascending movement of participation,

---

259. Augustine, *Serm.* 341.16 (PL 39:1498); Kizewski, "God-Talk," 309.
260. Augustine, *Gn. litt. lib. imperf.* 2.5 (CSEL 28.1:461).
261. Augustine, *Enarrat. Ps.* 121.5 (CCSL 40:1805).

hence, indicating how participation, which is spiritually constituted by faith, is grounds for God-Talk. He says,

> The city "which is being built is a city: whose partaking is in Being-Itself." To what am I telling you to hold fast? To that which Christ became for you; for he is Christ, and Christ himself is rightly understood in the words "I am Who am," as He exists in the form of God. In that nature wherein "he did not think it robbery to be equal to God" (Phil 2:6), there he is Being-Itself. But that you may partake of Being-Itself, He first participated in your nature. The Word was made flesh so that flesh might participate in the Word.[262]

It is within the humanity of Christ existing as the *city of God*, the Church, that transcendent meaning of Being-Itself can be properly understood and talked about. Faith in the Word takes primacy in biblical exegesis. The primacy of the Word's descent makes accessible to the human mind the transcendent meaning of divine revelation of his name by means of limited human words: "*He Who Is has sent me to you*, because at the present you waver and through the mutability of things and the variety of temporal things cannot know the meaning of the Selfsame. Since you cannot ascend, I descend."[263] In the "I" of his person, Christ reveals to us the name of God "Who Is."

Words and Silence in Prayer

Augustine does not only speak of conceptual speech about God but also of mystical utterances to God in prayer. His thoughts on speaking to God presupposes the primacy of Truth and Love illuminated by faith. For Augustine, "speech" can either be vocal or interior: "I believe you notice at the same time that even when a person merely strains his mind toward something, although we utter no sound, yet because we ponder the words themselves, we do speak within our own minds."[264] Whether vocal or silent, "speech serves us only to remind, since the memory in which the words inhere, by recalling them, brings to mind (*commemorare*) the realities themselves, of which the words are signs."[265] With regard to prayer,

---

262. Augustine, *Enarrat. Ps.* 121.5 (CCSL 40:1805).
263. Augustine, *Enarrat. Ps.* 121.5 (CCSL 40:1804–6).
264. Augustine, *Mag.* 1.2 (CCSL 29:159).
265. Augustine, *Mag.* 1.2 (CCSL 29:159).

the purpose of speech is not to remind God of what he forgot, but is for a "recollective" correspondence of our minds to the condescended presence of the Spirit of Christ in the heart.

Augustine prioritizes interior prayer because for him, the Light of Truth and Spirit of Love is not found in the exterior but in the interior of human mind and heart: "God should be sought and prayed to precisely in the silent depths of the rational soul, which is called 'the inner man.' . . . *Know you not that you are the temple of God and that the Spirit of God dwells in you?* (1 Cor 3:16) and *Christ dwells in the inner mind?* (Eph 3:14–17)."[266] Speaking to God vocally or silently must proceed from the heart since the heart is the center of the descending and ascending movement of participation in God: "Therefore, whether we cry to the Lord with the voice of the body—when occasion demands it—or in silence, we must cry from the heart."[267] For Augustine, it is fitting that vocal prayer is used for worship "that men may hear and, by being reminded, may with one accord dedicate themselves to God."[268] In prayer of worship, the words of the people of God, which are of "one accord," signifies the unity of their interior act of "being reminded," i.e., a communal return to the indwelling of Love. Augustine's emphasis on the cry of the heart indicates the limitation of words for articulating the reality they signify, i.e., the *caritas* to which they ascend. According to Thomas Hand, "prayer" for Augustine "is the articulation of love."[269] The use of words in prayer is not to remind God of something he does not know but for expressing our desire. Like Cyprian, Augustine explains that the primacy of the words used by Christ to teach us how to pray is the "form" for expressing our desire properly to him: "The words employed by our Lord Jesus Christ

---

266. Augustine, *Mag.* 1.2 (CCSL 29:158): "Deus autem in ipsis rationalis animae secretis, qui homo interior vocatur, et quaerendus et deprecandus est; haec enim sua templa esse voluit. An apud Apostolum non legisti: *Nescitis quia templum Dei estis, et spiritus Dei habitat in vobis*; et: *In interiore homine habitare Christum*? Nec in propheta animadvertisti: *Dicite in cordibus vestris, et in cubilibus vestris compungimini: sacrificate sacrificium iustitiae, et sperate in Domino*?"

267. Augustine, *Enarrat. Ps.* 118.29.1 (CCSL 40:1763): "Clamor ad Dominum, qui fit ab orantibus, si sonitu corporalis vocis fiat, non intento in Deum corde; quis dubitet inaniter fieri? Si autem fiat corde, etiam silente corporis voce; alium quemlibet hominem potest latere, non Deum. Sive ergo cum voce carnis, quando id opus est, sive cum silentio, ad Deum, cum oramus, corde clamandum est."

268. Augustine, *Mag.* 1.2 (CCSL 29:159).

269. Hand, *St. Augustine on Prayer*, 9.

in his prayer constitute the form for the expression of our desires."²⁷⁰ The words of Christ the *Magister* about God takes "formal primacy."

Conclusion

The variegated forms of analogy of participation, which emerge from our study as Origen's "resemblance," Gregory of Nyssa's "ακολουθία," Augustine's "*communio*," and Maximus's "assimilation" will shape our approach to Ratzinger's analogy of participation in the subsequent chapters. Understanding the Stoic roots of Origen's primacy of love and Augustine's comprehensive approach to primacy of love not only provides the patristic foundations for how Ratzinger speaks of the primacy of Christ, but also sets the stage for clarifying our theologian's contribution to the conversation. The specific referential continuity demonstrated in our study of the patristic patrimony that Ratzinger quotes revolves around how the question of truth, the logic of spiritual life, and the analogy of Scripture points to the primacy of Christ. Irenaeus's and Augustine's "analogy of Scripture," Gregory of Nyssa's "restraint of words," and Cyprian's "primacy of Christ's prayer" focuses the Christocentic nature of the investigation. For these Fathers, Christ the "Image" of God grounds our participation as his image, serves as the primal logic of spiritual life and gives us the reason to both talk about and talk to God.

---

270. Augustine, *Serm* 56.4 (CCSL 41:156).

PART TWO

Ratzinger's Primacy of Christ

Chapter 3

Analogy of Faith and Reason in Ratzinger's Theology

THE INTERVENING DEVELOPMENTS OF the Fourth Lateran Council's and Bonaventure's insights on the patristic use of analogy play a significant role in the understanding of the patristic patrimony present in Ratzinger's primacy of Christ. On account of Ratzinger's habilitation study on *The Theology of History of St. Bonaventure,* Bonaventure has a prominent role in our consideration of Ratzinger's primacy of Christ. Hence, in this chapter, a survey of the statement of the Fourth Lateran Council on analogy, Bonaventure's development of patristic analogy, and the modern question propelling Ratzinger's use of analogy precede our study of how Ratzinger synthesizes the analogy of faith and reason with the primacy of Christ.

Fourth Lateran Council

What Augustine stated in his *De Trinitate* about the presence of a greater dissimilitude in every similitude between God and man (XV.20.39), the Fourth Lateran Council of 1215 recapitulates in a new way. In the second *Constitution,* the Council addressed Joachim of Fiore's lack of real analogy in the way he spoke of the consubstantial unity of the Trinity. The Council clarifies that "between creator and creature there can be noted no similarity so great that a greater dissimilarity must not be noted between them [*quia inter creatorem et creaturam non potest tanta similitude notari, quin inter eos maior sit dissimilitudo notanda*]."[1]

1. Fourth Lateran Council, *Constitutiones* 2 [232].

In his *libellus,* Joachim of Fiore accused Peter Lombard of ascribing to God "a *quaternitas,* that is to say three persons and a common essence as if [the common essence] were a fourth person."[2] What Joachim rejects is description of the consubstantial unity of the Trinity as "supreme reality" (*quaedam summa res*).[3] The Council condemns Joachim's reduction to a *quaternitas,* Peter Lombard's teaching of a certain Trinitarian "supreme reality." The basis for the condemnation was Joachim's claim that in the one substance of the Trinity the three persons are not truly and properly one but collectively and analogously.[4] Joachim's error stems from his meaning of "analogous" unity. He drew a strict likeness between the Trinitarian unity and the unity of "many persons [into] one people."[5] Thus, he reduced analogy of "unity" in God and in creatures to the existing similarity alone, without including the Christian distinction that in every similarity, there is a great dissimilarity between God and creatures.[6] In his *Regensburg Lecture*, his *On the Way to Jesus Christ* and his conversation with Peter Seewald in *God and the World*, Benedict XVI makes reference this teaching of the Fourth Lateran Council as the faith's authoritative statement preserving the role of reason in human capacity for God.[7] As James Schall rightly noted, "[Benedict XVI] cited this authority [of the Fourth Lateran Council] for philosophic reasons, almost as if to say what Chesterton said, that oftentimes the purpose of authority in the Church is to save reason in the world."[8]

---

2. Fourth Lateran Council, *Constitutiones* 2: "Unde asserit, quod ille non tam Trinitatem quam quaternitatem adstruebat in Deo, videlicet tres personas et illam commune essentiam quasi quartam."

3. In his *Sentences,* Peter Lombard says, "Quoniam quedam smma res est Pater et Filius et Spiritus sanctus, et illa non est generans neque genita nec procedens" (For there is a certain supreme reality which is the Father and the Son and the Holy Spirit, and it neither begets nor is begotten nor does it proceed) (Lombard, *Libri VI sententiarum* I dist. 5 [1:42–51]) [Tanner, *Decrees of the Ecumenical Councils*, 1:231].

4. Fourth Lateran Council, *Constitutiones* 2: "Verum unitatem huiusmodi non veram et propriam, sed quasi collectivam et similitudinariam esse fatetur."

5. Fourth Lateran Council, *Constitutiones* 2.

6. See Kizewski, "God-Talk," 433–37.

7. See Benedict XVI/Ratzinger, "Regensburg Lecture," 27; *On the Way*, 69; *God and the World*, 272.

8. Schall, *Regensburg Lecture*, 65.

Bonaventure

Bonaventure's concepts of similitude and illumination are the two main expressions of the patristic analogy, which Ratzinger encounters in his study of Bonaventure's theology of history.

Similitude

In Bonaventure, there are different levels of similitude. The first two levels which suggest univocal similitude include: similitude by agreement in every way according to nature, as the persons of the Trinity are similar to one another; and similitude by participation in some universal as man and ass are similar in animal.[9] These first two levels do not describe the kind of similitude between God and man. The similitude of *univocation* establishes the great dissimilarity between God and creature to the extent that creation has nothing univocally in common with the Creator. However, the next two levels, which properly suggest *analogy* include: similitude according to proportionality, as the sailor and the charioteer agree according to a comparison to that which rules; and similitude according to order, as an exemplar to its effects.[10] These two levels describe the kind of similitude between God and man whereby there is a comparison between the Creator and the creatures he governs, and a similitude between the archetype of creation and its effects according to the order of proportionality. In the ratio of proportionality, the *vestiges* are similar to the exemplar from a distance while the *image*, i.e., man, has close similitude to the exemplar.[11] In the end, Bonaventure's notion of similitude implies the caution of the Fourth Lateran Council. He builds his similitude of proportionality on the similitude of univocation, which emphasizes the greater dissimilarity between God and creatures.

Like Augustine, Bonaventure finds the image of God expressed in the human soul. Bonaventure describes this image of God as the "expressed similitude" because in the order of proportionality, the soul is supremely ordered to God.[12] He supports his logic by calling to mind the words of Augustine that the rational soul is "*capax Dei* and can be a

9. Bonaventure, *Sent. I* d.35, q.1, c. ad 2 (1:601B).

10. Bonaventure, *Sent. I* d.35, q.1, c. ad 2 (1:601B). See also Kizewski, "God-Talk," 567.

11. Bonaventure, *Sent. II* d.16, a.1, q.1 (2:394).

12. Bonaventure, *Sent. I* d.3, p.1, a.1, q.2 (1:72).

participant [in him]."¹³ The agreement between God and human beings has an expressed similitude because it is a close and immediate likeness. Justin Kizewski describes Bonaventure's notion of "expressed similitude" as "a near univocal likeness" or "a very great analogical likeness."¹⁴ For Bonaventure, man's likeness to God as his expressed similitude is present from the origin of man in such a way that the similitude consists in the intrinsic comparison between the divine and human nature, as well as between the divine and human person.¹⁵ In his study of Bonaventure's theology of history, Ratzinger discovers how Bonaventure presents the death and resurrection of Christ as the full historical expression of the intrinsic and primal similitude between God and man. Ratzinger says, "The middle movement (*mittelsatz*), which Bonaventure designated again in mysterious ambiguity as 'assumptio,' revolves around the Cross: Christ here assumes wholeheartedly to the end, human likeness to the divine likeness, true humanity united together with his" with the exception of sin.¹⁶ The Cross of Christ is the central manifestation of how man is the expressed likeness of God in a fully historical way.

Primacy of Logos in Analogy of Speech

Among the various Christological titles, Bonaventure has a preference for Christ as *Word* (*Logos*) in the order of faith and reason.¹⁷ Ratzinger learns from his teacher, Gottlieb Söhngen that "Bonaventure deserves to be known as the classical theologian of the analogy of faith, just as Thomas Aquinas has long been appreciated as the classical philosopher and theologian of the *analogia entis*."¹⁸ In Bonaventure's analogy of word,

   13. Reference made to Augustine, *Trin*. 14.8.11 (PL 42:1068).

   14. Kizewski, "God-Talk," 568.

   15. Bonaventure, *Sent. II* d.16, a.1, q.1 (2:395).

   16. Benedict XVI/Ratzinger, *Offenbarungsverständnis*, 244: "Er ist ... die substantielle similitudo Dei. Der Mittelsatz, den Bonaventura wiederum in geheimnisvoller Doppelsinnigkeit als "assumtio" bezeichnet, rundet sich am Kreuz: Zur Gottgleichheit nimmt Christus hire in lezter Ernsthaftigkeit die Menschengleichheit, das wahre Menschsein mitsamt seiner von der Sünde cerursachten Elendigkeit hinzu."

   17. Cf. Egbulefu, "Bonaventure in Vatican II," 88; Bonaventure, *Sermones de Tempore* 36.4: "Radix enim omnis cognitionis in via est Verbum incarnatum et radix onmis cognitionis in patria est Verbum increatum."

   18. Söhngen, "Bonaventura als Klassiker der analogia fidei," 99; *Die Einheit in der Theologie*, 426–32; cf. Benedict XVI/Ratzinger, *Offenbarungsverständnis*, 157: "An welchem Punkt des Gesamt-systems sitzt die Analogie bei Bonaventura? Für diese

he synthesizes the analogy of being[19] and analogy of faith in the primacy of the speech form of the *Logos*.[20] Bonaventure places priority on the descending movement of the analogy of faith because God first manifested himself historically in the form of speech, i.e., in his *Logos*. Therefore, *Logos* takes primacy in the discussion of the analogy between God and man. Bonaventure builds on Augustine's dialogical character of word, which prioritizes the interior *logos* over its outward manifestation in voice. However, Bonaventure makes more explicit the full historical implication of the analogy between human intelligible word and the divine *Logos*.[21] We saw in Augustine how the notion of image fundamentally refers back to God.[22] Similarly, for Bonaventure, the *similitude* of word

---

wichtigere Frage hat Gottlieb Söhngen einen bedeutsamen Beitrag geleistet. Seine Antwort gipfelt in dem Satz: 'Wenn wir ... nach einem klassiche Theologen der analogia fidei fragen ... so hat keiner mehr Anrecht auf diesen Titel als Bonaventura.'" See also Kucer, *Truth and Politics*, 44: "In accordance with this Bonaventurian approach, Söhngen perceives the similarities between God and creation as situated within an analogy of faith." The later Karl Barth responded positively to Söhngen's Bonaventurian position.

19. Bonaventure, *Itin*. 5.2 (5:308B): "Esse primum nomen Dei"; cf. *Hex*. 10.10 (5:378B).

20. Benedict XVI/Ratzinger, *Offenbarungsverständnis*, 157: "Das heißt: Die Analogielehre Bonaventuras ist in seinem System so angelegt, dass nach seiner Lehre die Seinsanalogie, mit der alles Seiende auf den Gott hinüberdeutet, dessen erster Name ja gerade nach Bonaventura 'Sein' heißt, in der tatsächlichen heilsgeschichtlichen Lage erst zu sprechen beginnt durch die Glaubensanalogie, mit der Gott offenbarend zu uns herüberredet."

21. Benedict XVI/Ratzinger, *Offenbarungsverständnis*, 134. Commenting on how Bonaventure build on Augustine's analogy of word, Ratzinger says, "Die eigentliche heilsgeschichtliche Offerbarungsvorgang also, ist mit in die Logosspekulation, in the Metaphysik der Trinität hineingenommen. Man kann diesen Vorgang doppelt beurteilen: Man kan sagen, die Offenbarung und mit ihr die Heilsgeschichtlche werde hier bis in den Urbezirk des Metaphysischen hinaufgehoben; man kann aber auch umgekehrt sagen, die Trinität selbst werde hier heilsgeschichtlich gesehen und die Logos formel erhalte hier heilsgeschichtlichen Klang. Es handelt sich dabei um eine Entwicklung, die zwar an Augustine anknüpft, aber weit über ihn hinausführt. Augustin sagt zwar an der von Bonaventura angeführten Stelle, *Trin* 15.11, 20 (PL 42:1072), dass sich der Vorgang der Fleischwerdung des ewigen Wortes vergleichen lasse mit dem Vorgang der Lautwerdung unseres inneren Wortes, aber die Analogie, die gemeinsame ratio verbi, liegt für ihn nur beim inneren Wort. Deshalb ist es ein durchaus neuer Schritt, wenn Bonaventura nun das menschliche Wort in allen seinen Stufen zum Analogen des Gott-Logos erklärt." While Augustine focused on the interior dimension of the analogy of speech, Bonaventure expands the analogy to embrace both the interior and exterior, the metaphysical and the historical.

22. See chapter 2 (96) [x-ref].

to *Logos* points to the return of the expressed similitude back to God through the instruction of the divine Word.[23] Ratzinger concludes that for Bonaventure, "the entire world as one vast movement of God's utterance, regains its true meaning only in the moment when Christ reversed its movement and transformed it into a returning-back to the Father of lights."[24]

Analogy of Light

In his work on *The Theology of History in St. Bonaventure*, Ratzinger confirms the influence of Bonaventure in his reception of Augustine's illumination analogy. Peter Kucer comments, "in accordance with Bonaventurian thought, Ratzinger describes human capacity for truth not simply according to an Aristotelian theory of truth but also by taking into account Augustine's illumination theory."[25] The key to understanding Bonaventure's biblical synthesis of faith and reason is through his Augustinian analogy of light.

Light of Faith and Reason

Ratzinger describes Bonaventure's reception of Augustine's illumination theory as follows:

> For Augustine, God is Light that illuminates the human mind from above (*von oben*).[26] Bonaventure scholasticized this claim, as he inserts it into the overall schema (gesamtschema) of the illumination of the human mind, which is in three to four layers:

---

23. Bonaventure, *Sent. I* d.27, p.2, q.4 (1:489B): "Propter similituenem expressam" and "propter instructionem nostram." Man's express similitude to God and his reception of instruction by the divine Word refers back to the one utterance of the divine *Logos*.

24. Benedict XVI/Ratzinger, *Offenbarungsverständnis*, 159: "Die ganze Welt als seine einzige große Ausdrucksbewegung von Gott her, die aber erst ihren wahren Sinn ewinnt in dem Augenblick, in dem Christus diese Bewegung umkehr und zur Rückkehrbewegung zum 'Vater der Lichter' verwandelt."

25. Kucer, *Truth and Politics*, 69. Ratzinger speaks of Bonaventure's attempt to "achieve a synthesis" between Aristotelian active intellect and Augustine's illumination theory, which holds together an active intelligibility of objects via the abstraction of their essences, and the "the immediate divine illumination of the human spirit" respectively (Benedict XVI/Ratzinger, *Theology of History in Bonaventure*, 73).

26. Bonaventure, *Hex.* 5.1 (5:353A).

Man receives knowledge (*Licht*) from what is beyond (*über*) him, what is in him, what is outside (*außer*) of him.[27] ... But then the "superior light" (*lumen superius*) receives a new meaning: it becomes an additional special illumination and a special knowledge, and beyond the common human knowledge. Perhaps the most actual demonstration of this development is in the treatise on the *The Return of the Arts to Theology*.[28] There he defines this "superior light" (*obere Licht*) as the "light of grace and the Holy Scripture" (*Licht der Gnade und der Heiligen Schrift*).[29]

First, the origin of cognitive illumination is not from man but from "what is beyond him." Like Augustine, Bonaventure first affirms the transcendent God as the source of the illumination of reason. Second, the illumination, which comes from "what is in [man]" is a reference to the analogy of reason pertaining the universal principles of truth.[30] This light of reason enables the mind to know the first philosophical principles. Bonaventure calls the basic principles of knowledge the "uniform wisdom."[31] Bonaventure's uniform wisdom, which corresponds to Augustine's "light of reason" does not enable the mind to grasp God immediately. In this first level of illumination, there is no revelation.

---

27. The three layered Schema is in Bonaventure, *Sc. Chr.* q.4, f.31 (5:20AB), and the four layered in Bonaventure, *Red.* 1 (5:319A).

28. Bonaventure, *Red.* 1 (5:319A). See also 5 (5:321B): "Quartum autem lumen, quod illuminat ad veritatem salutarem, est lumen sacrae scripturae, quod ideo dicitur superius, quia ad superior ducit *manifestando, quae sunt supra rationem,* et etiam quia non per inventionem, sed per inspirationem a patre luminum descendit" (The fourth light that illuminates the saving truth, is the light of the sacred Scriptures, which is said to be higher because it leads to what is superior manifesting what is beyond reason, and also because it does not come through invention but it descends through inspiration by the Father's light).

29. Benedict XVI/Ratzinger, *Offenbarungsverständnis*, 307: "Für Augustin ist Gott das Licht, das 'über' dem menschlichen Geist leuchtet, 'von oben' in ihn hineinleuchtet. Bonaventura scholastisiert diese Aussage, indem er sie in ein Gesamtschema der menschlichen Erleuchtungen einfügt, das dreibis viergliedrig ist: Der Mensch empfängt Erkenntnisse ('Licht') von dem, was über ihm, was in ihm, was außer ihm ist, und schließlich auch von dem, was unter ihm ist. Damit bekommt aber das 'lumen superius' einen neuen Sinn: Es wird zu einer Sonder-Eleuchtung und zu einer Sonder-Erkenntnissen. Am deutlichsten vielleicht zeichnet sich diese Entwicklung ab in dem Traktat von der 'Heimführung der Künste zur Theologie': Dort wird dieses 'obere Licht' definiert als das *Licht der Gnade und der Heiligen Schrift*."

30. See chapter 2 (83) [X-REF].

31. Bonaventure, *Hex.* 2.9-10 (5:337F).

Third, the illumination from what is outside of the mind refers to the reflections of the Creator in his creation. This outside light, which Bonaventure identifies as "omniform wisdom" (*sapientia omniformis*)[32] corresponds with Augustine's light of beauty in creation.[33] As regards the *sapientia omniformis*, Bonaventure speaks of a certain "revelation" of the glory of the Creator.[34] This kind of intellectual revelation of God in creation is what Paul has in mind in his Letter to the Romans when he writes: *Deus enim illis revelavit* (Rom 1:19).[35] Bonaventure finds in Scripture the notion of revealed light of reason. However, he highlights the limits of this light as well. *Sapientia omniformis* runs the risk of fixation on the literal meaning of creation and forgetting that created things are signs of spiritual reality to be traced back to the Creator.[36] Finally, there is the light of grace, which is superior to the other natural illuminations. Bonaventure calls this *superior light*, which corresponds the Augustine's "light of faith," the *multiform sapientia* (the manifold wisdom) of God (Eph 3:8–10).[37] For Bonaventure, the light of faith is what enables the spiritual understanding of the mysterious language of Holy Scripture.[38] With this divine light, what "is veiled (*velata*) for the proud is revealed (*revelata*) for the little."[39] Bonaventure's light of faith corresponds with the spiritual unveiling of Scripture, whereby the sign-character of the entire creation and the figures of the Old Testament are spiritual analogies of Christ of the New Testament.[40]

Bonaventure's synthesis of faith and reason consists in the broad ranging meaning of the term "revelation." Revelation, which embraces both the limited light of reason and the superior light of faith are both operative in biblical exegesis. Ratzinger observes that "at no time does Bonaventure refer to the Scriptures themselves as 'revelation.' He speaks

---

32. Bonaventure, *Hex.* 2.21 (5:340A).

33. See chapter 2 (86) [X-REF].

34. Bonaventure, *Apol. Paup.* c.3, 8–10 (8:246F); c.8, 19–20 (8:293A); c.10, 4 (8:305A). Bonaventure speaks of the light of creation in terms of literal understanding of biblical faith in creation.

35. Bonaventure, *Hex.* 5.22 (5:357B); 2.20 (5:339F); cf. Benedict XVI/Ratzinger, *Theology of History in Bonaventure*, 85.

36. Bonaventure, *Hex.* 2.21 (5:340A).

37. Bonaventure, *Hex.* 2.11 (5:338A).

38. Bonaventure, *Hex.* 2.19 (5:339B).

39. Benedict XVI/Ratzinger, *Theology of History in Bonaventure*, 60–61.

40. Cf. Benedict XVI/Ratzinger, *Theology of History in Bonaventure*, 78, 84–85.

of *revelare* and *facies revelata* primarily when a particular understanding of Scripture is involved, namely that *manifold divine wisdom*."[41] In other words, in Bonaventure, the question of revelation is not simply about Scripture itself as much as it is about its interpretation. Revelation and illumination are analogous terms. Commenting on the kind of revelation required for proper biblical exegesis, Bonaventure affirms that the limited light of reason, which understands the literal language of the universe needs the light of faith to understand creation through the knowledge of the creator. In his *Itinerarium mentis in Deum*, he articulates the synthetic order of the light of faith and reason as follows:

> He who does not allow himself to be illuminated by the glory of created things is blind; he who does not awaken to their call is deaf; he who does not praise God for all his works is mute; he who does not discover the First Principle from all these signs is a fool. Therefore, open your eyes, call upon your spiritual ears; loosen your lips and apply your heart so that you may see, hear, praise, love, serve, glorify, and honor your God in all creatures lest the entire universe raise itself up against you. . . . But [the earth] will be the foundation of glory for the wise who can say with the Prophet: . . . "How great are your deeds O Lord. In Wisdom you have made them all; the earth is full of your creations" (Pss 91:5; 103:24).[42]

While creation is a ladder to the vision of God, one needs the light of Christian faith to see God's logic of creation. Ratzinger concludes that in Bonaventure's faith analogy, "*revelation is synonymous with the spiritual understanding of Scripture*; it consists in the God-given act

---

41. Benedict XVI/Ratzinger, *Theology of History in Bonaventure*, 62. In his *Milestones*, Ratzinger describes how his studies on Bonaventure's theology of history helped him to contribute to the discussions on the relationship between Scripture and Tradition during the Second Vatican Council. He says, "I was helped by the knowledge I had gained while studying Bonaventure's concept of revelation. I found that the basic direction taken by the Fathers of Trent in their conception of revelation had essentially remained the same as in the High Middle Ages. . . . Revelation, which is to say, God's approach to man, is always greater than what can be contained in human words, greater even than the words of Scripture. . . . Both in the Middle Ages and at Trent it would have been impossible to refer to Scripture simply as "revelation," as is the normal linguistic usage today. Scripture is the *essential witness* of revelation, but revelation is something alive, something greater and *more*: proper to it is that fact that it *arrives* and *is perceived*" (Benedict XVI/Ratzinger, *Milestones*, 123–27).

42. Bonaventure, *Itin.* c.2, 15 (5:299B) [Benedict XVI/Ratzinger, *Theology of History in Bonaventure*, 86].

of understanding, and not in the objective letter alone. Only those who understand Scripture spiritually have a *facies revelata.*"⁴³ One engages in spiritual exegesis by means of analogy of Scripture, which Augustine describes as the unity of the Old and New Testaments. In this analogy of Scripture, the words and their meaning represent analogy of reason and analogy of faith respectively. Here, Bonaventure echoes the common patristic insight on the analogy of reason within *analogia scripturae.*

The Historical Character of Illumination

In Bonaventure's intellectual-spiritual notion of the light of revelation, the mind grasps God *immediately*.⁴⁴ Here, Bonaventure retains the heart of Augustine's illumination theory, *"Inter mentem et Deum nihil cadit medium."*⁴⁵ On account of the immediacy of divine revelation, Bonaventure's theory of revelation is personal but not individualistic. Illumination is the work of the Mediator between God and man, Christ the Light. While God also occasionally employs the mediation of the angels in revelation,⁴⁶ revelation remains entirely the work of God in history, which embraces the world.

However, the historical character of illumination consists in the historical process of its mediation by the Church as a whole, not by an individual. The personal nature of revelation is within the context of God's work in history. According to Ratzinger, by the time Bonaventure wrote his *Hexaemeron,* "the Canon was already set down for him as it stands today"⁴⁷ and "the [Church Fathers] are the bearers of a new spiritual revelation, without which the Scriptures simply would not be

---

43. Benedict XVI/Ratzinger, *Theology of History in Bonaventure,* 63; cf. Bonaventure, *Hex.* 2.19 (5:339B).

44. Bonaventure, *Sent. II* d.23, a.2, q.3, ad 7 (2:546): "Cum ipse sit immediatus rationali creaturae"; *Sent. III* d.1, a.1, q.1, ad.4 (3:11): "Pro eo, quod natura rationalis, eo ipso quod est imago Dei, nata ordinary ad ipsum immediate."

45. Augustine, *Ver. rel.* 55.113 (PL 34:172): "Religet ergo nos religio uni omnipotenti Deo; quia inter mentem nostram qua illum intelligimus Patrem, et veritatem, id est lucem interiorem per quam illum intelligimus, nulla interposita creatura est"; Augustine, *Enarrat. Ps.* 118.18.4 (PL 37:1553): "Deus itaque per seipsum, quia lux est, illuminat pias mentes, ut ea quae divina dicuntur vel ostenduntur, intellegant"; cf. Benedict XVI/Ratzinger, *Theology of History in Bonaventure,* 74.

46. Bonaventure, *Hex.* 3.32 (5:348B).

47. Bonaventure, *Brev.*, Pro. 1 (5:202B); Benedict XVI/Ratzinger, *Theology of History in Bonaventure,* 79–80.

effective as revelation."⁴⁸ For Bonaventure, the historical process of ecclesial mediation of revelation, which includes the Canonical and patristic spiritual exegesis, has both an allegorical and an anagogical dimension. While Joachim of Fiore proposed a third age of revelation by the Spirit separate from the New Testament and the time of Christ,⁴⁹ Bonaventure takes the *via media*. For him, the time of Christ is at the center of the historical progress of the ecclesial understanding of the hidden meaning of Scripture, which contains within itself a statement about a final future revelation, and which corresponds with the fullness of time.⁵⁰ Ratzinger says, "for Bonaventure, history consists of two corresponding movements from the very beginning—*egressus* and *regressus*. Christ stands as the turning point of these movements and as the center who both divides and unites."⁵¹ In anagogical exegesis, the analogy of hope explains the goal of the historical of process of divine illumination of biblical meaning. He calls the final revelation a formless illumination (*nulliforms*) because no intellectual form will be necessary for such perfect comprehension of the divine face: "*Non est cuiuslibet, nisi cui Deus revelat.*"⁵² In this most perfect and interior contact with God, sacrificial love is the highest analogy between God and man.⁵³ Only the saints have reached this level of full intimate revelation of Christ.

48. Bonaventure, *Hex.* 19.10 (5:421B).

49. One of the ideas of the Calabrian Abbot Joachim of Fiore that was rejected is "the limitation of the New Testament and the time of Jesus Christ to the second age. The New Testament is the *testamentum aeternum*" (Benedict XVI/Ratzinger, *Theology of History in Bonaventure*, 105).

50. Bonaventure, *Hex.* 2.17 (5:339A): "Scripturae intelligi non possunt nec mysteria, nisi sciatur decursus mundi et disposition hierarchia"; 13.6, 7 (5:388B, 389A): "Repleta est terra Scientia domini sicut aquae maris operientis (Isa 11:9). . . . Et hoc potissime refertur ad tempus novi testament, quando scripturae intelligetur, quae modo non intelliguntur. Tunc 'erit mons'; scilicet ecclesia contemplative, et tunc 'non nocebunt,' quando fugient monstra haeresum sapientiae usura." See Benedict XVI/Ratzinger, *Theology of History in Bonaventure*, 83–84.

51. Benedict XVI/Ratzinger, *Theology of History in Bonaventure*, 142–43.

52. Bonaventure, *Hex.* 2.30 (5:341B), 28 (5:340F). This is the wisdom that Paul taught to the perfect (see 1 Cor 2:6–10).

53. Benedict XVI/Ratzinger, *Theology of History in Bonaventure*, 93: "The crucified Christ had appeared to St. Francis in the form of a Seraph. From the time of his own meditation on Mount Alverna, this vision had never lost its power over Bonaventure. . . . The comprehension of Christ was realized here on the highest level of love, on the level of the Seraphim. . . . Accordingly, [Francis] must belong to the seraphic Church of the final age. Thus an extensive synthesis of hierarchical thought, mysticism, and history is revealed in the unusual double-form of that vision." See Bonaventure, *Itin.*, Pro.2 (5:295A–B); *Apol. Paup.* c.3, 10 (8:247A).

Grace and Nature

Bonaventure calls the light of grace, the fifth essence (*quinta essentia*), the fifth element that stands behind the other four encompassing them as the totality of being.[54] According to Ratzinger,

> One has ascertained the vital basic direction of Bonaventure's concept of grace if one knows that grace *for him is* "spiritual light" (*geistiges Licht*) from the original light of God (*Urlicht Gottes*), and that his teaching on grace is hence the transfer of "light metaphysics" (*Lichtmetaphysik*) into the spiritual-psychic (*Geistig-Geistliche*) light-theology.[55]

The key to Bonaventure's "intrinsic character of grace"[56] is the primacy of the *Logos* of faith in the analogy of light. He considers existence in its "ever-present state of becoming . . . inseparable from the light of grace, so that grace can never simply be grasped as an independent (*selbständige*) layer on the soul, but always only preceded (*vorhergeht*) by the subsistence (*Bestehen*) of a 'continuity' between God and man."[57]

In Bonaventure's primacy of the *Logos,* Ratzinger discovers a *personal* and historical approach to the analogy between the divine and human nature. In his discussion on grace and nature, Bonaventure maintains that "grace is lost through sin so that a fresh infusion of divine love is needed in order to restore the original life of the soul."[58] For Ratzinger, Bonaventure's soteriological notion of the soul implies that "at every moment, spirit surpasses pure nature" because "the immediacy of [the soul's] relation to God is so intimately essential to it that it cannot exist properly except in being preserved immediately by God. . . . There is no ahistorical naturalness of man."[59] Bonaventure's idea of the intrinsic

---

54. Bonaventure, *Sent.* II d.13 (2:310–29); a.2, q.2 (2:319). See also Benedict XVI/Ratzinger, *Offenbarungsverständnis*, 336.

55. Benedict XVI/Ratzinger, *Offenbarungsverständnis*, 336.

56. See Benedict XVI/Ratzinger, *Offenbarungsverständnis*, 306, 334–35.

57. Benedict XVI/Ratzinger, *Offenbarungsverständnis*, 336.

58. Benedict XVI/Ratzinger, *Dogma and Preaching*, 153; Bonaventure, *Sent.* II d.28, a.1, q.1 ad 2 (2:676B). In chapter 1, we saw in Irenaeus of Lyon that grace is needed to restore human likeness to God, which was lost during the fall; cf. Irenaeus, *Adversus Haereses* 5.6.1 (SC 153:76): "Si autem defuerit animae Spiritus, animalis est vere qui est talis et carnalis derelictus imperfectus erit, imaginem quidem habens in plasmate, similitudinem vero non assumens per Spiritum." See also Benedict XVI/Ratzinger, *Dogma and Preaching*, 153.

59. Benedict XVI/Ratzinger, *Dogma and Preaching*, 153.

nature of grace is historically soteriological. For him, Christ is the central *Logos* of history to the extent that in the logic of his Cross and Resurrection, he reveals suffering as crucial to the true logic of man's expression of his similitude to God.[60] Here is a historical expression of the primacy of Christ.

Paschal Synthesis of Similitude and Illumination Analogies

In Bonaventure, the light of Christ's resurrection is the center of all illumination analogies and the doctrinal role of the Church mediates this Light of lights. In the spirit of the medieval understanding of a university, Bonaventure considers theology as the harmonizing discipline of other sciences in their quest for the truth. In a sevenfold manner, he demonstrates how Christ is the "center" of all sciences. For him, Christ is the center of essence, nature, distance, doctrine, modesty, justice, and concord/harmony. Each of these themes corresponds respectively with the following science: metaphysics, physics, mathematics, logic, ethics, politics/justice, and theology.[61] The seven sciences correspond to Christ's (eternal) generation, (historical) incarnation, passion, resurrection, ascension, (final) judgement and beatification respectively.[62]

In Bonaventure's reduction of the human sciences to the seven Christological illuminations, theology demonstrates the harmony between the logic of the Cross and mathematical truth; i.e., between the light of faith and the light of reason. In mathematics, the center of the circle (earth) is the meeting point of "two lines crossing each other at right angle (the Cross)."[63] Mathematics corresponds to Christology,

---

60. Bonaventure, *Hex.* 1.27.28 (5:334); cf. Benedict XVI/Ratzinger, *Offenbarungsverständnis*, 244.

61. Bonaventure, *Hex.* 1.11 (5:331A): "Est autem septiforme medium, scilicet essentiae, naturae, distantiae, doctrinae, modestiae, iustitiae, concordiae. Primum est de consideratione metaphysici, secundum physici, tertium mathematici, quartum logici, quintum ethici, sextum politici seu iuristarum, septimum theology"; cf. Benedict XVI/Ratzinger, *Offenbarungsverständnis*, 242.

62. Bonaventure, *Hex.* 1.11 (5:331A).

63. Bonaventure, *Hex.* 1.24 (5:333B): "Medium enim, cum amissum est in circulo, inveniri non potest nisi per duas lineas se orthogonaliter intersecantes." Commenting on this quotation, Ratzinger says, "The lost center of the circle is found again by means of two lines that intersect at right angles, that is, by a cross. This means that by His Cross, Christ has definitively solved the geometry-problem of the world history. With His Cross He has uncovered the lost center of the circle of the world so as to give the

which reduces all human logic to their original likeness to the divine logic.[64] By the devil's logic of prideful disobedience to God, he "made man differ from God while promising to make him similar to him."[65] On the contrary, Christ's paschal logic of humble obedience to God "made man similar to [Christ] himself, that is, to God."[66] Describing Christ's resurrection as the illumination of the paschal logic, Bonaventure says that "Christ opened the tomb, and this represents the opening of the scroll, and he removed the shroud, and this represents the manifestation of mysteries."[67] The light of Christ's resurrection reveals how the Cross of Christ reduces all human logic to its original likeness to the divine logic. It is under the parallel sciences of mathematics-passion and (doctrinal) logic-resurrection that Bonaventure synthesizes his similitude and light analogies.

Joseph Ratzinger

In the midst of a neo-pagan world, Joseph Ratzinger draws from the patristic and medieval analogy, tools for engaging the modern world with a courageous treatment of the Gospel message on the primacy of the *logos-love*.

Modern Opposition of Philosophy and Theology

Ratzinger saw in the modern thought a shift from the medieval classical complementarity between philosophy and theology to an opposition of one against another. Thomas Aquinas made the distinction between

---

true direction and meaning to the movement of the individual life and to the history of mankind as such" (Benedict XVI/Ratzinger, *Theology of History in Bonaventure*, 146).

64. According to Ratzinger, "The idea that the end involves a certain return to the beginning" emerges several times in Bonaventure's works as "a unified progressive and ascending movement" (Benedict XVI/Ratzinger, *Theology of History in Bonaventure*, 147). See Bonaventure, *Perf. ev.* q.2, a.2, ad 20 (5:148A); *Hex.* 16.22 (5:406B). The concept of time in Bonaventure is both linear and circular.

65. Bonaventure, *Hex.* 1.27 (5:334A): "Ex quo enim diabolus fecerat hominem dissimilem Deo, cum tamen promisisset, similem se facturum." "When you eat it . . . you will be like God" (Gen 3:5).

66. Bonaventure, *Hex.* 1.27 (5:334A): "Necesse fuit, Christum esse similem homini, ut faceret hominem similem sibi sive Deo."

67. Bonaventure, *Hex.* 1.30 (5:334B).

philosophy as the search of unaided reason for reality's ultimate questions and theology as faith seeking understanding.[68] However, Ratzinger observes that "since the late Middle Ages, philosophy has been paired with 'pure reason' while theology has been coupled with faith."[69] Martin Heidegger and Karl Jaspers represent the modern philosophical arguments against a methodological synthesis between philosophy and theology. Ratzinger comments,

> For Heidegger, philosophy is by nature questioning. Whoever believes he has the answers already is no longer capable of philosophizing. Since the philosophical question is folly in the eyes of theology, Christian philosophy is a sham. Jaspers shares the opinion that he who supposes himself in possession of the answer has failed as a philosopher: the open movement of transcendence is interrupted in favor of an imagined ultimate certainty.[70]

Modern philosophy rejects the Christian proposal that faith stimulates rather than obstruct authentic questions.

Meanwhile, in theology, Martin Luther and early Karl Barth represent a rejection of philosophy. According to Ratzinger, with his battle cry, *sola Scriptura*, "Martin Luther inaugurated a new era of antagonism to philosophy for the sake of the unadulterated Word of God.... In our century, Karl Barth sharpened this protest . . . with his contestation of *analogia entis*," which he considered the invention of the Antichrist and an obstruction to the possibility of his becoming Catholic.[71] Luther's and Barth's opposition of the use of philosophy in theology is more specifically a rejection of the use of analogy in theology because they simply wanted to exclude the question of metaphysics. For Ratzinger, the Barth's rejection of *analogia entis* is fundamentally a rejection of "the ontological option of Catholic theology for its synthesis of the [Greek] philosophical idea of being and the biblical concept of God."[72] However, Barth's theological attempt to rid philosophy of metaphysics spills over to a progressive Kantian philosophical replacement of metaphysics with history.[73] Thus,

68. Benedict XVI/Ratzinger, *Nature and Mission of Theology*, 16.
69. Benedict XVI/Ratzinger, *Nature and Mission of Theology*, 17.
70. Benedict XVI/Ratzinger, *Nature and Mission of Theology*, 17.
71. Benedict XVI/Ratzinger, *Nature and Mission of Theology*, 18–19.
72. Benedict XVI/Ratzinger, *Nature and Mission of Theology*, 19.
73. Benedict XVI/Ratzinger, *Nature and Mission of Theology*, 21: "One may well say that these developments in theology have been among the principal influences at

the philosophical and theological debate, which fundamentally hinges upon the rejection of the use of analogy faces the crisis of discontinuity between Greek philosophical ontology, biblical faith and the progressive nature of history. As we saw, under the direction of Gottlieb Söhngen, Ratzinger finds in Bonaventure a medieval development of a Christocentric synthesis of ontology, biblical faith and history common in the writings of the ancient authors.

Analogy of Light in the Primacy of Christ

Ratzinger synthesizes both faith and reason with the Johannine and Augustinian epistemology, which considers Christ as the Light, and faith and reason as the two analogous emission of light from the Light. Ratzinger says, "The Word-made-man did not simply enter a world that knew nothing whatsoever about him. He sent his radiance ahead of himself into the world and thus awakened the yearning of humanity. He is the light, the enlightening of every man that comes into the world (John 1:9)."[74] Kucer recognizes that Ratzinger's presentation of the analogy of being is explicitly Christological.[75] Given our focus on Ratzinger's primacy of Christ, our consideration of his contributions to the modern analogy debate will be in the context of his Christocentric synthesis of the light of faith and the light of reason. As we did with Augustine, we will use the three properties of being—truth, goodness and beauty—to investigate his theory of illumination. Benedict XVI refers to the Fourth Lateran Council's principle of "analogy and its language" as the magisterial statement undergirding his reflections on faith and reason.[76]

Primacy of Truth in the Light of Reason

Ratzinger's contribution to the modern debate on the analogy of faith and reason concerns "the question of truth." For him, the truth is essentially uncreated; no created reality is identical to the truth. However, we saw in both Augustine and Bonaventure how illumination analogy,

---

work in the progressive replacement of metaphysics by history, which has taken place in philosophy since Kant."

74. Benedict XVI/Ratzinger, *On the Way*, 72; *Beiträge zur Christologie*, 1002.
75. Kucer, *Truth and Politics*, 58.
76. Benedict XVI/Ratzinger, "Regensburg Lecture," 27, 29.

which pertains to the cognition of the truth explains man's capacity for the transcendent God. As Ratzinger says, it is "the fundamental conviction of the Christian faith that in the beginning was Reason and thus, Truth: it brings forth man and human reason in the first place as beings capable of the truth."[77] Reason and Truth are uncreated because in the beginning they pre-existed prior to creation, and as a creation of the true Being, human reason is capable of ascent to its Creator. The grounds for reason's capacity for ascent to the truth is the existing analogy between the transcendent nature of "pure intelligibility" and the light of created reason. Our consideration of Ratzinger's primacy of truth in the light of reason are under the following themes: (1) Primacy of *logos* in Christianity and ancient religions, (2) the notion of person in faith and philosophy, (3) primacy of reason in speech about God, and (4) primacy of reason in faith and politics.

Primacy of logos in Christianity and Ancient Religions

According to Ratzinger, "Jesus is not merely an enlightened man but rather the Son, the Word itself, toward which all other illuminations and other words tend."[78] In harmony with the patristic positive approach to reason, Ratzinger finds both in the God of faith and the God of the philosophers, a common ground for explaining the analogy of faith and reason. He says, "In an environment teeming with gods . . . the early Christianity boldly and resolutely made its choice and carried out its purification by deciding *for* the God of the philosophers and *against* the gods of the various religions."[79] In antiquity, the dialogue between Christianity and ancient gods was not interreligious but "inter-philosophical."[80] The common ground for such dialogue was the primacy of the God of reason (*logos*); "the highest being of whom [the] philosophers speak."[81] Ratzinger

77. Benedict XVI/Ratzinger, *Church, Ecumenism, and Politics*, 155.
78. Benedict XVI/Ratzinger, *On the Way*, 70.
79. Benedict XVI/Ratzinger, *Introduction to Christianity*, 137.
80. Carola, "Non-Christians in Patristic Theology," 34: "On the question of religion and the way of salvation, philosophers, not pagan priests, were the Church Fathers' partners in dialogue—to use a modern expression. The Christian apologists were those primarily engaged in this *inter-philosophical* exchange that ranged from a severe critique of pagan polytheism to an investigation of the origins of philosophical truths."
81. Benedict XVI/Ratzinger, *Introduction to Christianity*, 138.

finds in Justin Martyr's idea of the *seeds of the logos*,[82] a fine depiction of Christ's primacy in the philosophical dialogue between Christianity and ancient religions:

> Christ—Justin argues—is according to the Word of the Gospels "the *Logos*," i.e., Reason (*die Vernunft*), Meaning (*der Sinn*): thus everything rational and meaningful is also Christian, because yes Reason, Meaning and Christ are one and the same. Every splinter of Reason, every splinter of Meaning, which can be found in the world, are therefore fragments (*Scherben*) of the one Meaning, who is Christ. The reasonable and the meaningful found before and outside of Christ in the world, thus is to Christ as a fragment is to the whole: He is the whole of what was already previously found in scattered (*versprengten*) parts in the world. Whoever connects Christianity and Greek reason, does not chain heterogeneous elements to one another, but brings together what by nature has long belonged together. Justin's descendants lived by these thoughts and deepened it.[83]

The Christian measure of the truth of God is only the *Logos*, who is "Being itself; what the philosophers have expounded as the ground of all being [and] as the God above all powers."[84] The presence of reason or meaning within cultures are fragmentary knowledge of Being itself proclaimed fully in the Christian faith. When Ratzinger speaks of *Scherben des einen Sinnes* (fragments of the one Meaning), certainly, he is not referring to a fragmentation or disintegration of Being into the rational part

---

82. Carola, "Non-Christians in Patristic Theology," 35. Carola considers Justin's concept of the *seeds of the logos* to be a principle of natural illumination: "This seminal *logos* is the principle of natural revelation. It accounts for the innate religious and moral sense that human beings possess. Constituted by the seminal *logos*, human reason can attain to a knowledge of God's existence and the universal moral law" in a very limited and imperfect way.

83. Benedict XVI/Ratzinger, *Glaube in Schrift und Tradition*, 236 (my translation): "Christus—so argumentiert Justin—ist nach dem Wort des Evangeliums 'der Logos,' d.h. die Vernunft, der Sinn: Also ist alles, was vernuft-haft, was sinn-haft ist, auch christlich, weil ja Vernunft, Sinn und Christus ein und dasselbe sind. Alle Vernunftsplitter, alle Sinnsplitter, die in der Welt anzutreffen sind, sind demnach Scherben des einen Sinnes, der Christus ist. Das Vernünftige und Sinnhafte, das vor und außerhalb von Christus in der Welt anzutreffen ist, Verhält sich demnach zu Christus wie Splitter zum Ganzen: Er ist das ganz, was vorher in versprengten Teilen schon in der Welt anzutreffen war. Wer also Christentum und griechische Vernunft verbindet, kettet nicht heterogene Elemente aneinander, sondern bringt zusammen, was vom Wesen her längst zusammengehörte."

84. Benedict XVI/Ratzinger, *Introduction to Christianity*, 138.

of creation, but the metaphysical and analogous reflection of the Word in created reason. Ratzinger is using the term *Scherben* to underscore what is "partial" about the Greek philosophical knowledge of Christ. As Justin says, "So it is not that we [Christians] hold the same opinions as others, but what all others [the Greek philosophers] say is an imitation of ours."[85] The philosophers have a partial knowledge of Christ the *Logos*, while Christians know Christ in a full way. The ontological grounds for the Christian analogy of faith and reason consists in the similitude between the creative Being and the created being. Thus, Ratzinger uses the Christian option for the God of *logos* over the god of myths, to explain how faith and philosophy are the two analogous ways of speaking about God.

With regard to the relationship between Christianity and the Jewish faith, Ratzinger considers the same God of *logos* as the God of the Old Testament prophets. In agreement with "contemporary scholarship," he finds "quite amazing parallels in chronology and content between the philosophers' criticism of the myths in Greece and the prophets' criticism of the gods in Israel."[86] While Greek philosophy and Jewish prophets have two very distinct movements and aims, however, they shared an analogous "movement of the *logos* against the myth."[87] In his Regensburg Address, Benedict XVI describes this "close analogy" between the demythologization of Hellenism and the Jewish faith as follows:

> The mysterious name of God, revealed from the burning bush, a name which separates this God from all other divinities with their many names and simply asserts being, "I am," already presents a challenge to the notion of myth, to which Socrates's attempt to vanquish and transcend myth stands in close analogy. Within the Old Testament, the process which started at the burning bush came to new maturity at the time of the Exile, when the God of Israel, an Israel now deprived of its land and worship, was proclaimed as the God of heaven and earth and described in a simple formula which echoes the words uttered at the burning bush: "I am." This new understanding of God is accompanied by a kind of enlightenment, which finds stark

---

85. Justin Martyr, *Apologia* 1.60.10 (PTS 38:117); cf. Carola, "Non-Christians in Patristic Theology," 36. Carola insists that in Justin, "The *sperma tou logou* is neither the *logos* himself nor a part of him sown in human beings, but rather an imitation of the *logos*."

86. Benedict XVI/Ratzinger, *Introduction to Christianity*, 139.

87. Benedict XVI/Ratzinger, *Introduction to Christianity*, 139.

expression in the mockery of gods who are merely the work of human hands (cf. Ps 115).[88]

In this quotation, Benedict sees a "close analogy" in the parallel between the Greek and the Old Testament challenge of the notion of myth. At the center of this close analogy is coincidence of the biblical "I am" and the Greek "Being itself." In the Hellenistic period, "biblical faith encountered the best of Greek thought at a deep level, resulting in a mutual enrichment evident especially in the later wisdom literature."[89] Ultimately, the *Logos* of the Prologue of John's Gospel is the full manifestation of the analogy of reason as the grounds of the synthesis between the biblical faith and Greek philosophical *logos*.

In the Johannine *Logos*, where Christianity locates the unity of the Old and New Testament—*analogia scripturae*, Ratzinger also grounds his concept of the analogy of being. Therefore, the synthetic notion of *analogia entis* within *analogia fidei*, which we saw in Clement of Alexandria, Origen, Gregory of Nyssa, and Bonaventure is also fundamental to Ratzinger's synthesis of faith and reason in the primacy of truth. For Ratzinger the cause of the breakup of the ancient religions was the gulf between the God of faith and the God of the philosophers, the dichotomy between reason and piety.[90] If ancient Christianity rejected the *logos* of philosophers and went the purely religious route, it would have collapsed like other ancient religions.[91] Rather with the question of the truth at stake, Christianity proclaimed Christ as the *Logos*.

The notion of "person" in faith and philosophy

Not only did the Christian faith decide in favor of the *logos* of philosophers but it also transformed it from a pure intellectual *logos* to a personal one. Ratzinger comments,

> Christian faith gave a completely new significance to this God of philosophers, removing him from the purely academic realm and thus transforming him.... This God of philosophers, whose pure eternity and unchangeability had excluded any relation with the changeable and transitory, now appeared to the eye of

---

88. Benedict XVI/Ratzinger, "Regensburg Lecture," 20–21.
89. Benedict XVI/Ratzinger, "Regensburg Lecture," 22.
90. Benedict XVI/Ratzinger, *Introduction to Christianity*, 139.
91. Benedict XVI/Ratzinger, *Introduction to Christianity*, 139.

faith as the God of men, who is not only thought of all thoughts, the eternal mathematics of the universe, but also *agape*, the power of creative love.[92]

Faith and philosophy as the two analogous ways of comprehending the Supreme Being converges in the tension between a transcendent and a relational God. Christianity transforms the Greek philosophical notion of person into the proper analogy for the synthesis of the divine transcendence and his presence in human history. For Ratzinger, it is not in the *logos* of "thought alone" but in the *logos* of "creative love" that Christianity found the personal synthesis of the relationship between God and man. "Certainly, love, as Saint Paul says, 'transcends' knowledge and is thereby capable of perceiving more than thought alone (cf. Eph 3:19); nonetheless it continues to be love of the God who is *Logos*."[93] Furthermore, with its highly nuanced concept of *persona*, Christianity exposes the limitations of the philosophical notion of *logos* as pure thought, and proclaims the person of Christ as the answer to the philosophical question of truth. Truth is not only transcendent but also relational.[94]

The full meaning of the Christian concept of person appears in the history of thought within the context of the development of the Trinitarian doctrine. Conscious of the modern opposition of theology and philosophy, Ratzinger insists that the existential meaning of Christian personalism is not merely "a theological exception" to be divorced from the totality of philosophy and human thought.[95] On the contrary, the Christian notion of person contributes to the pre-Christian philosophy by calling "the *totality* of human thought into question [in order to] set it on new paths."[96]

In antiquity, "philosophy had been limited exclusively to the level of essences."[97] The novelty of Christian personalism consists in an "intellectual transformation . . . foreign to the Greek and Latin mind" that the concept of person "is not understood substantially but existentially."[98] For

92. Benedict XVI/Ratzinger, *Introduction to Christianity*, 143.
93. Benedict XVI/Ratzinger, "Regensburg Lecture," 27.
94. Benedict XVI/Ratzinger, *Introduction to Christianity*, 148: "It becomes apparent that truth and love are originally identical; that where they are completely realized they are not two parallel or even opposing realities but one, the one and only absolute."
95. Benedict XVI/Ratzinger, *Dogma and Preaching*, 191.
96. Benedict XVI/Ratzinger, *Dogma and Preaching*, 191.
97. Benedict XVI/Ratzinger, *Dogma and Preaching*, 191.
98. Benedict XVI/Ratzinger, *Dogma and Preaching*, 190.

Ratzinger, Boethius's definition of person as "the individual substance of a rational nature" is inadequate because it remains on the level of Greek thought, which is the level of substance.[99] The level of substance is incapable of explaining things concerning either the Trinity or Christology. In contrast, Ratzinger considers the formula of Richard of Saint Victor to be closer to the revealed truth because it "rightly notes that 'person' in the theological sense lies not on the level of essence but rather on the level of existence."[100] Richard of Saint Victor "defines person as *spiritualis naturae incommunicabilis existential*, a distinct and incommunicable existence of spiritual nature."[101] For Ratzinger, the Christian contribution to the concept of person is the shift from the Greek idea of pure and eternal self-thinking thought to "the relativity of the existence that is inherent in the concept of Logos."[102]

Beyond the Greek notion of God in terms of idea and meaning (essence), Ratzinger choses to explain the reasonableness of the Christian notion of person with the *relativity* inherent in the Johannine concept of *Logos*. For him, "*relatio* stands beside the substance as an equally primordial form of being."[103] Aristotle considered the category of *relatio* to be among the "accidents," which are separate from the form of the real (substance). However, Augustine says, "in God there is no accidental but rather only substance and relation."[104] Scripture presents an "experience of the God who is not only *logos* but also *dia-logos*, not only idea and meaning but speech and word in the reciprocal exchanges of partners in

---

99. Benedict XVI/Ratzinger, *Dogma and Preaching*, 191. Ratzinger considers Thomas's philosophical treatment of the whole matter of "person" as more faithful to Boethius and as if it were a theological exception. He comments, "This seems to me to be the limitation of Saint Thomas in this matter as well, that he proceeds in theology on the existential level with Richard of Saint Victor but treats the whole matter as if it were a theological exception, whereas in his philosophy he remains to a great extent faithful to the other approach of pre-Christian philosophy with Boethius's concept of person."

100. Benedict XVI/Ratzinger, *Dogma and Preaching*, 191.

101. Benedict XVI/Ratzinger, *Dogma and Preaching*, 191.

102. Benedict XVI/Ratzinger, *Dogma and Preaching*, 188.

103. Benedict XVI/Ratzinger, *Introduction to Christianity*, 183.

104. Augustine, *Trin.* 5.5.6 (CCSL 50:210–11): "Neque secundum accidens, quia et quod dicitur Pater, et quod dicitur Filius, aeternum atque incommutabile est eis. Quamobrem quamvis diversum sit Patrem esse et Filium esse, non est tamen diversa substantia, quia hoc non secundum substantiam dicuntur, sed secundum relativum; quod tamen relativum non est accidens quia non est mutabile."

conversation."[105] Thus, in the relationship between Greek philosophical notion of person and that of Christian theology, faith's introduction of a pure relativity is not a divorce from philosophy but a contribution to the history of human thought. By faith, the human logic of person rises from the ascending idea of *logos* to the descending analogy of relativity. The analogy of faith does not oppose the analogy of reason but elevates it to the fullness of *Logos*.

In Ratzinger, the person of Christ is the center of the biblical account of the primordial form of *relatio*. In John's Gospel, the existing paradox between verses 5:19 (*The Son can do nothing of his own accord*) and 10:19 (*I and the Father are one*) demonstrates both oneness of substance and "pure relativity" of persons.[106] By his very nature, Christ is "the One Sent" in a unique sense. In the Christian notion of person, Christ's personhood, which subsists in the person of the Son takes primacy because his humanity manifests in a historical existence, the transcendent nature of person as "pure relativity." If God who is pure act is also pure relativity, philosophy finds in the biblical "dia-logic" of Christ a transformation of *relatio* from an accidental to an *original* form of being. As the revelation of the original idea of "man," "in which the orientation of man first becomes evident . . . Christ is not the ontological exception but, rather, based on his exceptional position [primacy]," the Christo-logical concept of person is the original and new understanding of person.[107] The biblical primacy of Christ illuminates the limits of Greek philosophical notion of person in order to complete it genuinely. In the concept of person, the unifying analogy between its philosophical and theological approach consists in the newness and primacy of Christ's dia-logical notion of person.

We have already seen in Augustine and Bonaventure the roots of Ratzinger's dialogical or speech form of *logos*, which the person of Christ illuminates with the concept of pure relativity. In the intrinsic relativity of truth, the analogy of light as an expression of the patristic primacy of *logos*, finds its full expression in the Christian notion of person. In Ratzinger's philosophical articulation of the Christian notion of person, we also see reflections of the patristic ascending and descending movement in analogy. The *logos* of Greek philosophy is by ascent of thought

---

105. Benedict XVI/Ratzinger, *Introduction to Christianity*, 183.
106. Benedict XVI/Ratzinger, *Dogma and Preaching*, 187.
107. Benedict XVI/Ratzinger, *Dogma and Preaching*, 192.

in search of the *essence* of Being, while the *Logos* of faith descends as the Word in *relation* to being. The descending movement of the analogy of faith confirms, orders and expands the ascending movement reason.

Logos-speech

Fundamental to the use of analogy in Ratzinger's theology is the understanding of *logos* as both "reason" and "speech." In his Regensburg Address, Benedict XVI echoes the Justin Martyr's insight on the significance of reason in speaking well of God, whereby participation in the seeds of the *logos* explains the ability of philosophers to speak well of the truth.[108] For Benedict, the same *logos* is fundamental to the mode of the propagation of faith: "Whoever would lead someone to faith needs the ability to speak well and to reason properly."[109] In the word *logos,* reason and speech are one and the same thing: "*Logos* means both reason and word."[110] To propagate the truth of God with unreasonable speech (e.g., threats) is self-contradictory because God acts, σὺν λόγῳ, with *logos*."[111] The Pontiff affirms reason as the basic analogy between God's nature and human nature: "Not to act in accordance with reason is contrary to God's nature."[112] We saw earlier how in Ratzinger, the analogy of reason confirms the providential nature of the meeting of the biblical message of John's Prologue and Greek philosophy: *In the beginning was the Logos.* The analogy of faith and reason consists in the similitude between the ascending *logos* and the descending *Logos.*

Primacy of reason in faith and politics

In Ratzinger's critical approach to the political, we find a demonstration of his synthetic approach to the primacy of reason. Like Origen, Ratzinger prioritizes reason in his explanation of the relationship between faith and politics. For him, reason should be the primary navigator of politics, and Christian faith has much to contribute towards "the path of

---

108. Justin Martyr, *Apologia* 2.13.3 (SC 507:362). See chapter 1 (22) [x-ref].
109. Benedict XVI/Ratzinger, "Regensburg Lecture," 13.
110. Benedict XVI/Ratzinger, "Regensburg Lecture," 17.
111. Benedict XVI/Ratzinger, "Regensburg Lecture," 13.
112. Benedict XVI/Ratzinger, "Regensburg Lecture," 14.

reasonable politics."[113] The *Logos* of faith ensures the centrality of reason in politics by prioritizing the truth over and above state and religion.

According to Ratzinger, Christ changed the ancient concept of "state religion" when he said, "Render to Caesar the things that are Caesar's and to God the things that are God's" (Matt 22:21).[114] As we saw in Augustine's critic of Varro, the ancient state religion claimed supreme sacredness; a kind of divine state.[115] However, by placing itself resolutely on the side of truth, Christianity was well equipped to challenge the well-established dominant custom of the city of Rome, which claimed a uniqueness in world politics. The teaching of Christ, which separated the religious from the state "represents the source and the abiding basis for the Western idea of freedom."[116] Christian teaching takes away totalitarian authority from the hands of the state such that both the state and religion operate within a limited radius of activity. While the Church and state have different instrumental roles at the service of the truth, neither the Church nor the state can claim total authority over the truth.[117] As Ratzinger says, "Enlightenment is essentially dependent on the notion that the truth is absolute, or we can just say: divine."[118] In the right relationship between the truth and state, and the truth and the Church, "the truth remains essentially independent" of the Church and the state, and the Church and state remains "instrumentally subordinate to it"[119] in their own distinct ways. Thus, Christian *Logos* reduces any institutional and political claim to the possession of the truth to a myth.

For instance, about the political kingdoms that lay claim on man's total freedom, Ratzinger says, "even though their propaganda says that their goal is man's complete liberation, the abolition of all ruling authority, they contradict the truth of man and are opposed to his freedom because they force man to fit into what he himself can make."[120] The myth

---

113. Benedict XVI/Ratzinger, *Church, Ecumenism, and Politics*, 144.

114. Benedict XVI/Ratzinger, *Church, Ecumenism, and Politics*, 155–56.

115. See chapter 2 (89) [X-REF].

116. Benedict XVI/Ratzinger, *Church, Ecumenism, and Politics*, 156.

117. Benedict XVI/Ratzinger, *Church, Ecumenism, and Politics*, 157: "Where the church itself becomes the state, freedom is gone. But freedom is lacking also in places where the church is abolished as a public and publicly relevant authority, because there again the state claims to be the sole basis for morality."

118. Benedict XVI/Ratzinger, *Church, Ecumenism, and Politics*, 149.

119. Benedict XVI/Ratzinger, *Church, Ecumenism, and Politics*, 155.

120. Benedict XVI/Ratzinger, *Church, Ecumenism, and Politics*, 144.

of divine state, which promises man's complete liberation contradicts the nature of human freedom because the object of human longing for freedom is a reality that transcends man, i.e., the divine truth. Human freedom resides in a reality beyond human productivity. When a political system forces man to find its freedom in the object of his productivity, he contradicts the very object of man's freedom.[121] In Ratzinger's argument for the primacy of reason over political myth, we hear echoes of Origen's primacy of reason in politics. The comparison consists in how they both affirm that faith supports the centrality of reason in politics. For Origen, it was the law of nature, which faith protects that takes priority over political laws.[122] In Ratzinger, it is the truth about human freedom that takes priority over the political myth of liberation. Faith elevates the political by holding it accountable to reason, and by replacing "the myth of earthly paradise or utopian state" with "the objectivity of reason."[123]

Primacy of Goodness in Moral Illumination

Like Augustine, Ratzinger considers moral illumination as a function of the light of reason, which primarily centers on the question of the truth in the more practical dimension of reason. For Ratzinger, "In the rationality of creation is to be found not only a mathematical but also a moral message. The first step in recognition (illumination) comes through what we call the *conscience*."[124] Ratzinger uses Augustine's notion of memory (*anamnesis*) to explain the priority of goodness in moral illumination. His theory of moral illumination hinges on the essence of conscience. In other to explain how the essence of conscience does not preclude the transcendence of the subject in opposition to the objectivity of the truth,

---

121. Benedict XVI/Ratzinger, *Church, Ecumenism, and Politics*, 144.

122. Cf. Origen, *Contra Celsum* 5.37 (PG 11:1237B): "As there are, then, generally two laws presented to us, the one being the law of nature, of which God would be the legislator, and the other being the written law of cities, it is a proper thing, when the written law is not opposed to that of God, for the citizens not to abandon it under pretext of foreign customs; but when the law of nature, that is, the law of God, commands what is opposed to the written code, observe whether reason will not tell us to bid a long farewell to the written code, and to the desires of its legislators, and to give ourselves up to the legislator God, and to choose a life agreeable to His Word." See comments in chapter 2.

123. Benedict XVI/Ratzinger, *Church, Ecumenism, and Politics*, 146.

124. Benedict XVI/Ratzinger, *God and the World*, 139–40.

Ratzinger makes the distinction between the ontological and the practical levels of conscience.

First, our theologian speaks of the priority of "an original memory of the good and true (the two are identical) implanted in us."[125] This "*anamnesis* of the origin [of man] results from the godlike constitution of our being" that constitutes a remembering of the Creator.[126] The objective grounds of conscience prioritizes the analogy of the imprint of God's goodness in the human heart. Our primordial sense of goodness is the wisdom that illuminates our exercise of good moral judgment. Ratzinger's definition of the essence of conscience is in harmony with Ronald Nash's explanation of Augustine's ethics, i.e., "the principles of ethics also are universal and are known by reason."[127] Like Augustine's notion of memory, Ratzinger's concept of *anamnesis* is more fundamentally biblical than Platonic. Ratzinger says,

> The word anamnesis should be taken to mean exactly what Paul expressed in the second chapter of his Letter to the Romans: When Gentiles who have not the law do by nature what the law requires, they are a law to themselves, even though they do not have the law. They show that what the law requires is written on their hearts while their conscience also bears witness (Rom 2:14ff).[128]

The awakening of man's original *anamnesis* of the good and true is by analogy an interior illumination of the moral voice in the rational creature. It vindicates the mission of human nature created to seek the good. Ratzinger concludes, "Paul can say: the Gentiles are a law to themselves—not in the sense of a modern liberal notions of autonomy that preclude transcendence of the subject, but in the much deeper sense."[129] The modern liberal notion of autonomy needs to change from an absolute understanding of the subject to a self-surpassing meaning of the subject relative to the transcendent One.

Given the human tendency to forget his Creator, Ratzinger highlights the significance of the "we" of the Church, which analogously mediates man's *anamnesis* of the object of his original goodness. Ratzinger

---

125. Benedict XVI/Ratzinger, "Conscience and Truth," 535.
126. Benedict XVI/Ratzinger, "Conscience and Truth," 535.
127. Nash, *Light of the Mind*, 81.
128. Benedict XVI/Ratzinger, "Conscience and Truth," 534.
129. Benedict XVI/Ratzinger, "Conscience and Truth," 535.

says, "The *anamnesis* instilled in our being needs, one might say, assistance from without so that it can become aware of itself. But this 'from without' is not something set in opposition to *anamnesis* but ordered to it," bringing to fruition what is proper to it.[130] The modern problem consists in the lack of analogical understanding of the essence of conscience. A consequence of the lack of metaphysics in ethics and morals is the absolutized notion of the subject and of authority. For Ratzinger, the modern man's absolutized notion of the subject prevents him from understanding the reasonableness of the teaching authority of the papal primacy over the faithful. He says "The Pope cannot impose commandments on faithful Catholics because he wants to or finds it expedient."[131] Rather, the papal teaching authority derives its power from the *anamnesis* of the new "we" whereby as one Body in Christ, the ecclesial memory becomes the memory of one "I," i.e., the "I" of Christ. On account of the primacy of man's original recollection of the good and the true, Ratzinger defends the primacy of the conscience before the Pope.[132] He says, "The true sense of this teaching authority of the Pope consists in his being the advocate of the Christian memory."[133]

Furthermore, there is the act of moral judgment in the *conscientia*, which follows the essential *anamnesis* of the intrinsic goodness of being.[134] The conscience is considered free only when it proceeds from the priority of formation in the truth. The objectivity of *anamnesis* is the basis of recognizing an erroneous conscience. While on "the level of practical judgment, it can be said that even the erroneous conscience binds," the binding nature of an erroneous conscience "does not signify a canonization of subjectivity."[135] For Ratzinger, "the guilt" of acting from an erroneous conscience lies not in the act of the present judgment itself but "but to the neglect of my being which made me deaf to the internal

---

130. Benedict XVI/Ratzinger, "Conscience and Truth," 536.

131. Benedict XVI/Ratzinger, "Conscience and Truth," 536.

132. On account of the primacy of man's original recollection of the good and the true, Ratzinger defends Henry Newman's toast to conscience before the Pope. Henry Newman concluded his section five of his *Letter to the Duke of Norfolk* as follows: "If I am obliged to bring religion into after-dinner toasts (which indeed does not seem quite the thing), I shall drink—to the Pope, if you please—still, to Conscience first, and to the Pope afterwards" (Newman, "Letter to the Duke of Norfolk," 246).

133. Benedict XVI/Ratzinger, "Conscience and Truth," 537.

134. Benedict XVI/Ratzinger, "Conscience and Truth," 535.

135. Benedict XVI/Ratzinger, "Conscience and Truth," 538.

promptings of truth."¹³⁶ In order words, the problem of an erroneous conscience lies in the neglect of the analogy of being. For Ratzinger, the question of conscience, which hangs on truth as the grounds of freedom, is a law written in the hearts of all, and must be protected by the state and Church laws in a way corresponding to the objectivity of truth.

Finally, Ratzinger's primacy of Christ in moral illumination is biblical. He makes the distinction between the christologically informed ethics of the New Testament and the ethics informed by the Old Testament Decalogue. For him, "the original purpose that Decalogue served [was] to remind us of the deepest part of our reason."¹³⁷ In the christologically informed ethics, Christ the *Logos*-made-man who wants to awaken our very reason to himself bring to full maturity the deepest part of our reason.¹³⁸ Therefore, natural ethics of the present in the inner logic of the Decalogue confirms the primacy of the *Logos*, which brings it to full maturity. The analogy of being confirms the analogy of Scripture.

Primacy of the Form of Beauty in Aesthetic Illumination

There are two ways in which Ratzinger articulates his Christological synthesis of faith and reason in the analogy of beauty: via natural law, and paschal glory.

NATURAL LAW

Like Augustine and Bonaventure, Ratzinger considers the human capacity for perceiving physical beauty to be a function of the light of reason and describes truth as illuminated through the beauty of being. Beauty is capable of radiating the truth of being in a way distinct from theoretical instruction. Augustine's theory of aesthetic illumination operative in Ratzinger was already anticipated by Origen:

> If then a man can extend his thinking as to ponder and consider the beauty and the grace of all the things that have created in the in the Word, the very charm of them will so smite him, the grandeur of their brightness will so pierce him as with a *chosen dart*—as says the prophet—that he will suffer from the dart

---

136. Benedict XVI/Ratzinger, "Conscience and Truth," 538.
137. Benedict XVI/Ratzinger, *On the Way*, 164–65.
138. Benedict XVI/Ratzinger, *On the Way*, 164.

Himself a saving wound, and will be kindled with the blessed fire of His love.[139]

Ratzinger's description of the experience of aesthetic illumination is very similar to Origen's. What Origen describes as the piercing wound that enkindles the fire of divine love, Ratzinger explains as the wound of an arrow that strikes man with the truth: "The encounter with beauty can become the wound of the arrow that strikes the soul and thus make it see clearly, so that hence forth it has a criteria, based on what it has experienced, and can now weigh the arguments correctly."[140] Ratzinger says, "Beauty is knowledge, indeed, a higher form of knowing, because it strikes man with the truth in all its greatness."[141] In the human experience of beauty, illumination takes the form of an encounter with the greatness of reality and the unifying intelligence of the Creator. Benedict XVI says,

> I think we should recover—and enable people today to recover—our capacity for contemplating creation, its beauty and its structure. The world is not a shapeless mass of magma, but the better we know it and the better we discover its marvelous mechanisms, the more clearly we can see a plan, we see that there is a creative intelligence.[142]

Highlighting the priority of the form of beauty in the glory of creation, Ratzinger speaks of "the "that" of creation," which "points to the power that was there at the beginning and that could say: *Let there be . . .* "[143] For our theologian, the "that" of creation professed by faith is the one and the same creative intelligence, which Albert Einstein spoke about when he said that in the laws of nature "there is revealed such a superior Reason that everything significant which has arisen out of human thought and arrangements is, in comparison with it, the merest empty reflection."[144] A scientific study of the laws of the order of nature leads reason to an encounter with the form of beauty.

139. Origen, *Canticum Canticorum*, Prol. (PG 13:67C): "Igitur si quis potuerit capaci mente conjicere et considerare horum omnium quae in ipso create sunt decus et speciem, ipsa rerum venustate percussus, et splendoris magnificentia ceu jaculo, ut ait propheta (Isa 49:29), electo terebratus, salutare ab ipso vulnus accipiet, et beato igne amoris ejus ardebit."

140. Benedict XVI/Ratzinger, *On the Way*, 37.

141. Benedict XVI/Ratzinger, *On the Way*, 35.

142. Benedict XVI/Ratzinger, *Transforming Power of Faith*, 33–34.

143. Benedict XVI/Ratzinger, *In the Beginning*, 22.

144. Benedict XVI/Ratzinger, *In the Beginning*, 23; Einstein, *Mein Weltbild*, 106.

In this way, the convergence of natural law with faith in creation rejects any form of Big Bang theory that reduces creation to the product of darkness and myth. The universe "comes from . . . the beauty that is identical with love."[145] The contemplation of the beauty of creation is oriented to glorification of the Creator, which faith expresses as an orientation toward the Sabbath worship of God.[146] Thus, Sabbath worship is the mark of the covenant of love between God and his people, expressed in the history of the Israel. For Ratzinger, in the meeting of the biblical Sabbath and the fact of creation, "we can say that God created the universe in order to enter into a history of love with mankind."[147] Ratzinger concludes with the Christological implication of the ontology of aesthetic illumination: "God created the universe in order to be able to become a human being and pour out his love upon us and to invite us to love him in return."[148] In Ratzinger, both faith and reason arrives at the primacy of Christ with regard to the question of the "that" of creation, which investigates the Creator's intention for creation.

Synthesis of Faith and Reason in the Paschal Glory

Ratzinger finds on the Cross of Christ, a synthesis of light of faith and reason in the inner beauty of being. The comparison is between the *encounter* of truth by reason in the law of nature and the *encounter* of truth by faith in the Crucified One. The reality that strikes and wounds by the arrow of beauty is what faith reveals fully and personally in the beauty of the suffering Christ. The fire of divine love awakened by beauty is what Christ reveals as sacrificial love.

Ratzinger acknowledges that aesthetic theology leans more toward the mystical than the theological because "being overcome by the beauty

---

145. Benedict XVI/Ratzinger, *In the Beginning*, 25: "Creation exists for worship."

146. Benedict XVI/Ratzinger, *In the Beginning*, 27; cf. *Spirit of the Liturgy*, 26: "The goal of creation is the covenant, the love story of God and man. . . . Man's response to God who is good to him is love, and loving God means worshipping him. If creation is meant to be a space for the covenant, the place where God and man meet one another, then it must be thought of as a space for worship. . . . Creation looks toward covenant, but the covenant completes creation and does not simply exist along with it. Now if worship, rightly understood, is the soul of the covenant, then it not only saves mankind but is also meant to draw the whole of reality into communion with God."

147. Benedict XVI/Ratzinger, *In the Beginning*, 30.

148. Benedict XVI/Ratzinger, *In the Beginning*, 30.

of Christ is a more real, more profound knowledge than mere rational deduction."[149] However, he cautions that "to despise the impact produced by the heart's encounter with beauty would impoverish us and dry up both faith and theology."[150]

If we take the question of truth away from aesthetics, we become blinded from the very form of beauty, which the Creator intends to communicate through creation. The Roman Centurion was able to acknowledge the Crucified One as the true Son of God because in his encounter with form of Christ's Passion, he came to the knowledge of truth.[151] In his second book on *Jesus of Nazareth*, Ratzinger highlights the significance of the Cross in Christ's revelation of the truth to the Greek pilgrims. He comments, "When asked by a group of Greek pilgrims for an opportunity to meet him, Jesus responds with a prophecy of the Passion, in which he points to his imminent death as 'glorification'—glorification that is manifested in great fruitfulness."[152] For Ratzinger, John's account of the Greek pilgrims' brief encounter with Jesus (cf. John 12:20–22) is an insight into the reasonableness of the glory of the Cross. They asked to see the face of Jesus, and Jesus directs them to the Cross. On the Cross "They will see his 'glory': in the crucified Jesus they will find the true God, the one they were seeking in their myths and their philosophy."[153] The paschal illumination is what Ratzinger means by "the light of the Cross."[154] According to our theologian,

> An initial awareness that beauty has something to do with pain was certainly present in the Greek world.... In his discourse in the *Symposium,* Aristophanes says that lovers do not know what they actually want from each other. It is obvious that the souls of both are thirsting for something other than amorous pleasure. But the soul cannot express this other thing.[155]

Ratzinger uses this classic image from Greek drama to make his point that the recognition of the truth in encounter with beauty involves "pain." Faith teaches us that the Cross is ultimately the manifestation of

---

149. Benedict XVI/Ratzinger, *On the Way*, 36.
150. Benedict XVI/Ratzinger, *On the Way*, 36.
151. Benedict XVI/Ratzinger, *Jesus of Nazareth*, 2:224.
152. Benedict XVI/Ratzinger, *Jesus of Nazareth*, 2:19.
153. Benedict XVI/Ratzinger, *Jesus of Nazareth*, 2:19.
154. Benedict XVI/Ratzinger, *Jesus of Nazareth*, 2:19.
155. Benedict XVI/Ratzinger, *On the Way*, 34–35; cf. *Symposium,* 192c–d.

the purpose of creation, which is, for the glorification and worship of the Creator. As Ratzinger says, "The Cross of Jesus replaces all other acts of worship as the one true glorification of God, in which God glorifies himself through him in whom he grants us his love, thereby drawing us to himself."[156] Through illumination of both faith and reason, the light of the Cross manifests the primacy of Christ.

Limitation of Reason

Just as Augustine was concerned about the errant Stoic philosophical presuppositions undergirding the Roman state's claim to religious power, so also is Ratzinger concerned about the errors of the philosophical presuppositions behind the modern propaganda for progress in politics.[157] Ratzinger's argument against the self-limitation of reason comes down to the Augustinian traditional claim that reason without the authority of faith is incapable of discovering the truth.[158] Ratzinger's consideration of the limits of the light of reason is in the context of his criticism of the self-limitation of reason in modern philosophy. Self-limitation of reason distorts the meaning of reason by failing to include the proper role of the divine in the human scientific endeavors.

The positivistic tunnel vision found in scientific professionalism is an example of self-limitation of reason. We saw in Bonaventure the medieval understanding of the harmonizing role of theology in the midst of the diverse specialized sciences of the university. While a nostalgic longing for a return to the medieval university is ludicrous, the modern discontinuity from the original meaning of university is self-contradictory. When reason forgets that the meaning of "university" consists in the participation of the various disciplines in the search for the one truth, reason limits itself only to "the pragmatic question [of] how it functions."[159] This reduction of reason to its function is what Ratzinger means by the "law of positivism."[160] When a political philosophy attempts to become wholly "positive," it revokes its own charter as philosophy; and as a result,

---

156. Benedict XVI/Ratzinger, *Jesus of Nazareth*, 2:223.
157. See chapter 2 (89) [x-ref].
158. See chapter 2 (91) [x-ref].
159. Benedict XVI/Ratzinger, *Church, Ecumenism, and Politics*, 150.
160. Benedict XVI/Ratzinger, *Church, Ecumenism, and Politics*, 151.

it abandons the question of truth as unscientific by the very university which it once brought forth.[161]

In his *Regensburg Lecture*, Benedict XVI describes the secular nature of positivism as the "exclusion of the divine from the universality of reason."[162] The secular, which "relegates religion into the realm of subcultures"[163] fundamentally rejects analogy of reason. What is of great concern to Ratzinger is how "positivistic reason and the form of philosophy based on it" have become the universal standard for validity of reason in the Western world.[164] For Ratzinger, the tunnel vision of positivistic reason, which "rejects the primacy of *Logos*" is operative within the form of materialism present in the Marxist ideology.[165] The "mutual ordering of Church and theology is foreign to both positivistic and Marxist thought."[166] As Peter Kucer notes, "Karl Marx transformed [Giambattista] Vico's hylozoistic formula by not simply defining truth with what is made (*verum quia factum*), but also by equating truth with that which is put into action" oriented to the future changing of the world.[167]

The logical consequence of positivistic philosophy is pluralism and relativism. When truth is something that man can produce scientifically, the truth is no longer "the measure of man but the product of man."[168] Truth becomes relative to what one makes of it. Anything contrary to the plurality and relativity of truth such as Church magisterium becomes absurdity and arrogant pretense. On the contrary, the ancient writers and Ratzinger propose the use of analogy as the antidote to pluralism and relativism because analogy preserves the *symphonia* of truth where there is a limitation of reason.[169]

For him, faith liberates philosophy from self-limitation of reason by offering to it the *Logos* as the very foundation and prerequisite for the possibility of reason's operation. Referring to reason in the feminine, Ratzinger writes,

161. Benedict XVI/Ratzinger, *Nature and Mission of Theology*, 77.
162. Benedict XVI/Ratzinger, "Regensburg Lecture," 58.
163. Benedict XVI/Ratzinger, "Regensburg Lecture," 58.
164. Benedict XVI/Ratzinger, "Regensburg Lecture," 58.
165. Benedict XVI/Ratzinger, *Church, Ecumenism, and Politics*, 151.
166. Benedict XVI/Ratzinger, *Church, Ecumenism, and Politics*, 155.
167. Kucer, *Truth and Politics*, 34. See also Benedict XVI/Ratzinger, *Introduction to Christianity*, 59–66.
168. Benedict XVI/Ratzinger, *Nature and Mission of Theology*, 77.
169. Benedict XVI/Ratzinger, *Nature and Mission of Theology*, 83–84.

> As reason sets out on her search, faith commissions her to recognize in the faith the prerequisite that makes her own operation possible and not to pursue her claim to comprehensiveness to the point of abolishing her own foundation, for that would mean that she was mistaking herself for divine reason for the divine reason and thereby abandoning communication with the divine reason on which her life depends.[170]

When reason rejects faith, it rejects its own foundation in two possible ways. It either limits itself to an operation devoid of a fundamental analogy of dependence on the divine reason or it confuses itself for the divine reason. Self-limitation of reason clearly shows a lack of the basic analogy between God and creature. Wherever there is a lack of analogy of reason, the irrational and the mythological become measures of reality; "whenever the Big Bang theory is seen as the primordial beginning of the universe, the measure and foundation of reality is no longer reason but the irrational."[171] Reducing reason to a byproduct of some irrational and mythological beginnings of the universe is limited. When the foundation of reason is itself unreasonable then reason cannot claim to be "a final court of appeal."[172]

Conclusion

In this chapter, we have seen how the dynamic way in which Ratzinger presents the relationship between *analogia entis* and *analogia fidei* reflects the Fathers' and Bonaventure's ease with moving between the two poles. Contrary to Karl Barth's protest against *analogia entis*, Ratzinger defended the *partial* nature of the Greek philosophical knowledge of Christ, thus confirming *analogia entis* as distinct from a full knowledge of Christ by *analogia fidei*. Origen's priority of reason and Augustine's illumination analogy helped our theologian to establish the distinction and relationship between the light of reason and the light of faith. The analogy of reason and natural law with which Ratzinger explains the correspondence of creation to God, depicts how Christ the Light and the *Logos* takes primacy in *analogia entis*. The value of our theologian's emphasis on the ontological grounds of the freedom of conscience is a

---

170. Benedict XVI/Ratzinger, *Church, Ecumenism, and Politics*, 149.
171. Benedict XVI/Ratzinger, *Church, Ecumenism, and Politics*, 149.
172. Benedict XVI/Ratzinger, *Church, Ecumenism, and Politics*, 150.

renewal of the use of analogy within the modern debate on moral ethics. His emphasis on the primacy of the truth emerges as his main contribution to the analogy of faith and reason debate. In conclusion, our thesis, which rejects any reduction of Ratzinger's analogy of faith and reason to a merely Platonic analogy, clarifies in this chapter how our theologian's use of the theory of illumination places its priority on Christ.

Chapter 4

Ratzinger's Image and Participation Analogy

IMAGE AND PARTICIPATION, WHICH concern the relationship between nature and grace, is critical to understanding Ratzinger's eschatology and ecclesiology. The insights of the ancient writers we have studied now serve as helpful tools for addressing the three specific concerns highlighted in the general introduction: (1) Peter McGregor's question as to whether Ratzinger applies the term "heart" to Christ and to believers in a univocal way; (2) Patrick Fletcher's investigation of the Augustinian influence on Ratzinger's eschatology as a question of Platonism; (3) Gabino Bilbao's question about the integrity of the human nature in Ratzinger's volitional notion of divinization.

Image

Bonaventure's similitude of proportionality, Augustine's analogy of speech, and Ireneaus's and Tyconius's image and recapitulation aid our investigations on Ratzinger's use of image analogy.

Image of the Trinitarian Dialogue

Like Augustine, the most characteristic expression of Ratzinger's analogy of image is Trinitarian love.[1] According to Ratzinger, "The true God is self-obligation in triune love and, thus, pure freedom. To be an image of this God, 'to become like him,' is man's vocation."[2] We have learned that Augustine's investigation of man as image of the Trinity unfolds from the

---

1. According to Erich Przywara, "the most characteristic mode of the Augustinian analogy is the doctrine of the *imago Trinitatis*" (Przywara, *Analogia Entis*, 266).
2. Benedict XVI/Ratzinger, *Church, Ecumenism, and Politics*, 255.

analogy of love in Book VIII of *De Trinitate*.[3] In a similar way, Ratzinger's Trinitarian notion of man as image proceeds from the analogy of love between the Father and the Son. For Ratzinger, the dialogue between the Father and the Son is where we find an expression of the triune love, and man as image reflects this dialogue.

In both Augustine and Ratzinger, man is the image of the spoken Word of the Father. For Ratzinger, the Incarnation reveals how "the *Logos* so humbles himself that he adopts a man's will as his own and addresses the Father with the 'I' of this human being; he transfers his own 'I' to this man and thus transforms human speech into the eternal Word, into his blessed *Yes, Father*."[4] This transformation of human speech to the Speech of the *Logos* is possible because human speech bears a trace of God's Speech, the *Logos*. When Ratzinger says, "The *Logos* . . . is the image of God after which we were created," he is referring to the "dia-Logos" or the *Logos*-Love of God as the primal Image after which the creature is called the image of God.[5] "Human beings are . . . the fruit of love."[6] The Trinitarian idea of *Logos*, which presents the Son in light of the divine dialogue is fundamental to Ratzinger's demonstration of the primacy of Christ using the notion of image. Man is the image of "the Son's identity [as] the complete subordination of the *I* to the *Thou*, the self-giving and self-expropriation of the *I* to the *Thou*."[7] The human being is image of the divine relationality as expressed in the identity of Jesus as the Son. As Ratzinger says, "To be the image of God implies relationality."[8] The concept of image guarantees that when human beings close in on themselves, they betray themselves.

Image as "Soul" or "Spirit"

In his reflections on the immortality of the soul, Ratzinger demonstrates how the notion of image is first and foremost an ontological question, not only a matter of grace. He says, "When immortality is thought of simply as grace, or indeed as the special destiny of the pious, then it takes

---

3. Merriell, *To the Image of the Trinity*, 25.
4. Benedict XVI/Ratzinger, *Behold*, 41.
5. Benedict XVI/Ratzinger, *Behold*, 67–68.
6. Benedict XVI/Ratzinger, *In the Beginning*, 57.
7. Benedict XVI/Ratzinger, *Behold*, 41.
8. Benedict XVI/Ratzinger, *In the Beginning*, 47.

flight into the realm of the miraculous and loses its claim on the serious attention of thinking people."[9] In defense of the physical resurrection of Jesus' body, he insists that "what is really in question is the core of the image of God and the realism of God's historical action."[10] While Ratzinger preserves the Platonic body-soul distinction necessary for understanding the biblical idea of the "intermediate state" between death and the Last Day, his definition of the soul remains relational and dialogical.

Ratzinger's eschatology presupposes a relational concept of human nature, which he equates with image: "To be the image of God implies relationality"[11] and "every man *is* directly in relation to God."[12] "It is not a relation-less being of oneself that makes a human being immortal, but precisely his relatedness, or capacity for relatedness to God."[13] Ratzinger equates *image*—capacity for relatedness to God—with the *soul*. He says, "such an opening of one's existence . . . constitutes what is deepest in man's being. It is nothing other than what we call *soul*."[14] Elsewhere he says, "Soul is nothing other than man's capacity for relatedness with truth, with love eternal."[15] Relatedness is a matter of being and the concept of image guarantees that man is being-in-relation to God. Ratzinger asserts, "the work of Thomas and the Council of Vienne has conceived [the body-soul] duality in such a way that it is not dualistic but rather brings to light the worth and unity of the human being as a whole."[16]

---

9. Benedict XVI/Ratzinger, *Eschatology*, 154.

10. Benedict XVI/Ratzinger, "Jungfrauengeburt und leeres Grab": "So wird sichtbar . . . dass vielmehr der Kern des Gottesbildes und der Realismus von Gottes geschichtlichem Handeln in Frage steht. . . . Und so geht es darum, ob wir uns dem Wort des Glaubens anvertrauen können, ob wir Gott trauen und ob wir auf dem Grund des Glaubens leben und sterben können." The nineteen-hundred-word text lacks paragraph and page numbers, although it was later published as *Skandalöser Realismus*. The English translation is in Fletcher, *Resurrection Realism*, 90.

11. Benedict XVI/Ratzinger, *In the Beginning*, 47.

12. Benedict XVI/Ratzinger, *Dogma and Preaching*, 141.

13. Benedict XVI/Ratzinger, *Eschatology*, 155.

14. Benedict XVI/Ratzinger, *Eschatology*, 155.

15. Benedict XVI/Ratzinger, *Eschatology*, 259.

16. Benedict XVI/Ratzinger, *Eschatology*, 159: "Even in the continuous 'wasting away' of the body, it is the whole man in his unity who moves towards eternity. It is in the life of the body that God's creature grows in maturity in expectation of seeing God's face." For further discussions on Ratzinger's Resurrection realism, see Fletcher, *Resurrection Realism*.

Ratzinger uses "soul" and "spirit" as synonymous terms. On many occasions, he prefers to use spirit because spirit conveys a more personal, holistic, and dialogical way of speaking of the human soul: "Spirit is at once personal and also the 'form' of matter. . . . The soul belongs to the body as 'form,' but that which is the form of the body is still spirit. It makes man a person and opens him to immortality."[17]

Image, Hominization and Evolution

In response to the problem of hominization in evolution theory, Ratzinger's hermeneutic key is the understanding of man as image of the Trinitarian dialogue. One of the crucial problems with the evolutionary understanding of creation is the question of when hominization (the Rubicon of anthropogenesis)[18] happens within the ascending evolution of material things. In other words, the understanding of man based on the historical evolution of species is an anthropology devoid of metaphysics. With the personal and dialogical notion of image, Ratzinger finds a synthesis of matter and spirit, and of history and metaphysics.

Our theologian describes spirit in terms of creature's capacity for recognizing God as the *Thou* and speaking to God as the image of his Word. He comments,

> The clay became man at that moment in which a being for the first time was capable of forming, however dimly, the thought "God." The first *Thou* that—however stammeringly—was said by human lips to God marks the moment in which spirit arose in the world. Here the Rubicon of anthropogenesis was crossed.[19]

The constitution of man from clay, which marks the moment of the appearance of the spirit describes man as the image of the *Creator Spiritus,* whose identity consists in the *I-Thou* dialogue of love between the Father and the Son.[20] What constitutes the creation of the spirit called man is

---

17. Benedict XVI/Ratzinger, *Eschatology,* 149.
18. Benedict XVI/Ratzinger, *Dogma and Preaching,* 142.
19. Benedict XVI/Ratzinger, *Dogma and Preaching,* 142.
20. Commenting on Pentecost as a feast of creation, Benedict speaks of the heart of the *Creator Spiritus* as the Love existing between the Father and the Son: "Lo Spirito Creatore ha un cuore. Egli è Amore. Esiste il Figlio che parla col Padre" (Benedict XVI/Ratzinger, "Homiliae," 505). Creation longs for the revelation of this divine dialogue made present in the Incarnation of the Son of God (cf. Rom 8:22).

the dialogue within the heart of the Creator Spirit. As Ratzinger says, "in the human being, God enters into his Creation,"[21] i.e., in the human being, the heart of the Creator Spirit, which consists in his dialogue of love touches creation in such a way that "the human being is directly related to God."[22] When Ratzinger says that "the image of God also means that human persons are beings of word and of love,"[23] he is referring to man as image of the dialogue between the Father and the Son.

We saw in Augustine and Bonaventure the interpretation of the biblical notion of image and similitude according to the dialogical meaning of *logos*. A similar analogy of word as speech is Ratzinger's hermeneutic key in response to the question of hominization. Reason as a speech form of *logos* is Ratzinger's way of interpreting the concept of image as man's self-identification in reference back to God. According to Ratzinger, "It is clear that spirit is not a random product of material developments but, rather, that matter signifies a moment in the history of spirit."[24] Evolution of species can only address what is clay in the history of the creation of man while the biblical dialogical notion of image addresses both what is history and what is spirit in the creation of man. Ratzinger wants to demonstrate how "the theory of evolution does not invalidate the faith, nor does it corroborate it. But it does challenge faith . . . to help man understand himself and to become increasingly what he is: the being who is supposed to say *Thou* to God in eternity."[25] It is in the analogy of speech that history and spirit meet.

Hominization is personal because it involves the discovery of the subject in the creature's first recognition of his maker. Ratzinger says, "The faith declares no more about the first man than it does about each one of us, and, conversely, it declares no less about us than it does about the first man."[26] However, to understand the full meaning of man's personal relation to God, man needs to look to the constitutions of Christ's personal life. As the perfect Speech of the Father, Christ is the revelation of what it means to be related to the Creator. Ratzinger's attempt to reconcile the metaphysical nature of faith in creation with the historical

---

21. Benedict XVI/Ratzinger, *In the Beginning*, 45.
22. Benedict XVI/Ratzinger, *In the Beginning*, 45.
23. Benedict XVI/Ratzinger, *In the Beginning*, 48.
24. Benedict XVI/Ratzinger, *Dogma and Preaching*, 141.
25. Benedict XVI/Ratzinger, *Dogma and Preaching*, 142.
26. Benedict XVI/Ratzinger, *Dogma and Preaching*, 141.

character of Darwin's theory of evolution is with an eye to the biblical and patristic primacy of Christ.

The Definitive "Meaning" of Image

In chapter 1, our consideration of the patristic patrimony on the notion of image demonstrated how Irenaeus and Tyconius used the concepts of *image and recapitulation* to address the primacy of the Incarnation in God's intention to create. Like Irenaeus and Tyconius, Ratzinger also addresses God's intention to create in light of the Incarnation. According to Ratzinger, "God created the universe in order to be able to become a human being and pour out his love upon us and to invite us to love him in return."[27] The Incarnation explains God's intention to create by restoring the lost meaning of image, which we understand in a preliminary way: "In the New Testament Christ is referred to as the second Adam, the definitive Adam and as the image of God. . . . He is the definitive human being and creation is, as it were, a preliminary sketch that points to him," the definitive human being, Jesus Christ our brother.[28]

In Ratzinger's view of Christ as the definitive image, he emphasizes that Christ is the restorer of the true meaning of image. The relationship between image and Christ is a question of meaning, i.e., the light of Christ takes priority in understanding the biblical meaning of image. What Scripture and the Fathers call "image" is a reference to the original meaning[29] of the universal nature of man. He says, "The Fathers of the Church therefore say that when God created man 'in his image,' he looked toward the Christ who was to come, and created man according to the image of the 'new Adam,' the man who is the criterion of the human."[30] Just as Irenaeus depicts Adam as "the scheme (*dispositionem*) or copy" of the Incarnation,[31] so also does Ratzinger understand man as

---

27. Benedict XVI/Ratzinger, *In the Beginning*, 30.
28. Benedict XVI/Ratzinger, *In the Beginning*, 48.
29. Benedict XVI/Ratzinger, *God and the World*, 114.
30. Benedict XVI/Ratzinger, *Jesus of Nazareth*, 1:138.
31. Irenaeus, *Demonstration apostolicae praedicationis* 32 (SC 406:128) [*Proof of the Apostolic Preaching*]: "Igitur hominem hunc recapitulans Dominus, eandem ipsi carnationis (σάρκωσις) accepit dispositionem (οἰκονομία) ex Virgine nascens voluntate et sapientia Dei, ut et ipse (eam quae) ad Adam (erat) similitudinem carnationis ostenderet et fieret (is qui) scriptus (erat) in initio homo secundum imaginem et similitudinem Dei."

image of the definitive Image: "It is true that Christ is the image of the living God and that only through him, the definitive man do we experience who and what God is."[32] Ratzinger considers recapitulation in light of typology (unity of the Old and New Testaments) and the analogous nature of image:

> Holy Scripture enables us to go a still further step if we again follow our basic rule—namely, that we must read the Old and New Testaments together and that only in the New is the deepest meaning of the Old to be found. In the New Testament Christ is referred to as the second Adam, as the definitive Adam, and as the image of God (cf. e.g., 1 Cor 15:44–48; Col 1:15). This means that in him alone appears the complete answer to the question about what the human being is. In him alone appears the deepest meaning of what is for the present a rough draft. He is the definitive human being, and creation is, as it were, a preliminary sketch that points to him.[33]

Here, Ratzinger is speaking of Christ, the Incarnate Word not the pre-existent Word. Our theologian situates his concept of the "definitive image of God" (Christ) within historical unity of Scripture. He presents Christ as the "deepest meaning" and illuminator of biblical history. For Ratzinger, our postlapsarian understanding of God's intention for creating man is only a rough draft or a copy of the original Adam. Christ, who is the second Adam fully illuminates the original meaning of Adam and defines perfectly what is only preliminary in the fallen Adam. Thus, by revealing the primordial Adam in himself, Christ affirms how the fall of Adam is in opposition with God original intention for creating him.

Ratzinger considers how biblical faith in creation paints a picture of a certain prehistory leading to the creation of man. He notes that biblical prehistory narrative speaks of the creation of man as "an immeasurably long path," and suggests that "the adventure of human existence appears as a kind of finale."[34] In other words, "it is at the end of history that the goal of history appears."[35] There is a sense in which man is the crown of

---

32. Benedict XVI/Ratzinger, *Beiträge zur Christologie*, 845 (my translation): "Gilt, dass Christus das Bild des lebendigen Gottes ist, dass wir also erst durch ihn, den definitive Menschen erfahren, wer und was Gott ist."

33. Benedict XVI/Ratzinger, *In the Beginning*, 48. Here, Ratzinger is speaking of Christ, the Incarnate Word not the pre-existent Word (cf. Aquinas, *ST* II-II, q.2, a.7).

34. Benedict XVI/Ratzinger, *God and the World*, 116.

35. Benedict XVI/Ratzinger, *God and the World*, 116.

creation precisely because God created him in his own image. Ratzinger's historical argument for the uniqueness of man's relationship to the Creator echoes Bonaventure's idea of how proportionality portrays image as *expressed similitude*. In Bonaventure, man as the image of God is the "expressed similitude"[36] because in the order of proportionality, the soul is supremely ordered to God. According to Ratzinger, "In the human being heaven and earth touch one another. In the human being God enters into his creation; the human being is directly related to God."[37] The analogy of image between God and man explains why "the Bible says that whoever violates a human being violates God's property (cf. Gen 9:5)."[38] The notion of image is grounds for the dignity of the human person. Demonstrating the historical nature of Christ's primacy, Ratzinger then concludes, "It is specifically said about Christ, who is the fulfillment of man's potential, that he has come at the end of time."[39] Ratzinger's notion of image is eschatological to the extent that it considers man to be oriented towards its future, which the Incarnation reveals.

Whatever Ratzinger says about image must be considered in light of the Incarnation. For instance, he says, "image of God also means that human persons are beings of word and of love, beings moving toward Another ... being that God made capable of thinking and praying."[40] The central role of the "prayer of Jesus" in Ratzinger's Christology recapitulates the dialogical sketch of his concept of image. In the prayer of Jesus, the disciples learned that to be fully human is to be in dialogue with God: "Peter had grasped and expressed the most fundamental reality of the person of Jesus as a result of having seen him praying, in fellowship with the Father."[41]

In conclusion, Ratzinger's Augustinian *dialogical concept of image* is central to his anthropology. The ontological integrity of Ratzinger's dialogical personalism becomes evident in the way that the analogous identity between "image" and the Trinitarian dialogue maintains the ever-greater difference between the two natures. The primacy of the

---

36. Bonaventure, *Sent. I* d.3, p.1, a.1, q.2 (1:72).
37. Benedict XVI/Ratzinger, *In the Beginning*, 44–45.
38. Benedict XVI/Ratzinger, *In the Beginning*, 45.
39. Benedict XVI/Ratzinger, *God and the World*, 116.
40. Benedict XVI/Ratzinger, *In the Beginning*, 48.
41. Benedict XVI/Ratzinger, *Behold*, 19.

definitive Adam relative to the preliminary image holds together both the similarity and difference conveyed by the notion of image.

Participation

Peter McGregor raised the question as to whether Ratzinger's use of the term "heart" has a univocal meaning when applied to Christ and when applied to the believers.[42] In this section, we will investigate how Ratzinger speaks of the uniqueness of Christ's heart relative to the hearts of believers as a question of the analogy of participation. The pneumatic and ecclesial character of his participation analogy proves to bear the stamp of Origen's *resemblance*, Gregory of Nyssa's *following* (ἀκολουθία), Augustine's *communion,* and Maximus the Confessor's *assimilation.*

Priority of Christ's Vision and Epistemic Participation

Ratzinger describes man's knowledge of God with the descending and ascending movements of Christian analogy. With the notion of Christ's immediate vision of God, he articulates the descending movement of Christ's primacy, and with the analogy of "resemblance," he indicates the ascending movement of participation. With the image of the heart, Ratzinger depicts a spiritual and personal epistemology of resemblance.

Christ's Immediate Vision

Scripture asserts that only the Son can see the face of the Father: *no one knows the Father except the Son; no one knows the Son but the Father* (Matt 11:27). The immediacy of the Son's knowledge of the Father constitutes the uniqueness of Jesus' knowledge of God. In his first book on *Jesus of Nazareth*, Benedict XVI uses the notion of Christ's immediate vision of God to express primacy. He says, "Jesus' teaching is not the product of human learning, of whatever kind. It originates from the immediate

---

42. McGregor, *Heart to Heart*, 172. McGregor asks, "What kind of meaning is Ratzinger seeking to communicate through the use of this term [heart]? Is he simply mimicking in an unreflective or equivocal way the use of the term in Sacred Scripture? Second, if the term has a definite meaning, is it univocal, whether it is applied to the Father, the Son, or to human persons; or does it have a different meaning when applied to human hearts, including the human heart of Jesus, than when it is applied to the heart of the Father."

(*unmittelbaren*) contact with the Father, from 'face-to-face' dialogue, from the vision of the one who rests close to the Father's heart."[43] Benedict articulates the immediacy of Christ's vision in comparison to the Moses' vision of God's back. For him, the comparison draws from the promise in Deuteronomy 18:5 of a prophet like Moses, which "implicitly contains an even greater expectation: that the last prophet, the new Moses, will be granted what was refused to the first one—a real, immediate vision of the face of God, and thus the ability to speak entirely from seeing, not just from looking at God's back."[44] In this quotation, Christ's "immediate vision" and his "ability to speak from" his immediate vision, indicate the *univocal* and the *analogical* parts of his primacy.[45] The immediate vision of Christ is univocal[46] because "God can be known, in a strict sense, only by himself,"[47] and *no one knows the Father except the Son*. The human speech of Christ is by definition analogous.

Pneumatic Resemblance

In Ratzinger's theology, man's ascending participation in the Word depends on the priority of Christ's descending speech about God. In his interview with Peter Seewald, *God and the World,* Benedict XVI addresses the epistemic participation as a function of man's resemblance of God:

> There is first of all a quite universal rule of knowledge expressed in this sentence about "no one knows the Father except the Son; no one knows the Son but the Father." It signifies that like can only be recognized by like. Where there is no inner

---

43. Benedict XVI/Ratzinger, *Jesus of Nazareth*, 1:7; *Jesus von Nazareth*, 1:31–32.

44. Benedict XVI/Ratzinger, *Jesus of Nazareth*, 1:5–6.

45. Cf. Kizewski, "God-Talk," 679: "Benedict refers to the 'immediate vision' of God and the capacity to speak from seeing. These anticipate both parts of this section—the one clearly is the beatific vision of Christ, the other is his analogous speaking."

46. Cf. Clement of Alexandria, *Strom.* 8.8 (GCS 2:95; PG 9:592): "And, again, of the things contained under these ten [Aristotelian] Categories, some are *Univocal*, as ox and man, as far as each is an animal. For those are Univocal terms, to both of which belongs the common name, animal; and the same principle, that is definition, that is animate essence." Commenting on the words of Jesus when found in the temple by his parents, Benedict XVI affirms the univocal nature of Christ's vision of the Father: "This is what the twelve-year old's answer makes clear: he is with the Father, he sees everything and everyone in the light of the Father" (Benedict XVI/Ratzinger, *Jesus of Nazareth*, 3:127).

47. Benedict XVI/Ratzinger, *God and the World*, 272.

correspondence to God, there is no possibility of knowing God. God can be known, in a strict sense, only by himself. Consequently, knowledge of God is bestowed on man, then that assumes that God draws man into a relationship of kinship and that there is then so much alive in man that *resembles* God that cognition and knowledge become possible. And then Jesus continues: "No one can know this except those to whom you choose to reveal it." In other words: Recognition and knowledge can only dawn within a community of will.[48]

Ratzinger claims that man's knowledge of God is only possible because of the existing resemblance between God and man. Ratzinger's notion of resemblance is spiritual, anabatic and love-centered. Like Origen, Ratzinger does not speak merely of the Platonic resemblance to God, which is about contemplating the divine forms, rather he speaks of a resemblance summed up in one word: charity. Like Origen, Ratzinger is convinced that the best way to become acquainted with God is through love and the highest degree of knowledge is Love.[49] Man knows God by love: When Ratzinger says that "recognition and knowledge can only dawn within a community of will" between God and man, he affirms the inseparableness of the knowledge of God from love of God.[50]

The "Heart" as an Epistemic Image

Ratzinger uses the image of the heart to express a more personal and Christocentric way of knowing and recognizing God. For him, the term "heart" conveys the epistemic center of man's holistic participation in God: "The word 'heart' has expanded beyond the reason and denotes a deeper level of spiritual/intellectual existence, where direct contact takes place with the divine."[51] As distinct from a solely intellectual cognition, Ratzinger considers a "spiritual-intellectual" way of knowing God as a

---

48. Benedict XVI/Ratzinger, *God and the World*, 272.
49. Benedict XVI/Ratzinger, *Church Fathers*, 38–39.
50. Benedict XVI/Ratzinger, *God and the World*, 272.
51. Benedict XVI/Ratzinger, *Behold*, 68. See also Ivánka, *Plato Christianus*, 326; Balthasar, *Heart of the World*, 14: "Both Biblically and philosophically (in the total human context, that is), the heart is conceived to be the real center of spiritual and corporeal man, and by analogy, it is also seen as the very center of God as he opens himself up to man (1 Sam 13:14).... For Stoicism, the heart is the seat of the ἡγεμονικόν, the guiding faculty in man. Going beyond this, New Testament theology adds, on the one hand, an incarnational element."

"deeper" form of cognition. This deeper way of knowing is due to the indwelling of the *Logos* in the human heart. Ratzinger uses Origen's Stoic idea of hegemonikon (ἡγεμονικόν) to explain how the heart is christologically the unifying center of the human person and of the whole humanity: "Origen goes on: It is the *Logos* which is at the center of us all—without our knowing—for the center of man is the heart, and in the heart there is the ἡγεμονικόν—the guiding energy of the whole, which is the *Logos*."[52] The *Logos* takes priority in the believers' spiritual knowledge of God. The "Purity of heart is what enables us to see" (cf. Matt 5:8).[53]

Since Ratzinger considers the term "heart" as a cognitive image, its application to Christ's knowledge must be univocal because Christ possesses an immediate vision of the Father. What the heart of Christ knows univocally about God, the hearts of believers receive from his words by analogy of participation. When Ratzinger says that "[Christ's] Heart calls to our heart,"[54] he indicates the descending movement of Christ's immediate knowledge of the Father's love effecting the ascending movement of the believer's participation in Christ's words about God. The believer's participation in the pierced heart of Christ is an encounter of the saving knowledge of God because it is not solely intellectual but spiritual and holistic. Ratzinger says, "The pierced heart of Jesus . . . saves the world by opening itself. . . . The Heart saves, indeed, but it saves by giving itself away."[55] What is salvific about encountering the heart of Christ is the knowledge of God's love as a self-giving love. Salvation consists not only of an intellectual knowledge of God, but also in a recognition of the newness of his love. For Ratzinger, the term "heart" is an epistemic image, which does not apply univocally to Christ and to believers, but conveys how believers participate in the Christ anabatically.

Becoming Like God and Discipleship

In Irenaeus, we saw a synthesis of both the ontological goodness and the soteriological perfection of man expressed in the analogy of image and likeness. While the concept of image confirms the goodness of human nature, likeness connotes what was lost as a consequence of sin. Christ

---

52. Benedict XVI/Ratzinger, *Behold*, 67.
53. Benedict XVI/Ratzinger, *Jesus of Nazareth*, 1:343.
54. Benedict XVI/Ratzinger, *Behold*, 69.
55. Benedict XVI/Ratzinger, *Behold*, 69.

saves by restoring the lost likeness. Therefore, the empirical desire for redemption from evil is a question of freedom, whereby the freedom man seeks involves his redemption by way of becoming like God. Like Irenaeus, Ratzinger's comments on the notion of likeness falls under the soteriological dimension of the concept of participation. Ratzinger says, "If man is to be free, he must be 'like God.' Wanting to be like God is the inner motive of all mankind's programs of liberation. The yearning of freedom is rooted in man's being, right from the outset he is trying to become *like God*."[56] Becoming like God is a question of human longing for "liberation" or salvation. Ratzinger asks, "What is 'human freedom'? Can man become free without truth, i.e., in falsehood? Liberation without truth would be a lie, it would not be freedom but deception."[57] Human freedom is a matter of restoring the truth, goodness and beauty of creation, which Christ alone accomplishes. Ratzinger considers any liberation of man, which does not enable him to become divine as a betrayal of his boundless yearning.[58] He says, "An anthropology of liberation will have to face the question: what is meant by *becoming like God, becoming God*."[59] When Ratzinger speaks of "becoming like God," he means salvation by spiritual participation.

For Ratzinger, evil is not equally primal as the goodness of being is primal. Rather, there is only one principle of being, the Creator, who is good; and on account of freedom, "evil comes only from a subordinate source," thus making man curable of evil.[60] Participation by way of likeness is soteriological. And yet, the theory of evolution calls to question the need for soteriology: "Many think that in light of the history of evolution, there is no longer room for the doctrine of the first sin that then would have permeated the whole human history. And as a result, the matter of Redemption and of the Redeemer would also lose its foundation."[61]

Gregory of Nyssa's explanation of participation as *following* (ακολουθία) God or seeing his back, which is one of Ratzinger's favorite patristic depictions of true discipleship,[62] is for him a concept describing

56. Benedict XVI/Ratzinger, *Behold*, 33.
57. Benedict XVI/Ratzinger, *Behold*, 33.
58. Benedict XVI/Ratzinger, *Behold*, 35
59. Benedict XVI/Ratzinger, *Behold*, 34.
60. Benedict XVI/Ratzinger, *Saint Paul*, 94.
61. Benedict XVI/Ratzinger, *Saint Paul*, 90.
62. See Benedict XVI/Ratzinger, *On the Way*, 26–27: "Personally, I always find particularly moving the commentary on this passage (Exod 33) that Gregory of Nyssa

"a new direction of one's life ... surrendered to the will of another, so that being with him and being at his disposal are now the really important content of a human existence."[63] Like Gregory, Ratzinger uses the concept of *following* to demonstrate Christ's primacy. He considers following Christ to be how we know and see the face of God. To follow Christ is to follow the perfected man and learning from him how God intends for his creature to participate in him. As Ratzinger says, "In the last analysis, following Christ is nothing other than man's becoming man by integrating into the humanity of God."[64] In more specific and concrete terms, Christ describes the meaning of following God by his own Cross: *If any man would come after me, let him deny himself and take up his cross and follow me* (Mark 8:34). The paschal focus of the notion of following explains the meaning of Christian martyrdom. Understood fundamentally as self-renunciation and self-sacrifice, participation by following, which "expresses the basic law ... of man's authentic humanization" highlights the primacy of Christ's humanity.[65]

According to Ratzinger, "[Peter] is uncompromisingly put back in his place: *Get behind me!* (Mark 8:32–33)" by his master because "[he] had attempted, as it were, to stop following and to take the lead, determining for himself which way to walk."[66] In Scripture, *following* is the essence of discipleship: "The essence of discipleship is depicted in the Gospels in a few stereotyped words of Jesus: *Follow me*."[67] In John's Gospel, "to follow means to recognize Jesus' voice and to follow that voice through the confusion of voices with which the world surrounds us"[68]: *When he [the Shepherd] has brought out all his own, he goes before them, and the sheep follow him, for they know his voice* (John 10:4). The voice of the *Logos* takes primacy because it communicates the true way of being and becoming man. What he speaks about man comes entirely from his

---

gives. Being able to see God only from the back." See also Benedict XVI/Ratzinger, *Transforming Power of Faith*, 80.

63. Benedict XVI/Ratzinger, *Dogma and Preaching*, 126: "To follow really means to go behind, to move in the direction prescribed, even if this direction is completely contrary to one's own wishes. Precisely because the word 'follow' is meant so literally, it affects the innermost depths of man."

64. Benedict XVI/Ratzinger, *Dogma and Preaching*, 129.

65. Benedict XVI/Ratzinger, *Dogma and Preaching*, 128.

66. Benedict XVI/Ratzinger, *Dogma and Preaching*, 126.

67. Benedict XVI/Ratzinger, *Dogma and Preaching*, 126.

68. Benedict XVI/Ratzinger, *Dogma and Preaching*, 128.

immediate vision of the face of the Creator, "not just from looking at God's back."[69]

Eschatological Participation

Ratzinger speaks of "participation" in the context of his extensive study on eschatology. The contentious eschatological elements of participation are expressed in the themes of immortality of the soul and resurrection on the Last Day. In his book *Resurrection Realism*, Patrick Fletcher demonstrates Ratzinger's change of heart, from his earlier anti-Platonic suspicion of the body-soul dualism to his more mature movement away from the modern anti-Platonic stance: "Ratzinger began as a suspicious 'anti-Platonist,' but gradually came to embrace the contributions of Greek philosophy to a Christian understanding of resurrection."[70] Focusing on Platonism, Fletcher suggests a discontinuity between the earlier views of Ratzinger's resurrection realism and Augustine's approach: "Ratzinger's early treatment of Platonic thought and his dismissal of Greek anthropology is less nuanced and rigorous than Augustine's careful acceptance of certain elements of Platonic philosophy."[71]

However, where Fletcher sees a discontinuity, a continuity can be seen in two ways: (1) Ratzinger's dialogical vision of the body-soul duality is in continuity with Augustine's dialogical notion of image and participation; (2) in his *Behold the Pierced One* and *Eschatology*, Ratzinger's development of the patristic anthropology of the heart is consistent with his dialogical eschatology of participation in the *Introduction to Christianity*.

---

69. Benedict XVI/Ratzinger, *Jesus of Nazareth*, 1:5–6.
70. Fletcher, *Resurrection Realism*, 72.
71. Fletcher, *Resurrection Realism*, 83–84: "One could say that Ratzinger rejects some of those elements of Platonic anthropology that Augustine accepts (e.g., the body-soul schema), and even appears close to accepting the immateriality of beatitude (a Platonic idea rejected by Augustine). It is clear from Ratzinger's discussion in *Einführung* that his understanding of Platonic anthropology in that work has little in common with Augustine's understanding of it. For Augustine, the existence of a body and a soul need not automatically lead to the notion that the body is the soul's prison. Augustine freely used these concepts, and distinguished them in order to unite them in the resurrection."

Immortality of the Soul and the Resurrection of the Body

Ratzinger's personal vision of the immortality of the soul remained simply Christian, and thus analogically involving the meeting of the biblical faith and Greek philosophy. In his work on *Introduction to Christianity* (1968), Ratzinger's brief reflections on eschatology maintained a personal and dialogic view of immortality and resurrection of the body. With regard to immortality he says, "It is a question of a 'dialogic' immortality; that is, immortality results not simply from the self-evident inability of the indivisible to die but from the saving deed of the lover who has the necessary power: man can no longer perish because he is known and loved by God."[72] The saving deed of God's love for man, which enables participation in him renders the question of immortality dialogic. The dialogue of God with man is what defines life everlasting: "If the dialogue of God with man means life, if it is true that God's partner in the dialogue himself has life precisely through being addressed by him who lives forever, then this means that Christ, as God's Word to us is himself 'the resurrection and the life.'"[73] For Ratzinger, the dialogic view of eschatology is what Christianity brings to its inter-philosophical dialogue with the Greek isolation of the body from the soul. He comments,

> It should be noted here that even in the formula of the Creed, which speaks of the resurrection of the body," the word "body" means in effect "the world of man" (in the sense of biblical expressions like "all flesh will see God's salvation," and so on); even here the word is not meant in the sense of a corporality isolated from the soul.[74]

With regard to resurrection on the Last Day, the primacy of the Word's flesh defines "the communal character of human immortality," because in his body, the whole of mankind and all flesh are related.[75] Ratzinger's concept of participation in the resurrection on the Last Day bears the stamp of Augustine's ecclesial idea of *Totus Christus*, head and body,[76] whereby the communion of saints will be the judge of men. In

---

72. Benedict XVI/Ratzinger, *Introduction to Christianity*, 350.

73. Benedict XVI/Ratzinger, *Introduction to Christianity*, 352.

74. Benedict XVI/Ratzinger, *Introduction to Christianity*, 350–51.

75. Benedict XVI/Ratzinger, *Introduction to Christianity*, 351.

76. Augustine, *Enarrat. Ps.* 30.2.3 (CCSL 38:192): "Hoc autem corpus nisi connexione caritatis adhaereret capiti suo, ut unus fieret ex capite et corpore, non de coelo quemdam persecutorem corripiens diceret: *Saule, Saule, quid me persequeris?* quando

his *Introduction to Christianity*, Ratzinger anchors the anthropological, soteriological and ecclesial/eschatological dimensions of the resurrection in his Augustinian dialogical view of man.

Similarly, in his later work on *Eschatology* (1977), Ratzinger's detailed analysis of both the Judaic and Greek foundations of the Christian doctrine on the "intermediate state" of the soul between death and the Last Day was for the purpose of preserving the personal and holistic view of man's participation in eternity. His later criticism of modern anti-Platonism, which rejects the possibility of an "intermediate state" between the separation of the body and the soul[77] at death and the reunion of the body and soul on the Last Day is fundamentally in continuity with his earlier attempt to preserve a holistic and personal analogy of spiritual participation of the creature in the Creator. The key to the continuity of his thought is his dialogical understanding of the human soul. In the *Foreword* to his *Eschatology*, he says, "I am not concerned with an empty abstraction or with 'Platonism' but with a strictly theological interpretation (in the sense of what Jesus taught) of our life beyond death."[78] Thus, Ratzinger's earlier and later eschatological view of participation is neither concerned with Platonism nor is it inconsistent.

In his book *Dogma and Preaching*, Ratzinger's skepticism about Greek dualistic body-soul distinctions was to preserve a personal and holistic vision. He speaks of salvation as a spiritual participation that allows both the "whole man" (body and spirit) and the "whole world" to share in God: "Wholeness is understood here in a double sense: it is the *whole* man who enters into salvation, and it is the *whole* world that shares

---

eum iam in coelo sedentem nullus homo tangebat, quomodo eum Saulus in terra saeviens adversus Christianos aliquo modo iniuria percellebat? Non ait: Quid sanctos meos, quid servos meos? sed, *quid me persequeris,* hoc est, quid membra mea?" See chapter 2 (114).

77. According to Fletcher, "Ratzinger's chief antagonist on the issue of resurrection [was] Gisbert Greshake" (Fletcher, *Resurrection Realism*, 82). "[Ratzinger's] argument over the resurrection with Greshake (as well with Greshake's sometime coauthor, Gerhard Lohfink) began with [Ratzinger's] *Eschatologie* in 1977, although woven in 'Jenseits des Todes' (1972) Ratzinger had attacked the idea of 'resurrection in death' without naming it directly" (85). Fletcher further clarifies that Ratzinger's "dispute with Greshake was originally about the body-soul distinction and the intermediate state," which Greshake later modifies (87). "Greshake and Lohfink rejected an intermediate state in order that resurrection might happen in death" (88).

78. Benedict XVI/Ratzinger, *Eschatology*, xx. "Platonism" means different things at different times, even when used by the Ratzinger.

in it."⁷⁹ Ratzinger's concern is to present a notion of salvation faithful to Scripture. He says, "Scripture attributes much less importance to the dualism of body and soul in man than Greek philosophy does" because "the 'dualism' of the Bible (if we can still use the word at all in that context) . . . is personalistic, not ontological."⁸⁰ The root of the biblical soteriology is less concerned about the body-soul dyad and more concerned about the Creator-creature analogy.⁸¹ Ratzinger's ideas about eschatology emphasize the biblical vision of salvation as less concerned with abstract distinctions.⁸² He comments,

> Salvation, therefore, does not simply result from the autonomous departure of an intellectual substance that is now detached from matter and continues to exist on its own and can have only a very incidental residual connection to the material parts that once clung to it; rather, it is the salvation of the *man*, of this particular creature of God, which despite its incontestable ontological stratification is nevertheless a genuine unity, a single work of the Divine Master. This completely different sort of opposition, Creator-creature (instead of soul-body), is the root of the biblical doctrine of salvation and defines the holistic approach that seems so foreign to Greek philosophy.⁸³

When the Creator-creature relation concerns salvation, it must be a matter of participation. Ratzinger's dialogical and personal notion of image always grounds his analogy of participation. His eschatology presupposes his Augustinian dialogical notion of human nature, not a substantialistic⁸⁴ anthropology.

---

79. Benedict XVI/Ratzinger, *Dogma and Preaching*, 268.

80. Benedict XVI/Ratzinger, *Dogma and Preaching*, 268.

81. Benedict XVI/Ratzinger, *Dogma and Preaching*, 269.

82. Benedict describes how the unification of body and soul is a constitutive element of salvation, whereby "the challenge of *eros* can be said to be truly overcome." He says, "Man is truly himself when his body and soul are intimately united; the challenge of *eros* can be said to be truly overcome when this unification is achieved. Should he aspire to be pure spirit and to reject the flesh as pertaining to his animal nature alone, then spirit and body would both lose their dignity. On the other hand, should he deny the spirit and consider matter, the body, as the only reality, he would likewise lose his greatness" (Benedict XVI/Ratzinger, *Deus Caritas Est* 8).

83. Benedict XVI/Ratzinger, *Dogma and Preaching*, 269.

84. Benedict XVI/Ratzinger, *Einführung*, 319: "Was wir in einer mehr substantialistischen Sprache 'Seele haben' nennen, werden wir in einer mehr geschichtlichen, aktualen Sprache bezeichen *Dialogpartner Gottes sein*."

The "Heart" as an Image of the Whole

The image of the "heart" allows Ratzinger to speak of eschatology in a more *personalistic* and less *substantialistic* language (*subtantialistischen Sprache*).[85] In his *Dogma and Preaching*, Ratzinger uses the phenomenon of the heart to support his holistic view of the body. In reference to Romano Guardini's address on the image of the heart,[86] Ratzinger depicts the heart as a place of unity of body and spirit. In the bodily activities of sharing a meal together and sexual union, the material ingesting of food and the biological process of sexual inclination take on spiritual form of fellowship of human persons, and the act of self-giving respectively. Fellowship and self-giving in love are deeds of the heart. In the unifying character of the heart, "Matter receives light and clarity from the brightness of the spirit, which permeates and illuminates its dullness; spirit receives depth, maternal warmth, and strength through the corporeal-earthly elements that is wedded to it."[87] While the phenomenon of sexual union points to the self-giving of the *whole* man or woman to God, the phenomenon of table fellowship indicates the unity of the *whole* humanity in salvation. In the human experience of sexual union and table fellowship, which are expressions of human love, Ratzinger suggests that the principle of corporeality always communicates the spirit as "being-for-another" and "being-with-the-whole" cosmos.[88]

In his later work on *Eschatology*, Ratzinger refers to Gregory of Nyssa's homily on the beatitudes as "a magnificent witness to continuity with antiquity, but also to the transmutation of thought of the ancient world."[89] Ratzinger focuses how Gregory links the beatitude, *blessed are the pure of heart, for they shall see God*, to a statement from Jesus' high-priestly prayer, *This is eternal life, that they know you*.[90] Our theologian intends to show that eternal life, which consists in the vision of God is a function of a pure and undivided heart, not an abstract endeavor: "His promise is

---

85. Benedict XVI/Ratzinger, *Einführung*, 319.

86. See Guardini, *Christliches Bewußtsein*, 185–96, esp. 187.

87. Benedict XVI/Ratzinger, *Dogma and Preaching*, 267.

88. See Benedict XVI/Ratzinger, *Introduction to Christianity*, 245: "Christian faith is not based on the atomized individual but comes from the knowledge that there is no such thing as the mere individual, that on the contrary, man is himself only when he is fitted into the whole: into mankind, into history, into the cosmos, as is right and proper for a being who is *spirit in body*."

89. Benedict XVI/Ratzinger, *Eschatology*, 151.

90. Benedict XVI/Ratzinger, *Eschatology*, 151.

that we will attain the vision of God, which is life, not through speculative thinking but by the purity of an undivided heart in faith and love."[91] Highlighting the biblical epistemology of the heart, Ratzinger maintains his emphasis on a dialogical concept of epistemic participation: "Man is defined by his intercourse with God."[92]

Origen's and Augustine's contributions to Ratzinger's notion of participation explain the unifying image of the heart present in our theologian's eschatological and ecclesial primacy of Christ. In our consideration of the cognitive value of Ratzinger's image of the heart, we saw how Ratzinger uses Origen's Stoic idea of ἡγεμονικόν to explain how the heart is christologically the unifying center of the human person and of the whole humanity. While Origen did not use the expression, the "Heart of Christ," his notion of participation in the heart and his Stoic concept of the Logos as ἡγεμονικόν find their proper analogy in Ratzinger's primacy of the Heart of Christ.

Ratzinger's eschatological vision of participation bears the stamp of Augustine's ecclesial idea of *Totus Christus*, head and body.[93] By participation in the Heart of the risen Christ, the believer already shares in the reality of his future as member of the Body of Christ. As an eschatological reality, "*Heaven* means *participation* in this new mode of Christ's [resurrected] existence and thus fulfillment of what baptism began in us."[94] Ratzinger says,

> The perfecting of the Lord's body in the *plērōma* of the "whole Christ" brings heaven to its true cosmic completion. Let us say it once more before we end: the individual's salvation is whole and entire only when the salvation of the cosmos and all the elect has come to full fruition. For the redeemed are not simply adjacent to each other in heaven. Rather, in their being together as the one Christ, they *are* heaven.[95]

Participation in the "whole Christ" constitutes the meaning of "resurrection of the body" because "in their [the believers'] being together as

91. Benedict XVI/Ratzinger, *Eschatology*, 152. Fletcher did not consider Gregory of Nyssa's contribution to Ratzinger's resurrection realism because the limit of his work focused on the Augustinian influence. Our work proposes a broader spectrum of patristic influence. See chapter 2 (89).

92. Benedict XVI/Ratzinger, *Eschatology*, 152.

93. Augustine, *Enarrat. Ps.* 30.2, 3 (CCSL 38:192). See chapter 2 (114).

94. Benedict XVI/Ratzinger, *Eschatology*, 236.

95. Benedict XVI/Ratzinger, *Eschatology*, 238.

the one Christ, they *are* heaven."⁹⁶ Thus, the image of the "heart" allows Ratzinger to speak of the relationship between Christ and believers in a more personal way. The image of the heart of Christ, which takes primacy in salvation is his way of using an image language to convey the analogy of participation in the "whole Christ." With the image of the heart, which harmonizes the body-soul duality and conveys relationally, the ontological is not opposed to the personal, and the individual finds unity with the whole of history. In the body of the whole Christ, the soul experiencing the "intermediate state" of the separation body and soul in death, retains within itself the matter of his life and tends impatiently towards the risen Christ. We shall further discuss the ecclesial implication of Ratzinger's primacy of Christ's heart, which he articulates with Augustine's concept of communion.

Communion

Central to Ratzinger's concept of participation is the *communio* analogy. One of his main contributions to the communion concept is its practical application to the ecclesial structure of the Church as a society. His *communio* ecclesiology developed in response to the inadequate "ecclesiology of communion" adopted by the *conciliar*⁹⁷ vision. He describes the conciliar ecclesiology of communion as follows:

> Those who speak today of an "ecclesiology of communion" generally mean two things: (1) they intend to contrast a pluralist, or "federalist" ecclesiology, so to speak, with a centralist conception of the Church; and (2) they want to emphasize the interconnectedness of the local Churches in the give-and-take

---

96. Benedict XVI/Ratzinger, *Eschatology*, 238.

97. Benedict XVI/Ratzinger, *Theology of the Liturgy*, 359: "In 1965, the last year of Vatican II, a review had been founded that was supposed to be the permanent voice, so to speak, of the Council and its spirit, which therefore was called *Concilium*." In his book on *Joseph Ratzinger,* Maximillian Heinrich Heim gives a more detailed account of Ratzinger's "productive collaboration and separation from Concilium." See Heim, *Joseph Ratzinger*, 174–83. Before switching to the international journal *Communio*, "from 1965 to 1972, Ratzinger himself belonged to the editorial board of *Concilium*, as a member of the section for dogmatic theology" (Heim, *Joseph Ratzinger*, 179). Heim identifies the *Concilium*'s reduction of the truth to sociology as the reason for Ratzinger's separation from the journal.

of their exchanges as well as the pluralism of their cultural forms of expression in worship, discipline, and doctrine.[98]

Clearly, our theologian rejects a politically horizontal approach to the meaning of communion. In contrast, Ratzinger sought a spiritual approach. A study on the *structural* ecclesiology of communion *per se* is beyond the scope of our study. In this section, we are concerned with demonstrating how the primacy of Christ shapes the spiritual analogy of communion in Ratzinger's theology. In considering the biblical, philosophical and ecclesial elements that constitute Ratzinger's use of participation as communion, we will demonstrate how the Christological method of the ancient authors helps our theologian to offer a more spiritual Christian concept of *communio*.

Covenant and Communion

In the Christian κοινωνία, one finds the meeting of the Old Testament notion of "covenant" and the Greek idea of κοινωνία. For Ratzinger, the Old Testament's preference for using "covenant" to explain the relationship between God and man was set in opposition to polytheism in order to preserve the transcendence and unity of God.[99] While "covenant" was in "repudiation of the idea of actual "communion" between God and man," the pagan world, on the other hand, placed the idea of communion at the

---

98. Benedict XVI/Ratzinger, *Theology of the Liturgy*, 360–61. For more information on Ratzinger's rejection of a sociological interpretation of the Church as *communio*, see the Kasper-Ratzinger debate on the relationship between the universal Church and the local Churches. In this debate, Ratzinger gave a spiritual and ontological interpretation of the communion of the Church while Walter Kasper was more concerned with the social and historical implications of an ontological interpretation of the Church as communion. See Kasper, "Friendly Reply to Cardinal Ratzinger"; Benedict XVI/Ratzinger, "Response to Walter Kasper." According to Ratzinger, "If one strips away all the false associations with church politics from the concept of the universal church and grasps it in its true theological (and hence quite concrete) content, then it becomes clear that the argument about church politics misses the heart of the matter" (Benedict XVI/Ratzinger, "Response to Walter Kasper," 11). Using the Augustinian eschatological *totus Christus*, Derek Sakowski endeavoured to clarify how "the 'universal Church' is not an abstract species, with various 'particular' Churches as concrete individuals. . . . To be 'concrete' is not to be confused with being empirically verifiable" (Sakowski, *Ecclesiological Reality of Reception*, 43).

99. See Benedict XVI/Ratzinger, *Pilgrim Fellowship of Faith*, 74, 75.

center of their religious longing.[100] For Ratzinger, Plato's idea of κοινωνία captures the Hellenistic root of the Christian notion of communion:

> Thus in the *Symposium*, Plato talks about the reciprocal communion between gods and men (ἡ περὶ θεούς καὶ ἀνθρώπους κοινωνία). According to him, communion with the gods also brings about fellowship among men. He notes that this communion is the ultimate intention and the most profound content of all sacrifices, of worship as such. In this connection he coins a marvelous phrase that we might refer to as a presentiment of the Eucharistic mystery when he says that worship is entirely concerned with the wholeness and healing of love.[101]

In the Christian κοινωνία, one finds both the Old Testament concept of "covenant," which highlights the distinction between the divine transcendence and human limitations, and the Greek κοινωνία, which emphasizes the analogy or the similitude between God and creature.

However, Ratzinger insists on the limitations of the Platonic idea of κοινωνία on two grounds. First, "the real object of longing for pagan mysticism is not communion, but union; the end here is, not relationship, but identity."[102] Second, "Plato is talking, not about God, but about the gods and Hellenistic mysticism prefer to talk about divinity rather than about God."[103] In the end, Christian κοινωνία is not merely a synthesis of the Old Testament "covenant" and Greek κοινωνία, but introduces a new reality in Christ. This new reality consists in a κοινωνία between the Trinity and creatures because man bears the image of God's *caritas* and dialogue. Once again, the notion of image as relationality grounds the Christian analogy of communion.

Christological Pneumatology of Communion

In his 1998 article on *The Holy Spirit as Communion*[104] (which was later published in his book *Pilgrim Fellowship of Faith*), Ratzinger demonstrates

---

100. Benedict XVI/Ratzinger, *Pilgrim Fellowship of Faith*, 75.

101. Benedict XVI/Ratzinger, *Pilgrim Fellowship of Faith*, 75; cf. Plato, *Symposium* 188 b–c.

102. Benedict XVI/Ratzinger, *Pilgrim Fellowship of Faith*, 75; cf. Plato, *Symposium* 188 b–c.

103. Benedict XVI/Ratzinger, *Pilgrim Fellowship of Faith*, 76.

104. Benedict XVI/Ratzinger, "Holy Spirit as Communio," 324.

how Augustine's Pneumatology considers *communio* ecclesiology to be analogous to the mode of the being of the Holy Spirit. He says,

> The definition of the Spirit as "communion," which Augustine thus derives from the expression "Holy Spirit," has for him . . . clearly a fundamentally ecclesiological sense. . . . Becoming a Christian means becoming "communion" and, thus, entering into the mode of the existence of the Holy Spirit.[105]

The mode of the existence of the Holy Spirit is "communion," and to be a Christian—being in communion with Christ—is to participate in becoming communion. Thus, ecclesial participation as "communion," which is a pneumatological derivation from the Trinitarian analogy of communion explains ecclesial participation as the spiritual capacity to communicate and unite with God.

For Ratzinger, Augustine finds the connection between Christology and Pneumatology in the Johannine image of Christ as the giver of the gift of "living water."[106] While Jesus was conversing with the Samaritan woman at the well, he presents himself as the giver of the *"gift of God,"* which is the gift of the "living water": *If you know the gift of God and who it is who is saying to you, "give me a drink," you would have asked him and he would have given you living water* (John 4:7–14). The *gift* of living water that Christ gives is the *caritas* of Holy Spirit, poured out on the Cross in the form of the Eucharist: "Christ is the spring of living water—the crucified Lord is the spring that makes the world fruitful. The source of the Spirit is the crucified Christ. Yet from him every Christian also becomes a spring of water."[107] Thus, in Ratzinger, the Cross is the fundamental locus of spiritual communion between God and human persons.

Primacy of the Incarnation in Ecclesial Participation

Ratzinger's ecclesial communion between God and creature is consistent with the *assumptio hominis* of Athanasius and other Greek Fathers, which identifies the humanity of the Word as the locus of participation. In Ratzinger's explanation of how believers participate in the heart of Christ, we saw how Christ's assumption of a human heart reveals the heart of

---

105. Benedict XVI/Ratzinger, *Pilgrim Fellowship of Faith*, 42.

106. Benedict XVI/Ratzinger, *Pilgrim Fellowship of Faith*, 47.

107. Benedict XVI/Ratzinger, *Pilgrim Fellowship of Faith*, 47. Romans 5:5 is also a key verse for Augustine's Pneumatology.

God as divine charity. We saw how Augustine capitalized on the unifying identity of the Holy Spirit as *caritas* between the Father and the Son for his analogical explanation of the communion in the Body of Christ.[108]

In his book *Pilgrim Fellowship of Faith*, Ratzinger builds on Augustine's Christocentric Pneumatology and draws a Spirit-centered analogy between Trinitarian Love (the highest form of communion) and ecclesial κοινωνία. Like Augustine who synthesizes Hilary of Poitiers's *communicatio unitatis* and John Chrysostom's Eucharistic incorporation, Ratzinger adopts a synthetic concept of κοινωνία as God's assimilation of the human beings into the eternal communion of his love in the Eucharistic body of Christ. According to Ratzinger,

> [God] is a dialogue of eternal love.... Because he is relationship, he is able to open himself up and establish a relationship of his creature to himself.... The Incarnate Son is the "communion" between God and men.[109] ... To use Saint Paul's expression: the Church insofar as she is the Church, is the "body of Christ" (that is, in fact, men's partaking of the communion between man and God, which is what the Incarnation of the Word is [cf. 1 Cor 10:16–17]).[110]

As one can readily see, the Incarnation of Christ is the ladder on which the divine self-communication descends and the human person ascends to participation in God. In reference to the Pauline text, which is fundamental to Hilary's and Augustine's Eucharistic analogy, Ratzinger restricts the notion of participation to the ascending movement of the analogy of communion. For Ratzinger, there is a distinction between communion and participation. Participation is "men's partaking of the communion between man and God, which is what the Incarnation of the Word is."[111] In other words, in participation, there is a priority of the Incarnational communion.

---

108. See chapter 2 (109).

109. Benedict XVI/Ratzinger, *Pilgrim Fellowship of Faith*, 76.

110. Benedict XVI/Ratzinger, *Pilgrim Fellowship of Faith*, 77: " The cup of blessing which we bless, is it not a participation [*koinonia*; Vulgate, *communication*] in the blood of Christ? The bread which we break, is it not a participation [*koinonia*; Vulgate, *participation*; Neo=Vulgate, *communicatio*] in the body of Christ? Because there is one bread, we who are many are one body, for we all partake of the one bread (1 Cor 10:16–17)."

111. Benedict XVI/Ratzinger, *Pilgrim Fellowship of Faith*, 77.

There are three distinct uses of κοινωνία in Ratzinger's Eucharistic ecclesiology. First, there is the communion of God and man in the Incarnation of the Word. This communion takes primacy on account of the uniqueness of Christ's humanity. Second, there is the ecclesial κοινωνία, which is properly called a participation of the believers in the Incarnational communion between the Father and the Son. While we can speak of participation as a form of communion, we cannot reduce communion to the concept of participation. Sacramentally speaking, the divine-human κοινωνία in the Incarnation is not a participation but an assumption, a transubstantiation or a pulling, so to speak of humanity "from their creaturely anchorage, grasped at the deepest ground of their being, and changed into the Body and Blood of the Lord."[112] For Ratzinger, liturgical participation emphasizes the priority of God's action, which consists in the words and deeds of the Incarnate Word. He comments, "The word 'part-icipation' refers to a principal action in which everyone has a 'part.' . . . The real 'action' in liturgy in which we are all supposed to participate is the action of God himself."[113] Eucharistic participation draws the believers into the Body and Blood of the God-man communion, transforming them into the likeness of the inner divine dialogue.

Finally, participation of believers in Christ communicates the *gift* of the Trinitarian unity between men and their brethren. For Ratzinger, "The man who takes this bread is assimilated to *it,* is taken into it, is fused into this bread and becomes bread like Christ himself."[114] Becoming bread like Christ means "entering into that state in which human existence is opened up to God and which is at the same time the necessary condition for the opening up of the inner being of men for one another."[115] It is the divine communion that shapes the human communion with his brethren: "The path toward the communion of men with one another goes by way of communion with God."[116] An encounter with the humanity of Christ, which is the original and definitive humanity is an encounter with the truth of all men. In the Eucharist, the *I* of Christ "breaks up man's

---

112. Benedict XVI/Ratzinger, *Theology of the Liturgy*, 107.

113. Benedict XVI/Ratzinger, *Theology of the Liturgy*, 107.

114. Benedict XVI/Ratzinger, *Pilgrim Fellowship of Faith*, 78; cf. Augustine, *Conf.* 7.10.16.

115. Benedict XVI/Ratzinger, *Pilgrim Fellowship of Faith*, 79.

116. Benedict XVI/Ratzinger, *Pilgrim Fellowship of Faith*, 79.

entire self and creates a new 'we.' Communion with Christ is necessarily also communication with all who belong to him."[117]

Therefore, for Ratzinger, "communion" is a synthetic analogy describing God's unique descent to humanity, humanity's spiritual ascent to the transcendent God, and humanity's union with one another. With the priority of the Incarnation in Ratzinger's concept of participation, Eucharistic communion becomes the place where participation in the communion of God and man finds its full expression.

Communion as Participation in Suffering

Ratzinger's notion of participation draws upon Augustine's *communio sanctorum*. In Augustine, the Spirit as the gift of *caritas* communicates unity to the Church through the "universal society of saints": "The presentation of the little ones to receive the spiritual grace is the act not so much of those by whose hands they are borne up as of the universal society of saints ... by whose holy and perfectly united *caritas* they are assisted in receiving the communion of the Holy Spirit."[118] In Augustine's theology of the heart, we saw that through the communion of the saints, the cry and anguish of Christ's heart unifies the hearts of all people who participate in his gift of self-giving love.[119] In the same way, while reflecting on the eschatological nature of ecclesial communion, Ratzinger speaks of participation through the "suffering members" of Christ's body called the saints:

> Since Christ's body truly belongs to him, encounter with Christ takes place in encounter with those who are Christ's, because they are his body. And so our destiny, our truth, if it is really constituted theologically, christologically, depends upon our

---

117. Benedict XVI/Ratzinger, *Pilgrim Fellowship of Faith*, 78; *Theology of the Liturgy*, 268.

118. Augustine, *Ep.* 98.5 (PL 33:362). See chapter 2 (111).

119. Augustine, *Enarrat. Ps.* 119.7 (CCSL 40:1783): "Who among us cries from the ends of the earth? Neither I, nor you, nor he, but the Church. It is the entire inheritance of Christ that cries toward God from the ends of the earth.... All the saints form only one man in Christ (*omnes sancti unus homo in Christo*), since holy unity is in Christ. And this one man exclaims: *From the ends of the earth I have cried out to you, when my heart was in anguish*." See chapter 2 (113).

relation to Christ's body and notably to its suffering members. To this extent, the "saints" are our judge.[120]

The communion of the saints is what constitutes a valid participation in the body of Christ. According to Ratzinger, "Christ does not stand facing us alone. It was alone that he died, as the grain of wheat, but he does not arise alone, but as a whole ear of corn, taking with him the communion of the saints. Since the Resurrection, Christ . . . is—as the Church Fathers say—always *caput et corpus*."[121]

The communion of saints shows how communion consists in participation in the suffering of the body of Christ. It presents the logic of sacrifice as "the transforming of death to love":[122] "Death may remove [man] from the biosphere, but the life that reaches beyond it—real life—remains. This life which John calls *zōē* as opposed to *bios*, is man's goal. The relationship to God in Jesus Christ is the source of a life that no death can take away."[123] Referring to the writings of the Jewish Philosopher Philo of Alexandria, Ratzinger grounds the logic of participation in the suffering of Christ on analogy of faith and reason. Explaining the Hebrew and the Hellenistic roots of Christian idea of "participation" as communion, Ratzinger observes that "Philo, for his part, diverges from traditional Hebrew terminology and within the context of concepts from Hellenistic mysticism, talks about 'communion' between God and the pious man in worship."[124]

While explaining priestly "consecration" (anointing) as a participation in the Father's priestly consecration of Christ (cf. John 17), Ratzinger sees Philo as an anticipation of the paschal communion between the Father and the apostles:

> Jesus himself is the priest sent into the world by the Father; he himself is the sacrifice that is made present in the Eucharist of all times. Somehow Philo of Alexandria had correctly anticipated this when he spoke of the Logos as priest and high priest (*Leg. All.* 3.82; *De Somn.* 1.215; 2.183). The meaning of the Day of

---

120. Benedict XVI/Ratzinger, *Eschatology*, 207.
121. Benedict XVI/Ratzinger, *Theology of the Liturgy*, 266.
122. Benedict XVI/Ratzinger, *Theology of the Liturgy*, 267.
123. Benedict XVI/Ratzinger, *Jesus of Nazareth*, 2:85.
124. Benedict XVI/Ratzinger, *Pilgrim Fellowship of Faith*, 75.

Atonement is completely fulfilled in the "Word" that was made flesh "for the life of the world" (John 6:51).[125]

Philo takes a step further from Platonic κοινωνία and identifies the Old Testament notion of priestly sacrifice of "atonement" with the Hellenistic Logos. Ratzinger names Philo's *Odes of Solomon* as one of the earliest appearances of the synthesis of *logos* and *sacrifice—λογικὴ λατρία*. The significance of Philo's contribution towards the synthesis of Greek *reason* and Jewish *sacrifice* is foundational for the philosophical and biblical grounds for what Christ reveals on the Cross as true worship.

Thus, Ratzinger insists that Christ's synthesis of *logos* and *sacrifice* is the full meaning of Scripture. For him, Hebrews 5:7 presents Jesus' priestly act of atonement as a summation of the "loud cries and tears" throughout human history, and offering this act to God in exchange for the manifestation of his glory within us: *In the days of the flesh, Jesus offered up prayers and supplications, with loud cries and tears, to him who was able to save him from death, and he was heard for his godly fear*.[126] When Jesus prays Psalm 43 on the Mount of Olives and Psalm 22 on the Cross of Calvary, he unites humanity's "loud cries and tears" to his priestly self-offering to the Father.[127] On the Mount of Olives, Jesus prays the words of Psalm 43:5: *My soul is sorrowful, even unto death* (Mark 14a:33–34); and he dies crying out and praying Psalm 22: *My God my God, why have you forsaken me* (Matt 27:46).

The metaphor, which Ratzinger uses to convey communion as participation in suffering, is image of the "heart." In both Augustine and Ratzinger, the "suffering heart" of the saints is synonymous to their "cry of prayer."[128] The prayer of the Eucharist is the highest expression of the suf-

---

125. Benedict XVI/Ratzinger, *Jesus of Nazareth*, 2:88–89.

126. Benedict XVI/Ratzinger, *Jesus of Nazareth*, 2:162.

127. Benedict XVI/Ratzinger, *Jesus of Nazareth*, 2:201: "Jesus uses passages from the Psalms to speak of himself and to address the Father. Yet these quotations have become fully personal; they have become the intimate words of Jesus himself in his agony. It is he who truly prays these psalms; he is the real subject."

128. See Carola, *Augustine of Hippo*, 284–85. Commenting on Augustine's theology of tears, Carola says, "Augustine himself had been a sinful son who benefitted from his own mother's tears. In fact the Bishop of Hippo attributes the first moments of his adult conversion to his mother's intercession [cf. Augustine, *Conf.* 5.7.13 (CC 27:64)]. The contrite tears which he himself was later to shed in the house garden at Milan are nothing less than the crowning complement to the copious tears which Monica had shed for many years." Ratzinger considers Monica as the figure of the Church in Augustine's conversion: "Es bleibt uns noch en gewichtiges Erlebnis darzulegen, das uns

fering heart because "*blood* in connection with the Eucharist also stands for self-giving (*Hingabe*) . . . as we can see right before our eyes in the pierced heart of Christ."[129] In the bread, which indicates a bodily communion with Christ, Eucharist and *communio* are synonymous terms: "The concept of *communio* is anchored first and foremost in the most Blessed Sacrament of the Eucharist, which is why, in the language of the Church, we still describe the reception of the sacrament . . . simply as *going to communion*."[130] In the believers' communion of the body and blood of Christ, participation in suffering takes place in their hearts as participation in the prayer of the one man. McGregor explains the relationship between the image of the heart, the Eucharist and the Church as follows: "The Eucharist is the *symbolon* of . . . the believer's heart, the Father's heart and the heart of Jesus in the heart of the Church."[131] For Ratzinger, the Eucharist is "the heart of the Church"[132] because it is the sacrament of participation in the suffering heart of the body of Christ. The Eucharist is the heart of the Church precisely because it is communion understood in this way.

Volitional Assimilation

In his commentary on Jesus' prayer on the Mount of Olives, Ratzinger articulates the volitional dimension of participation with the concept of assimilation (*aufnahme*). He highlights the prayer of Jesus at the Mount of Olives as the most insightful glimpse into how the believer is assimilated into the divine freedom through the union of the human and divine wills of Christ. For him, this prayer "gives us a true glimpse into the inner being of God himself."[133]

---

bereits zweimal in Augustins Bekehrungsweg entgegengetreten ist: Die Begegnung mit seiner Mutter Monnica. Sie ist nicht nur 'mater carnis,' sondern als Magd Gottes trägt sie mehr noch als die leiblichen die geistlichen Geburtswehen um ihren Sohn, ja von ihrem Herzblut ward durch ihre Tränen tagtäglich für ihn geopfert. So ist es klar, dass von hier aus das bild der mütterlichen Kirche für ihn das eindrucksvollste und lebendigste wird" (Benedict XVI/Ratzinger, "Volk und Haus Gottes," 70). The tears of the saints are concrete expression of their prayers.

129. Benedict XVI/Ratzinger, *Theology of the Liturgy*, 361–62.
130. Benedict XVI/Ratzinger, *Theology of the Liturgy*, 361.
131. McGregor, *Heart to Heart*, 371.
132. Benedict XVI/Ratzinger, *Behold*, 75.
133. Benedict XVI/Ratzinger, *Jesus of Nazareth*, 1:344.

Primacy of Christ's Human Will in Descending Assimilation

In chapter 2, we saw how Maximus explained divinization with the analogy of "assimilation," a process that involves "no faculty, of any sort for being assimilated, because then it would no longer be grace but the revelation of an activity latent within the potentiality of nature."[134] We further explained that for Maximus "God is beyond participation,"[135] and the descent of God's grace is no participation but an assimilation, since participation involves no change in God, only a change in the creature. In a similar way, Ratzinger describes assimilation as a descending analogy prior to the believer's ascending participation. He says, "In the prayer on the Mount of Olives . . . it is the Son speaking here, having *assimilated* (*aufgenommen*) the fullness of man's will into himself and transformed (*umgewandelt*) it into the will of the Son."[136] Assimilation is a descending act of the Son through his humanity, which is our original humanity. The result of the descending movement of *assimilation* is the ascending participation of *transformation* since man's disobedience is not assimilated but transformed in the humanity of Christ.

In the same chapter 2, we also saw in Maximus the Confessor how the volitional unity of the divine and human will "depends on a *prior*, unconstrained, free act of the divine person, who steers the struggle from above and on the voluntary character of that person's 'ineffable self-immolation.'"[137] We concluded that Maximus indicates the primacy of Christ by refusing to attribute γνώμη (deliberation) to the human will of Christ. In other words, as the savior, Christ does not possess a hypostatic realization of nature the way we do because, while ours involves deliberation in the freewill, the humanity of Christ takes priority of perfection. Similarly, in his commentary on the prayer of Jesus on the Mount of Olives, Ratzinger indicates how the human will of Christ takes priority of perfection because it is the will of the Son's humanity.

---

134. Maximus the Confessor, *Ad Thalassium* 22 (PG 90:321A). See chapter 2 (119).

135. Maximus the Confessor, *Capita de charitate* 3.22 (PG 90:1024) [*Selected Writings*].

136. Benedict XVI/Ratzinger, *Jesus of Nazareth*, 2:162. Philip Whitmore translates *aufgenommen* as "subsumed." But, we consider "assimilated" closer to the German sense of *aufnehmen*. "Gerade hier spricht der Sohn, der allen menschlichen Willen in sich *aufgenommen* und in Sohneswillen umgewandelt hat" (Benedict XVI/Ratzinger, *Jesus von Nazareth*, 2:184).

137. See chapter 2 [x-ref]; Balthasar, *Cosmic Liturgy*, 269; cf. Maximus the Confessor, *Opuscula* (PG 91:1048C).

He attributes the deliberative and resisting part of the dialogue to the weakness of our humanity being transformed in the humanity of Christ: "In Jesus' natural human will, the sum total of human nature's resistance to God is, as it were, present within Jesus himself. The obstinacy of us all, the whole of our opposition to God is present, and in his struggle, Jesus elevates our recalcitrant nature to become its real self."[138] Ratzinger makes the distinction between our "fallen human will" and our "transformed human will." Only our transformed human will, as opposed to our fallen human will, participates in God through the "perfect human will of Christ." Our "real self" or original humanity, which is *prior* to our fallen humanity is what Jesus' perfect will restores. In Christ, humanity's primordial will is what was able to say "Yes" to the will of the *Logos* because Christ's human will is the true human will: "What unites the two wills is the 'Yes' of *Christ's human will* to the divine will of the *Logos*."[139] The uniqueness of the will of Christ consists in its ability to expose the false nature of our human fallen will in light of the original and true human will.

However, Gabino U. Bilbao claims that in Ratzinger's Christology of the union of two wills "the consistency proper to the will of humanity, which corresponds with his [Christ's] human will tends to disappear."[140] He goes on to say, "In Ratzinger's reading of the influence of the *Logos* on humanity, its work of divinization on humanity tends not to emphasize that to speak of divinization neither means a change in substance nor an alteration of the same humanity."[141] On the contrary, Bilbao's concern is unfounded for two reasons. Firstly, the consistency of the human will consists in what Christ reveals about the primordial human nature, not what sin distorts in human nature. In the human will of Christ where one encounters what is truly consistent in nature, Christ reveals how the human will is intrinsically ordered to the divine will. Secondly, while explaining how Christ's human will assimilates the believer's will into the divine will, Ratzinger emphasizes no alteration in the human nature

---

138. Benedict XVI/Ratzinger, *Jesus of Nazareth*, 2:161.

139. Benedict XVI/Ratzinger, *Behold*, 92.

140. Bilbao, "Neocalcedonismo," 93: "La consistencia propria de la libertad de la humanidad, que se correspondería con su voluntad humana, tiende a desaparecer."

141. Bilbao, "Neocalcedonismo," 93: "En la lectura de Ratzinger del influjo del Logos sobre la humanidad, la divinizacíon que en ella se opera, se tiende a no subrayar que dicha divinizacíon no supone un cambio sustancial ni una alteración en la misma."

when he says, "In becoming attuned to the divine will, [the human will] experiences its fulfillment, not its annihilation."[142]

Human Nature as Ordered to the Divine Will

Ratzinger affirms that the personal union of Christ's human and divine wills reveals to us how the specific and consistent element of the human will consists in the fact that the natural will is ordered to God: "In Jesus ... the human will, as created by God is ordered to the divine will."[143] As God's creation, man is the image of God. The union of Christ's human will to the divine will is a perfect reflection of what it means to be God's image. Ratzinger speaks of the prelapsarian human will, which Christ comes to restore. While the human will is naturally ordered to God's will, it still needs the grace of Christ to accomplish its goal. Healing man's post-lapsarian will means restoring to him his pre-lapsarian will. The human will of Christ is the perfect image of the divine will because it is the human will of the Son. Ratzinger uses the volitional dimension of image as fundamental to the anthropological understanding of the union of the two wills of Christ. The grace of assimilation presupposes the natural ordering of the human will to the divine will. Assimilation understood in light of Ratzinger's primacy of Christ's will explains how he takes the human nature very seriously.

In Ratzinger's dialogical understanding of the concept of image, one cannot speak of a "pure human nature" but a relational nature, such that an affirmation of the integrity of human nature is simultaneously an affirmation of its relationality, and vice versa. The closer man is to God the more perfectly human he becomes because he is the image of God. Ratzinger's dialogical vision of the human person, which we have seen throughout this work, is the hermeneutic key to his volitional analysis of how the union of Christ's two wills is consistent with Christ's humanity. He highlights the personal dimension of Jesus' prayer on the Mount of Olives where he sees Scripture depicting a dialogue between two persons: the Son and his *Abba*. He says, "This brings us to one final point regarding

142. Benedict XVI/Ratzinger, *Jesus of Nazareth*, 2:160.

143. Benedict XVI/Ratzinger, *Jesus of Nazareth*, 2:160; *Jesus von Nazareth*, 2:182: "Es gibt in Jesus den 'Naturwillen,' der menschlichen Natur, aber es gibt nur *einen* 'Personwillen,' der den 'Naturwillen' in sich aufnimmt. Und dies ist ohne Zerstörung des eigentlich Menschlichen möglich, weil von der Schöpfung her der menschliche Wille auf den göttlichen hingeordnet ist."

Jesus' prayer, to its actual interpretative key, namely, the form of address: 'Abba Father' (Mark 14:36)."[144] Quoting Joachim Jeremias's work *Abba*, he notes, "Jeremias shows that this word *Abba* belongs to the language of children—that it is the way a child addresses his father within the family. . . . *[Jesus] spoke to God like a child to his father. . . . Jesus' use of 'Abba' in addressing God reveals the heart of his relationship with God.*"[145] Ratzinger insists that the biblical narrative of the prayer on the Mount of Olives uses a non-substantialist language: "It is therefore quite mistaken on the part of some theologians to suggest that the man Jesus was addressing the Trinitarian God in the prayer on the Mount of Olives."[146] Rather, it is the Son drawing humanity into what he univocally ascents to, i.e., the will of the Father. Ratzinger's discourse on volitional union of the two wills on the Mount of Olives concerns the primacy of Christ's will and how we participate analogically to it. His concern is to convey how the personal assimilation of Christ's human will reveals the analogy between the Father-Son eternal dialogue and the God-man volitional dialogue.

Conclusion

In response to the three analogy questions navigating the inner trajectory of this chapter, we come to the following conclusions. Firstly, Ratzinger's understanding of the "heart" as a cognitive image addresses McGregor's question about how our theologian applies the term to Christ and human persons. Based on our analysis of Ratzinger's reference to the immediate vision of Christ, the term "heart" is an epistemic image, which does not apply univocally to Christ and to believers, but conveys how believers participate in the Christ in a holistic and personal way. Secondly, while Patrick Fletcher investigated the Augustinian roots of Ratzinger's eschatology as a question of Platonism, alternatively, we insist that Augustine's influence on Ratzinger's eschatology is a matter of dialogical personalism. We argued for consistency in Ratzinger's eschatology based on the contribution of Augustine's analogy of speech in Ratzinger's dialogical view of persons. Finally, Ratzinger's emphasis on how the grace of assimilation presupposes the natural order of the will, sheds light on Bilbao's question about the integrity of human nature in Ratzinger's

---

144. Benedict XVI/Ratzinger, *Jesus of Nazareth*, 2:161.
145. Benedict XVI/Ratzinger, *Jesus of Nazareth*, 2:162. See Jeremias, *Abba*, 62.
146. Benedict XVI/Ratzinger, *Jesus of Nazareth*, 2:162.

volitional understanding of divinization. Ratzinger's insistence on the redeemed human will as that which radiates more clearly what is consistent in human nature, explains his emphasis on the personal assimilation of Christ's human will as what reveals the analogy between the Father-Son eternal dialogue, and the God-man volitional dialogue. In the end, Augustine's *Totus Christus* is evidently a crucial hermeneutic key to the holistic vision of Ratzinger's anthropology, ecclesiology, eschatology and Christology is holistic. Indications of anointing Christology even surfaces in the Augustinian roots of Ratzinger's insights on "Communion as participation in suffering." Also, in Ratzinger's close association of the priestly consecration of Christ's suffering and death, one finds echoes of Origen's paschal-centered anointing Christology, which we saw in chapter 1.

Chapter 5

Ratzinger's Primacy of Christ in God-Talk

RATZINGER'S INSIGHTS ON GOD-TALK, which follows the patristic emphasis on the Christocentric unity of Scripture, Tradition and worship, also serve as a synthesis of the other two categories of analogy already covered.

The Limitation of Human Nature and Divine Transcendence

The Christian distinction, which characterizes the twofold aspects of *apophatic* theology is the basic principle of God-Talk operative in Ratzinger's insights on the themes of naming God, Scripture and revelation, prayer and liturgy. One way in which Ratzinger indicates biblical negative theology is through "the law of disguise."[1]

Ratzinger confirms that Scripture talks about the appearance of God in concealed terms in references to Israel, Nazareth, Cross and Church: "One could cite in this connection the series Earth-Israel-Nazareth-Cross-Church, in which God seems to keep disappearing more and more and, precisely in this way, becomes more and more manifest as himself."[2] Biblical talk about God suggests that one is able to recognize God in the least expected form because in "the peculiarity of the Christian form of

---

1. Benedict XVI/Ratzinger, *Introduction to Christianity*, 254.
2. Benedict XVI/Ratzinger, *Introduction to Christianity*, 256.

negative theology, the form determined by the Cross,"[3] God's humble mode of appearance in creation affirms his total transcendence from human recognition. The close union between the suffering Son of God with the suffering humanity is both a revelation and a concealment. In Nazareth and on the Cross, total dissimilarity and unknowability of God is vivid because they make the divinity of Christ most invisible and unrecognizable: "When [God] really did appear upon the scene, so other, so invisible in regard to his divinity, so unrecognizable, it was not the kind of otherness and strangeness that we had foreseen and expected, and he thus remained in fact unrecognizable."[4] The human mind knows and recognizes the intrinsic transcendence of God in those signs and indications of total absence of God. As Benedict XVI says in his *Infancy Narratives,* "In the Gospel accounts, the oneness of the one God and the infinite distance between God and creature is fully preserved. There is no mixture, no demi-god."[5]

In his *Regensburg Lecture,* Benedict XVI demonstrates how biblical apophatic theology provides the proper space for the analogy of God-Talk. He says,

> God's transcendence and otherness are so exalted that our reason, our sense of the true and good, are no longer an authentic mirror of God, whose deepest possibilities remain eternally unattainable and hidden behind his actual decisions. As opposed to this, the faith of the Church has always insisted that between God and us, between his eternal Creator Spirit and our created reason there exists a real analogy, in which—as the Fourth Lateran Council in 1215 stated—unlikeness remains infinitely greater than likeness, yet not to the point of abolishing analogy and its language. God does not become more divine when we push him away from us in a sheer, impenetrable voluntarism; rather, the truly divine God is the God who has revealed himself as *logos* and, as *logos,* has acted and continues to act lovingly on our behalf.[6]

---

3. Benedict XVI/Ratzinger, *Introduction to Christianity,* 255.

4. Benedict XVI/Ratzinger, *Introduction to Christianity,* 255. God makes his presence known through signs of lowliness: "The other sign that he [God] has adopted and that, by concealing him more, shows more truly his intrinsic nature, is the sign of the lowly, which, measured cosmically, quantitatively, is completely insignificant, actually a pure nothing" (Benedict XVI/Ratzinger, *Introduction to Christianity,* 256).

5. Benedict XVI/Ratzinger, *Jesus of Nazareth,* 1:52.

6. Schall, *Regensburg Lecture,* 27.

In chapters 1 and 2, we learned from Irenaeus and Augustine how the limitation of language does not amount to reason's incapacity for speaking about God.[7] While Irenaeus attributes the reason for human capacity to speak about God[8] to divine love, Augustine simply says, "We ought not to be silent about him."[9] Similar to Irenaeus and Augustine, Benedict explains how Christian apophatic theology is "not to the point of abolishing analogy and its language" because "God who reveals himself as *logos* (speech) . . . acts lovingly on our behalf."[10] On account of the unchangeable nature of truth, "the infinite dissimilarity [between human words and divine reality] still does not turn knowledge into ignorance, truth into falsehood."[11] Ratzinger's contribution to the positive nature of God-Talk is how it addresses the modern self-limitation of reason. Ratzinger's insights on the analogy of faith and reason underscores how the modern self-limitation of reason considers the receptivity of truth to be a form of weakness and a dogmatic imposition of the irrational upon reason. Instead of affirming the dissimilarity between God and creature as an apophatic reality, which creates the space for proper similarity, modern self-limitation of reason widens the gap to the extent of declaring God to be dead. Ratzinger proposes that "Christians [must] raise the standard of the primacy of truth" by adopting a posture contrary to that of modern philosophical errors.[12] He outlines three ways to raise the standard of the primacy of truth. First, instead of the modern self-limitation of reason, we must prioritize the analogy of reason in speaking well of God. Second, instead of presuming the makeability of truth, "we can only acknowledge in humility that we are unworthy messengers who do not proclaim ourselves but speak with a holy fear about something that is not ours but that comes from God."[13] Third, instead of relativizing moral life, we must speak of the *Logos* in both word and deed.

---

7. See chapters 1 (52) and 2 (128).
8. Irenaeus, *Adversus Haereses* 2.13.4 (SC 294:116).
9. Augustine, *Serm* 225.3.3 (PL 38:1098).
10. Schall, *Regensburg Lecture*, 27.
11. Benedict XVI/Ratzinger, *On the Way*, 69.
12. Benedict XVI/Ratzinger, *On the Way*, 70.
13. Benedict XVI/Ratzinger, *On the Way*, 70.

Naming God

The notion of faith and reason plays a significant role in Ratzinger's reflections on naming God; a confirmation of our discussion of "faith and reason" before "God-Talk." Like Clement of Alexandria and Gregory of Nyssa, Ratzinger comments on the analogical nature of naming God.[14] Clement makes the distinction between how reason can only *"declare about God"*[15] and the necessity of the "eminent grace" of the Son in naming God.[16] Similarly, Ratzinger makes the distinction between the philosophical declarations about God and the primacy of Christ in naming God.

Ratzinger considers naming God to be a fundamentally relational process. In his *Introduction to Christianity*, Ratzinger makes the distinction between the purpose of a concept and the purpose of a name. He comments, "The concept tries to perceive the nature of the thing as it is in itself. The name, on the other hand, does not ask after the nature of the thing as it exists independently of me; it is concerned to make the thing nameable, that is, 'invocable,' to establish a relation to it."[17] While "the philosopher [seeks] the concept of the highest Being," God's revelation of his name through faith "is not so much [an expression of] his inner nature as a making nameable" of himself.[18] God is invocable by human words because he first condescended "into coexistence" with us and "puts himself within [our] reach."[19] Thus, naming God presupposes revelation and relationship of faith. However, the philosopher who seeks the essence of the highest Being guarantees the reasonableness and meaning of God's name. Faith provides what is lacking in reason while reason guarantees the meaning of faith. "When John presents the Lord Jesus Christ as the real, living name of God,"[20] he shows how the descent of God's name is a function of the Incarnation, and how Christ takes priority in man's capacity to name God. In Christ, the *logos* of philosophy that stretches thought analogically toward the essence of Being loses itself into the *Logos* of Scripture, which condescends Being into being by the analogy

---

14. See chapter 1 (59, 64).
15. Clement of Alexandria, *Strom.* 6.17 (SC 446:362).
16. Clement of Alexandria, *Strom.* 5.13 (PG 9:124B).
17. Benedict XVI/Ratzinger, *Introduction to Christianity*, 134.
18. Benedict XVI/Ratzinger, *Introduction to Christianity*, 134.
19. Benedict XVI/Ratzinger, *Introduction to Christianity*, 134.
20. Benedict XVI/Ratzinger, *Introduction to Christianity*, 134.

of faith. Analogy of faith elevates the analogy of being into the logic of Christ. In Christ, by virtue of this prior relation of condescension, God makes himself nameable by human words.

In his Papal Audience delivered on January 16, 2013, Pope Benedict XVI says, "the phrase 'name of God' means God is the One who is present among men."[21] He sees the words ascribed to God's identity, i.e., his name, as a real analogical vehicle of his ontological presence within human nature and history without losing his transcendence. The use of name in the mediation of the real analogy between God and man, acknowledges "speech" as the central analogical bridge between the limitation of human words and the divine transcendence. For the Pontiff, Christ is the full revelation of this mediating "speech" as revealer of the "name" of God:

> The content of revelation and the Revealer coincide in him. Jesus shows us God's face and makes *God's name* known to us. In the Priestly prayer at the Last Supper, [Jesus] says to the Father: "I have manifested *your name* to men.... I made known to them *your name*" (cf. John 17:6; 6:26).... All this found fulfillment and completion in Jesus ... the abbreviated Word, the short and essential Word of the Father who has told us all about him. In Jesus the whole Word is present.[22]

Christ the Word is the one who makes God invocable by human words because "in him God has entered forever into coexistence with us."[23] God makes himself accessible to us by using human words to reveal his "name" to Moses in the burning bush, "thus made it possible to call on him, [and] had given a tangible sign of his 'being' among men."[24] However, "what has been meant since the episode of the burning bush by the idea of the name is really fulfilled in him who as God is man and as man is God."[25] Thus, on account of the primacy of *Logos*, the analogy of Scripture whereby the Old and the New Testament find unity contains the elevation of the analogy of being into the analogy of faith.

In the Hellenistic period, the encounter between the biblical faith and the best of Greek philosophy corresponds with coincidence of the

---

21. Benedict XVI/Ratzinger, *Transforming Power of Faith*, 81. The title of the catechesis is "Jesus Christ, *Mediator and Sum Total of Revelation*."

22. Benedict XVI/Ratzinger, *Transforming Power of Faith*, 81.

23. Benedict XVI/Ratzinger, *Introduction to Christianity*, 135.

24. Benedict XVI/Ratzinger, *Transforming Power of Faith*, 81.

25. Benedict XVI/Ratzinger, *Introduction to Christianity*, 135.

biblical "I am" and the Greek "Being itself."[26] In the Christian faith, philosophy's recognition of the name of Being itself guarantees the reasonableness of faith, by which the believer is capable of naming God the Father, the Son and the Holy Spirit. Thus, Christ is the synthesis of the philosophical and theological meaning of God's name.

God as "Father" and the Primacy of Christ's Prayer

In the first volume of his books on *Jesus of Nazareth*, Benedict XVI uses analogy to answer the question "why God the Father but not the Mother?"[27] For him, Scripture insists on addressing God as Father in opposition to the "mother-deities that completely surrounded the people of Israel and the New Testament Church."[28] These mother deities, which "create a picture of the relation between God and the world that is completely opposed to the biblical image of God" lack the necessary apophatic theology.[29] The title of God as Father rejects the inherent pantheism often present in other surrounding deities. As our theologian says, "These deities always, and probably inevitably, imply some form of pantheism in which the difference between Creator and creature disappears."[30] On the contrary, the biblical "image of the Father was and is apt for expressing the otherness of Creator and creature and the sovereignty of his creative act. Only by excluding the mother-deities could the Old Testament bring its image of God, the pure transcendence of God, to maturity."[31] Only within the Creator-creature distinction can one speak properly of God. By preserving the holiness or otherness of God, the name "Father" identifies the analogy of divine Fatherhood in greater dissimilarity with human fatherhood: "God's fatherhood is more real than human fatherhood, because he is the ultimate source of our being . . . because he gives us our true paternal home, which is eternal."[32] Benedict is not denying that there is a trace of God himself in the anthropology of fatherhood. On the contrary, he affirms the analogy but within its proper dissimilarity with the

26. Benedict XVI/Ratzinger, "Regensburg Lecture," 22.
27. Benedict XVI/Ratzinger, *Jesus of Nazareth*, 1:139–41.
28. Benedict XVI/Ratzinger, *Jesus of Nazareth*, 1:140.
29. Benedict XVI/Ratzinger, *Jesus of Nazareth*, 1:140.
30. Benedict XVI/Ratzinger, *Jesus of Nazareth*, 1:140.
31. Benedict XVI/Ratzinger, *Jesus of Nazareth*, 1:140.
32. Benedict XVI/Ratzinger, *Jesus of Nazareth*, 1:141–42.

inner mystery of God: "The pattern of relationship between father and son could not serve as an analogy, to pass on to us even a distant glimpse of the inner mystery of God, were there not a trace of God himself to be found in it."[33]

Benedict places priority on the descending movement of divine titles as prerequisite for a proper use of speech to God in prayer. He says, "The picture of God the Father that we find in the Bible is not a projection upward of our own experiences; rather, the contrary: we are told from on high, in quite a new way, what a father really is and what he could be and should be among us human beings."[34] Like Cyprian of Carthage, who considers the prayer of Jesus as the form of Christian prayer, Benedict considers Jesus' prayer to God as Father to be the formal title that most properly conveys the analogy between human words and divine reality. He asserts, "We make our petitions in the way that Jesus, with the Holy Scripture in the background, taught us to pray, and not as we happen to think or want. Only thus do we pray properly."[35] Moreover, "Jesus alone was fully entitled to say 'my Father,' because he alone is truly God's only-begotten Son, of one substance with the Father."[36] If there is anyone who knows how to properly name the reality of the divine relationship to his creatures, that person is the only begotten Son of the Father, and "only through communion with Jesus Christ do we truly become *children of God*."[37] As Benedict XVI says, "It is in fact in Jesus that man becomes able to approach God in the depth and intimacy of the relationship of a child to his father."[38]

The significance of the liturgical context of this title in Scripture is its preservation of the ecclesial origination of the title. While Jesus alone is fully entitled to call God "my Father," he taught his disciples to call God "our Father" because what Jesus has in a fully personal way, we share by analogy of ecclesial communion: "The Our Father is at once a fully personal and a thoroughly ecclesial prayer."[39] In the Lord's Prayer, our "I" takes on an ecclesial meaning in the "I" of Christ.

---

33. Benedict XVI/Ratzinger, *God and the World*, 272.
34. Benedict XVI/Ratzinger, *God and the World*, 275.
35. Benedict XVI/Ratzinger, *Jesus of Nazareth*, 1:140.
36. Benedict XVI/Ratzinger, *Jesus of Nazareth*, 1:140.
37. Benedict XVI/Ratzinger, *Jesus of Nazareth*, 1:141.
38. Benedict XVI/Ratzinger, *School of Prayers*, 9.
39. Benedict XVI/Ratzinger, *Jesus of Nazareth*, 1:141.

Naming the "Holy Spirit"

Relying on Augustine's *De Trinitate*, Ratzinger's commentary on how Scripture names the Third Person of the Trinity maintains the basic principle of God-Talk, i.e., speaking about God within the context of his total transcendence. With regard to the transcendence of God, the name "Spirit" and "Holy" affirms the Otherness and the intrinsic nature of God. According to Ratzinger, Augustine interprets the Johannine phrase *God is Spirit* (John 4:24) as a reference to "what makes God unknowable"[40] and wholly Other: "As we find in John 4:24: *God is Spirit*. Being a spirit and being holy is how the nature of God himself is described, what is characteristic about God . . . the word 'Spirit' expresses the otherness of God as against what is of the world."[41]

The analogy of the name "Holy Spirit" consists in the comparison between what two distinct entities have in common; and what the Father-Son has in common is being "holy," being "spirit." In the very name "Holy Spirit," there is no confusion with the Father and the Son because what is particular about the Third Person is not what is distinctly Father or Son but what the Father and the Son have in common, i.e., they are both holy and spirit.[42] Ratzinger concludes that the origin of Augustine's identity of the Holy Spirit as *the communion* is this: "If he [the Holy Spirit] is called by what is divine about God, what is shared by Father and Son, then his nature is in fact this, being *the communion* of the Father and the Son."[43] The Christological implication of the name of the Holy Spirit is that the name "Son" expresses how the Father communicates with the world his otherness, his being holy and spirit. Thus only by being partaker of Christ's Sonship to the Father can we partake in the Father's holiness and spirit, i.e., can we become *like* God. In the Son, the divine transcendence becomes accessible to the limitation of human words because in him the Father communicates his Holy Spirit.

---

40. Benedict XVI/Ratzinger, *Pilgrim Fellowship of Faith*, 41.
41. Benedict XVI/Ratzinger, *Pilgrim Fellowship of Faith*, 41, 42.
42. Augustine, *Trin.* 5.11–13.
43. Benedict XVI/Ratzinger, *Pilgrim Fellowship of Faith*, 41.

The Term "Son"

In the first volume of *Jesus of Nazareth*, Benedict XVI comments on how Jesus' use of the title "Son" demonstrates both God's original statement about man and God's speech about himself. While Jesus' self-identification as the "Son of Man" conveys God's definitive speech about the glory of man, the biblical meaning of the term "the Son" communicates God's talk about himself.

First, Jesus addressed himself mostly as the "Son of man": "Son of Man—this mysterious term is the title that Jesus most frequently uses to speak of himself. In the Gospel of Mark alone the term occurs fourteen times on Jesus' lips."[44] Benedict observes "in both Hebrew and Aramaic usage, the first meaning of the term 'Son of Man' is simply 'man.'"[45] This linguistic insight helps understand Jesus' statement: *The Sabbath was made for man, not man for the Sabbath. So the Son of Man is Lord even of the Sabbath* (Mark 2:27f). In the expression "Son of Man," God declares man as being meant for freedom in worship; and Jesus' claim as the Lord of the Sabbath is an expression of his primacy.[46] Jesus identifies himself as the illuminative center of worship. For Benedict, Jesus reveals the true meaning of worship in "the inner unity of Cross and glory, of earthly existence in lowliness and future authority to judge the world."[47]

The "Son of Man" is a title "with which Jesus both concealed his mystery and, at the same time gradually made it accessible, was new and surprising."[48] In accord with the "law of disguise," Scripture uses the term "Son of Man" in a way that conceals the divine source or origin of Jesus, and emphasizes his *kenosis*. In the Gospel of Mark, Benedict identifies the culmination of the kenotic meaning of the "Son of Man" as evident in the third prediction of the Passion: *For the Son of man also came not to be served but to serve, and to give his life as a ransom for many* (Mark 10:45). He demonstrated in great detail how the Old Testament prophecy in the Books of Daniel and the Isaiah anticipates the New Testament meaning of the Son of Man. These texts are not only prophesies about the kenotic aspect of the Son of Man, but also "they are sayings about Jesus' future

---

44. Benedict XVI/Ratzinger, *Jesus of Nazareth*, 1:321.
45. Benedict XVI/Ratzinger, *Jesus of Nazareth*, 1:324.
46. Benedict XVI/Ratzinger, *Jesus of Nazareth*, 1:325.
47. Benedict XVI/Ratzinger, *Jesus of Nazareth*, 1:325.
48. Benedict XVI/Ratzinger, *Jesus of Nazareth*, 1:324.

glory."[49] Therefore, in the living experience of his Cross, the Son of man also reveals in his future glory the true humanity. The title emphasizes the primacy of Jesus and the universal claim of his humanity: "The enigmatic term 'Son of Man' presents us in concentrated form with all that is most original and distinctive about the figure of Jesus, his mission, and his being. He comes from God and his is God. But that is precisely what makes him—having assumed human nature—the bringer of true humanity."[50] In the figure of the "Son of Man" God utters his original and definitive statement about man, about true being.

Second, Benedict says, "Jesus' prayer is the true origin of the term *Son*" and "the term 'Son,' along with its correlate 'Father (Abba),' gives us a glimpse . . . into the inner being of God himself."[51] Thus, our theologian asserts that the term "the Son" is God's statement about himself. But what exactly does God say about himself in the term Son? According to Benedict, "The mystery of Trinitarian love comes to light in the term 'the Son.'"[52] The title "the Son" is God's self-utterance about his identity as "Trinitarian love." The term expresses "the dialogue of love within God himself—the dialogue that God *is*."[53] By communicating himself as pure relation of love, "the Son" simultaneously identifies the prayer of Jesus as the locus of participation in the Trinitarian love. What the term "the Son" says about God "is perfectly one with the Paschal Mystery of love that Jesus brings to fulfillment in history."[54]

Human Words Become Divine Word

In his critique of the historical-critical method, Benedict XVI uses the relationship between the *historical method* and *analogy of faith* to explain the proper relationship between relationship between *human words* and *God's Word* in Scripture. Our theologian envisions "a synthesis between an exegesis that operates with historical reason and an exegesis that is guided by faith."[55]

49. Benedict XVI/Ratzinger, *Jesus of Nazareth*, 1:327.
50. Benedict XVI/Ratzinger, *Jesus of Nazareth*, 1:334.
51. Benedict XVI/Ratzinger, *Jesus of Nazareth*, 1:344.
52. Benedict XVI/Ratzinger, *Jesus of Nazareth*, 1:344.
53. Benedict XVI/Ratzinger, *Jesus of Nazareth*, 1:344.
54. Benedict XVI/Ratzinger, *Jesus of Nazareth*, 1:34.
55. Benedict XVI/Ratzinger, *Light of the World*, 172; *Behold*, 14; *Jesus of Nazareth*, 1:xv–xvii.

The Historical-Critical Method

Highlighting the importance of setting the limits of the historical method in exegesis, Ratzinger recalls how Gregory of Nyssa encountered in his interlocutor, Eunomius, a reduction of exegesis to solely a scientific endeavor: "Eunomius had maintained that it was possible to form a completely satisfactory concept of God which really grasped and accurately described God's being."[56] In chapter 2, we saw how Gregory confronts Eunomius on his inability to set the limits of reason in the face of the transcendence of the divine essence.[57] Similarly, Ratzinger calls attention to the lack of restraint operative in a reduction of exegesis to a purely historical-critical interpretation. Ratzinger comments,

> Is there not too much *physiologein* (to treat in a scientific way) in our exegesis and our modern way of dealing with Scripture? Are we not in fact treating it as we treat matter in the laboratory? ... And where in this process is the essence of interpretation which not only views the words as a dead collection of texts but hears the living Speaker himself in them?[58]

The reduction of exegesis to historical method demonstrates an overreach beyond the limits of the historical method. Ratzinger calls for a necessary restraint within the limits of historical science relative to biblical exegesis. The danger of overreaching beyond the limits of the historical method is the blurring of the Christian distinction between the limits of human words and the divine transcendence.

Limits

Benedict XVI recognizes two significant limits of a purely historical-critical method. First, one of the limits of the method is its treatment of the

---

56. Benedict XVI/Ratzinger, *New Song*, 64. Ratzinger says, "Eunomius had maintained that it was possible to form a completely satisfactory concept of God which really grasped and accurately described God's being. Gregory responded that Eunomius had tried to encompass the unfathomable nature of God in the span of a child's hand. Scientific thinking naturally aims at this kind of comprehension it tries to take things in hand so that we can have them at hand. 'It transforms each mystery into a *thing*. Gregory calls this *physiologein*, i.e., *to treat in a scientific way.*' But the mystery of theology is one thing and the science about natures is something else."

57. See Gregory of Nyssa, *Contra Eunomium* 3.5 (PG 45:601B).

58. Benedict XVI/Ratzinger, *New Song*, 65.

biblical words as human words instead of as God's speech: "Because it is a historical method, it presupposes the uniformity of the context within which the events of history unfold. It must therefore treat the biblical words it investigates as human words.... Its specific object is the human word as human."[59] Second, he recognizes that the historical method "considers the individual books of Scripture in the context of their historical period, and then analyze them according to their sources. The unity of all of these writings as one 'Bible,' however is not something it can recognize as an immediate historical datum."[60] Since the historical method "always has to begin by going back to the origin of the individual texts, which means placing them in their past context,"[61] it fragments more than it unites Scripture.

Possibilities

Within these limits of the historical method, Benedict acknowledges two corresponding inherent possibilities and values of the method. First, Benedict acknowledges that "on painstaking reflection, it [the historical method] can intuit something of the 'deeper value' the word contains. It can in some sense catch the sounds of a higher dimension through the human word, and so open up the method to self-transcendence."[62] A historical study of human words, which presupposes the self-transcendence of words, can possibly intuit the "deeper value" or "higher dimension" of the words. The capacity of human words for communicating meaning beyond itself explains the capacity for biblical words to echo a voice greater than human words and a meaning beyond the historical past in which it was written: "In these words from the past, we can discern the questions concerning their meaning for today; a voice greater than man's echoes in Scripture's human words."[63] Second, the historical-critical method "can examine the lines of development, the growth of traditions, and in that sense can look beyond the individual books [of Scripture] to see how they come together to form the one *Scripture*."[64] The study of

---

59. Benedict XVI/Ratzinger, *Jesus of Nazareth*, 1:xvi–xvii.
60. Benedict XVI/Ratzinger, *Jesus of Nazareth*, 1:xvii.
61. Benedict XVI/Ratzinger, *Jesus of Nazareth*, 1:xvii.
62. Benedict XVI/Ratzinger, *Jesus of Nazareth*, 1:xvii.
63. Benedict XVI/Ratzinger, *Jesus of Nazareth*, 1:xviii.
64. Benedict XVI/Ratzinger, *Jesus of Nazareth*, 1:xvii.

historical developments of traditions within Scripture begs for the unity of the books as one text, which only analogy of Scriptures can provide: "the individual writings [*Schrifte*] of the Bible point somehow to the living process that shapes the one Scripture [*Schrift*]."[65] In "the inner nature of the [historical] method points beyond itself and contains within itself an openness to complementary methods."[66] In so far as the historical method recognizes its inner openness to the analogy of Scripture and the analogy of faith, it is very valuable to biblical exegesis.

Analogy of Faith

Going beyond the limits of purely historical-critical method, Benedict seeks "to apply new methodological insights that allow us to offer a properly theological interpretation of the Bible."[67] Our theologian finds in the analogy of faith, an appropriately theological interpretation of Scripture. In Ratzinger, the analogy of faith—the intrinsic correspondences within the faith—assures the understanding of the inner meaning of Scripture. He demonstrates these inner correspondences within the faith in his discussions on the self-transcendence of biblical words, analogy of Scripture, Creed and dogma.

Inner Self-Transcendence of Words into God's Word

Significant to Benedict's explanation of the self-transcendence of human words of Scripture is the role of the common history sustaining the biblical authors. He says,

> It is necessary to keep in mind that any human utterance of a certain weight contains more than the author may have been immediately aware of at the time. When a word transcends the moment in which it is spoken, it carries within itself a "deeper value." This "deeper value" pertains most of all to words that have matured in the course of faith-history. For in this case the author is not simply speaking for himself on his own authority. He is speaking from the perspective of a common history that

---

65. Benedict XVI/Ratzinger, *Jesus of Nazareth*, 1:xviii.
66. Benedict XVI/Ratzinger, *Jesus of Nazareth*, 1:xviii.
67. Benedict XVI/Ratzinger, *Jesus of Nazareth*, 1:xxiii.

sustains him and that already implicitly contains the possibilities of its future, of the future stages of its journey.[68]

Since biblical words were written from the perspective of a common faith, the words carry within themselves the deeper value bestowed by the vision of faith within the authors historical time. The faith sustaining the biblical authors permeates the collective history of a pilgrim people led by a deeper subject: "The author does not speak as a private, self-contained subject. He speaks in a living community, that is to say, a living historical movement not created by him, nor even by the collective, but which is led forward by a greater power that is at work."[69] The formal author of Scripture is God, who is leading the faith that shapes the meaning of the words of the biblical authors, while "the People of God—the Church—is the living subject of Scripture" in which the words of Scripture is always present.[70]

Emphasizing the role of the Church in the self-transcendence of biblical words, Benedict affirms a fundamental principle present in the patristic patrimony: "Reading Scriptures must occur in the fire, that is, in the community of the Holy Spirit, in the living faith that connects us with the origin of the food."[71] Interpreting the Scriptures outside of the Spirit in which it was written does not reveal the true meaning of its words. In his book *A New Song*, Ratzinger demonstrates how the analogy of faith helps the reader to understand the inner self-transcendence of biblical words:

> If even human speech boundlessly transcends itself the greater it is and refers to the unsaid and inexhaustible beyond the words themselves, how much more must this be true of the word whose ultimate and real subject we believe to be God himself? Must we not once again develop methods that respect this inner self-transcending of the words into the word of God, methods that are open to grasping the experience of the saints with this word.[72]

The metaphysical grounds for the self-transcendence of human word is the analogy of being, a certain stretching of word beyond itself. But

---

68. Benedict XVI/Ratzinger, *Jesus of Nazareth*, 1:xix–xx.
69. Benedict XVI/Ratzinger, *Jesus of Nazareth*, 1:xx.
70. Benedict XVI/Ratzinger, *Jesus of Nazareth*, 1:xxi.
71. Benedict XVI/Ratzinger, *New Song*, 65.
72. Benedict XVI/Ratzinger, *New Song*, 64.

Ratzinger speaks of this ascending analogy within the faith community sustaining the self-transcendence of the biblical words. While philosophical reasoning is capable of articulating the existence of God, the jump beyond the limits of human word "into the word of God" requires faith. Thus, when our theologian speaks of the "inner self-transcendence of the words into the word of God," he is making a claim on *analogia entis* within *analogia fidei*.

Commenting on Hans Urs von Balthasar's *Christian Universalism* (*Christlicher Universalismus*), Ratzinger describes the Word's assumption of both the historical and ontological dimensions of the self-transcendence of biblical words as "*analogia entis* within *analogia fidei*."[73] The history of faith within which biblical words were written contribute to the self-transcendence of biblical words, which by nature is capable of stretching beyond itself: "God speaks as man: this means that God assumes also the multiple self-transcending forms of human word, which as human are embedded in human history as well as in its nature."[74] The language of being is always operative in a proper way within the language of faith: "The Word of God ... presupposes the word of man and however leads it to death, to decline, so as to let it become precisely an instrument of divine talk."[75] The human word needs to empty itself (*kenosis*) in order to become adequate instrument of the divine Word. Biblical words transcend themselves by way of *kenosis*. The universal claim of biblical words does not consist in a merely exterior presence of the history of religions in Scripture, but by the renunciation or purification of what is worldly in them.[76] In Ratzinger's comments on Balthasar's kenotic theory of the analogy of word, one can find an echo of Origen's idea that the poverty of biblical words validates them as appropriate instruments of divine Word.

---

73. Benedict XVI/Ratzinger, *Beiträge zur Christologie*, 1057: "Die analogia entis in der analogia fidei."

74. Benedict XVI/Ratzinger, *Beiträge zur Christologie*, 1055–56 (my translation): "Gott redet als Mensch—das bedeutet, dass Got auch die vielfältigen Selbstüberschreitungen des menschlischen Wortes übernimmt, das als menschliches eingebettet ist ebenso in des Menschen Geschichte wie in seine Natur."

75. Benedict XVI/Ratzinger, *Beiträge zur Christologie*, 1056: "So auch das Gotteswort: Es setzt Menschenwort voraus und führt es doch in das Absterben, in den Untergang hinein, um es erst so zum Werkzeug göttlichen Redens werden zu lassen."

76. Benedict XVI/Ratzinger, *Beiträge zur Christologie*, 1057: "Das heißt zur Auseinandersetzung mit der Religionsgeschichte, deren höchstes 'Wort' die überbietung des Wortes und seiner Positivität durch das Fahrenlassen aller Worte in der Negation des Welthaft-Irdischen ist."

Analogy of Scripture

Peter Kucer is right to suggest that in Ratzinger, the analogy of faith in a strict sense is a reference to the "correct reading of Scripture, where scriptural passages ought always be seen in relationship to other passages, in particular regarding the relationship of the Old Testament to the New Testament."[77] This strict sense of *analogia fidei* is distinct from a "fundamental *analogia fidei*," which we explained in the concluding section of chapter 2.[78] Like Augustine, who makes explicit reference to "analogy" when "it is shown that the two testaments, the Old and the New, are not opposed to each other,"[79] Ratzinger makes explicit reference to *analogia scripturae* when "the organic *continuity* of meaning exists between the Old and New Testaments. . . . A New Testament cut off from the Old is automatically abolished since it exists, as its very title suggests, because of the unity of both."[80] For Ratzinger, the unity of the Old and New Testaments is "Christological hermeneutic, which sees Jesus Christ as the key to the whole and learns from him how to understand the Bible as a unity."[81] Our theologian affirms *Dei Verbum* 12, which asserts as a fundamental principle of theological exegesis, attending to the content and to the unity of Scripture as a whole.[82] A dimension of the unity of Scripture, which Ratzinger considers essential is "Canonical exegesis," an expression of essential compliment to what the limits of the historical-critical interpretation. He says, "*Canonical exegesis*—reading the individual texts of the Bible in the context of the whole—is an essential dimension of exegesis. It does not contradict historical-critical interpretation, but carries it forward in an organic way toward becoming theology in the proper sense."[83]

The theological principle behind Ratzinger's analogy of Scripture is an echo of Augustine's priority of reality (*res*) over signs. In Ratzinger,

---

77. Kucer, *Truth and Politics*, 57.

78. According to Kucer, a fundamental analogy of faith is knowing through divine revelation, the ontological similarities between God and creation. See Kucer, *Truth and Politics*, 57.

79. Augustine, *Util. cred.* 3.5 (PL 42:68): "Secundum *analogiam*, cum demonstratur non sibi adversari duo Testamenta Vetus et Novum."

80. Benedict XVI/Ratzinger, "Biblical Interpretation in Crisis," 20.

81. Benedict XVI/Ratzinger, *Jesus of Nazareth*, 1:xix.

82. Flannery, *Vatican II*, 758.

83. Benedict XVI/Ratzinger, *Jesus of Nazareth*, 1:xix.

revelation takes priority over the letter of Scripture because the light of faith gives the proper meaning to the words: "Scripture *is* not revelation but, in any case, is only a part of this greater reality."[84] The presence of revelation, which essentially has to do with faith in Christ and the Church is the reality of Scripture.

Dogma and the Creed

Ratzinger considers "dogma itself as the ecclesial theology of the New Testament."[85] Dogma vindicates the words of Scripture by putting into words the "thing itself" (the *res*) as a way of preserving the meaning of Scripture from individual whims.[86] However, Ratzinger recognizes that the words of dogma are not the only possible way of articulating the matter of its content but "a form" of doing so: "One is not entitled to go too far in the direction of taking these words [of dogma] as the only possible ones and deducing that the matter can be stated only in this way and in no other."[87] For our theologian, the tentative nature of dogma consists in the "negative character of the language of theology, the purely tentative fashion in which it speaks."[88] The positive dogmatic statements about God preserve the mystery from what it is not. For instance, in the fourth-century dogmatic statement of faith, "*una essentia tres personae*," the concepts of substance and person "emphasizes the absoluteness of the relative, of that which is relation."[89] By absolutizing the relational, dogma uses the philosophical language of "person" in a new way. Relation becomes no longer an accident but a primordial form of being; thus, an analogy. While the philosophical words "substance" and "person" remain inadequate relative to the reality they convey, they enabled contact with the reality to take place.

Situating dogma within the history of the believing community, Ratzinger considers the Apostles' Creed to be the original and primitive form of what we today call "dogma." He says, "In the baptismal formulary [of the profession of faith], Christian doctrine stands before us in its

---

84. Benedict XVI/Ratzinger, *God's Word*, 53.
85. Benedict XVI/Ratzinger, *God's Word* , 62.
86. Benedict XVI/Ratzinger, *Introduction to Christianity*, 181.
87. Benedict XVI/Ratzinger, *Introduction to Christianity*, 181.
88. Benedict XVI/Ratzinger, *Introduction to Christianity*, 181.
89. Benedict XVI/Ratzinger, *Introduction to Christianity*, 180.

original shape, and thus, also in its primitive form, what we today call *dogma*."[90] The profession of faith as a dialogue of Christian assent to God and renunciation of evil provides the concrete and liturgical context for receiving dogmatic propositions. Dogma is a form of expressing the fruit of the dialogue between the believing community and God. Indicating the analogical character of Christian doctrine, Ratzinger speaks of the Creed as *symbolum*, which comes from συμβαλλειν—to come together.[91] As *symbolum*, the profession of faith facilitates the inner correspondence of faith commonly proclaimed and historically lived by the believing community.[92] In other words, dogma and the Creed are at the service of the analogy of faith since they facilitate the unity of the faith of the people of God. Dogma and the Creed do not constitute revelation itself but facilitate the unity of revelation. The Creed facilitates the unity of faith by underscoring that "faith comes from hearing," not from reading philosophical statements or from something thought up by oneself.[93] The receptive nature of the faith, which highlights the "we" dimension of what the Church professes demonstrates how the Church is the historical locus of the ongoing process of understanding the inner meaning of Scripture. For Ratzinger, having a personal relationship to Christ means "ceasing to build a wall around oneself, giving oneself over into the unity of the 'whole Christ,' the *totus Christus*, as Augustine beautifully puts it."[94] In the Creed, "when the Church says, 'I believe,' she is professing that she is a comprehensive 'I' that spans and unifies the ages."[95]

Thus, in Ratzinger's explanation of the analogical nature of dogma and the Creed, we find echoes of Bonaventure's illumination theory, whereby the historical character of illumination consists in the historical process of its mediation by the Church as a whole, not by an individual.

90. Benedict XVI/Ratzinger, *Introduction to Christianity*, 96.
91. Benedict XVI/Ratzinger, *Introduction to Christianity*, 97.
92. Benedict XVI/Ratzinger, *Introduction to Christianity*, 97.
93. Benedict XVI/Ratzinger, *Introduction to Christianity*, 91: "The assertion 'faith comes from what is heard' . . . illuminates the fundamental differences between faith and mere philosophy, a difference that does not prevent faith, in its core, from setting the philosophical search for truth in motion again. . . . In philosophy the thought precedes the word; it is after all a product of the reflection that one *then* tries to put into words; the words always remain secondary to the thought and thus in the last resort can always be replaced by other words. Faith, on the other hand, comes to man from outside, and this very fact is fundamental to it."
94. Benedict XVI/Ratzinger, *Dogma and Preaching*, 44.
95. Benedict XVI/Ratzinger, *Dogma and Preaching*, 44.

Describing the analogy between doctrine and Scripture in Irenaeus, Benedict says,

> For Irenaeus, the "rule of faith" coincided in practice with the Apostles Creed, which gives us the key for interpreting the Gospel, for interpreting the Creed in light of the Gospel. The Creed, which is a kind of Gospel synthesis helps us understand what it means and how we should read the Gospel itself.[96]

Scripture and doctrine find inner correspondence in the one historical process of revelation where "the Creed appears as the hermeneutic key to the Scriptures, which without any hermeneutic would ultimately have to remain silent."[97]

The priority lies in the *meaning* of Scripture, and Christ the Light spiritually illuminates God's talk about himself through the Church's talk about God. Revelation is the *Word* himself while Scripture is the material *words* referring to the Word. Ratzinger comments,

> Revelation is not a collection of statements—revelation is Christ himself. He is the *Logos,* the all-embracing Word in which God declares himself and that we therefore call the Son of God. This one Logos, of course, has communicated himself in the normative words, in which he presents to us what is distinctively his. Yet *the Word* is always greater than the *words* and is never exhausted by the words.[98]

Analogy of Scripture consists in the illumination of the written words by the Word himself. Revelation, who is Christ the Light, is always greater than the words of Scripture. Therefore, "there can never be an actual principle of *sola scriptura* in Christianity. . . . Scripture is not revelation but, in any case, is only a part of this greater reality."[99] Ratzinger's idea that "all words refer to the Word"[100] is a patristic idea, which we saw in Origen's abbreviated Word: "He is one, unique Word, formed of multiple sentence, each of which is a part of the same whole, of the same *Logos.*"[101]

---

96. Benedict XVI/Ratzinger, *Church Fathers*, 23.
97. Benedict XVI/Ratzinger, *God's Word*, 63.
98. Benedict XVI/Ratzinger, *On the Way*, 82.
99. Benedict XVI/Ratzinger, *God's Word*, 53.
100. Benedict XVI/Ratzinger, *On the Way*, 83.
101. Origen, *Commentary* 5.4 (GCS 4:102).

Biblical Use of Image Language and Conceptual Language

Scripture talks about God with both images and concepts. In comparison to conceptual language, Ratzinger considers biblical use of images to be more effective in certain aspects. For instance, according to Peter McGregor, "Ratzinger's theology of the Father's heart is found to be a symbolic theology, which regards the bodily image of the heart as giving us a greater insight into the nature of God's heart than do concepts."[102] Commenting on the Old Testament's use of bodily organs to describe who God is, Ratzinger says "The image language of the body furnishes us then, with a deeper understanding of God's dispositions toward man than any conceptual language could."[103] With regard to the Old Testament highly uncritical image of God who "*has* a heart," our theologian recognizes "how badly our basic image of God and our understanding of the Christian reality come to grief *on this very point*."[104]

Ratzinger's comparison of image language with conceptual language is analogy. To the extent that the biblical use of image and concepts are both forms of speech, they are by definition analogous to the divine Word. Both image and conceptual languages share the limitation of words relative to the divine mystery they communicate. The relationship between the biblical use of image and concept is analogous to faith and reason. Neither the divine images of the Hebrew faith nor the Greek philosophical concepts are sufficient for salvific knowledge of God. Rather, the language of the Word saves. Ratzinger gives an example of how the Old Testament use of bodily image corresponds to the analogy of faith. He says, "The pierced Heart of the crucified Son is the literal fulfillment of the prophecy of the Heart of God, which overthrows its righteousness by mercy and by that very action remains righteous."[105] Faith in the crucified Son provides knowledge of the heart of God.

Primacy of the Incarnate Word in Christian Prayer

The anthropological foundation of Ratzinger's thoughts on Christian prayer is the Augustinian analogy of speech, which we discussed in

---

102. McGregor, *Heart to Heart*, 5.
103. Benedict XVI/Ratzinger, *Jesus of Nazareth*, 1:139.
104. Benedict XVI/Ratzinger, *Introduction to Christianity*, 145.
105. Benedict XVI/Ratzinger, *Behold*, 64.

chapter 4. The notion of "image of the divine speech" is the basic ontology of Christian prayer. Man is a praying being because he participates ontologically in God whose nature is to speak, to hear, to reply: "Only because there is already speech, "Logos," in God can there be speech, "Logos" to God. Philosophically we could put it like this: the Logos in God is the ontological foundation for prayer."[106] Prayer does not contradict human nature or divine nature. Since "prayer is an act of being," opposition to prayer is a rejection of being.[107]

What is unique about Christian prayer is the incarnational assumption of human speech by the eternal Speech of God, which enables man to share in the internal speech of the Trinity. Ratzinger comments,

> Man could speak with God if he himself were drawn to share in this internal speech. And this is what the Incarnation of the *Logos* means: he who is speech, Word, Logos, in God and to God participates in human speech. This has a reciprocal effect, involving man in God's own internal speech. Or we could say that man is able to participate in the dialogue within God himself because God has first shared in human speech and has thus brought the two into communication with one another.[108]

Image and participation explains how Christian prayer breaks the alienation of man from God by analogy. Our theologian prioritizes the descending analogy of the divine speech as condition of participation through prayer. Ratzinger's argument for the reasonableness of prayer is fundamentally an argument for the Trinitarian analogy. The prayer of the Son is the compass guiding the Christian prayer; "apart from the Son, the Father remains ambivalent and strange" because "*Patrocentrism*, i.e., the Abba, presupposes the Christological character of prayer."[109] The name "Father" presupposes the eternal Son. The Father of all creation has made his Son the *firstborn of all creation* (Col 1:15) so that he may transpose into the followers of Christ, the benefit of sharing in the Sonship of Christ and capable of saying "Yes" to the Father.

For Ratzinger, what constitutes the reasonableness of the ecclesial dimension of Christian prayer is the analogy of communion, which we have discussed in the previous chapter. The Church plays a mediating

---

106. Benedict XVI/Ratzinger, *Feast of Faith*, 25.
107. Benedict XVI/Ratzinger, *Feast of Faith*, 27.
108. Benedict XVI/Ratzinger, *Feast of Faith*, 25–26.
109. Benedict XVI/Ratzinger, *Feast of Faith*, 28.

role in assisting her children to remember and learn what it means to be a praying being: "A Christological form of prayer which excludes the Church also excludes the Spirit and the human being himself."[110] In the ecclesial character of prayer, the believer receives through the Church, Christ's spiritual and transforming *gift* of speech that restores the believer back to his or her true self: "It is in the gift of speech, and not until then, that I am really restored to my true self; only thus am I given back to God, handed over by him to all my fellow men."[111]

Human Words Become Worship and Sacrifice

Fundamental to our theologian's reflections on liturgical God-Talk is his idea of participation, which confirms why our study of his theology demands a discussion on "participation" before "God-Talk." Explaining the meaning of "active participation" in liturgy, Ratzinger speaks of the concept of "*part*-icipation" as a reference to "a principal action in which everyone has a *part*."[112] Knowledge of what constitutes the "principal action" is essential to an active participation in the action.[113] For our theologian, the central *actio* of the liturgy is the Eucharistic prayer, which the Church Fathers called *oratio*: "the essence of the Christian liturgy is to be found in the *oratio*; this is its center and fundamental form."[114] He noted that "the word *oratio* originally means, not 'prayer' (for which the word is *prex*), but solemn public speech."[115] Thus, returning to the analogy of speech, which shapes Ratzinger's theology of the *Logos*, our theologian concludes that active liturgical participation is where "such [public] speech now attains its supreme dignity through its being addressed to God in full awareness that it comes from him and is made possible by him."[116] In the Eucharistic liturgy, there is a primacy of the action of God's Word, whereby "the action of God, which takes place through human speech, is the real 'action' for which all of creation is in

---

110. Benedict XVI/Ratzinger, *Feast of Faith* , 30.
111. Benedict XVI/Ratzinger, *Feast of Faith*, 30.
112. Benedict XVI/Ratzinger, *Theology of the Liturgy*, 106.
113. Benedict XVI/Ratzinger, *Theology of the Liturgy*, 106.
114. Benedict XVI/Ratzinger, *Theology of the Liturgy*, 106.
115. Benedict XVI/Ratzinger, *Theology of the Liturgy*, 106–7.
116. Benedict XVI/Ratzinger, *Theology of the Liturgy*, 107.

expectation."[117] With the Eucharistic prayer as the "form or center" of liturgical God-Talk, we see that *oratio* is *actio* in its fullest expression. We saw this inseparableness of "speech" and "action" in Cyprian of Carthage's reflections on the Lord's Prayer.

In his extensive writings on the theology of the liturgy, Ratzinger explains how the liturgy is the place where human words can become true worship and sacrifice to God. For him, "human words can become true worship and sacrifice only if they are given substance by the life and suffering of him who is himself the Word."[118] In the previous chapter, we spoke about the communion of the saints as participation in the suffering of the body of Christ. Communion as participation in suffering is the grounds for Ratzinger's reflections on how human words communicate divine reality in liturgy. The power of God's Word is manifest in his capacity to transform death into love. For Ratzinger, "the transformation of death to love . . . combines human words with the Word of eternal love, which is what the Son is, as he ceaselessly gives himself up in love to the Father."[119] In liturgy, the words of the Canon—Eucharistic prayer, which is the "principal action in which everyone has a *part*,"[120] the word of the *Logos* is the "true sacrifice." By "putting his words in our mouths, letting us pronounce them with him, he permits us and enables us to make the offering with him: his words become our words, his worship our worship, his sacrifice our sacrifice."[121] Therefore, the liturgy declares the primacy of Christ as the key to understanding the analogical relationship between the condescension of God's Word and the ascent of human words. Only by participating in the sacrifice of the *Logos* can our human words become worship.

Analogy in the Structure of the Liturgy

There are two ways in which Ratzinger explains the analogical character of the inner structure of the liturgy: (1) Word and response (*Wort und Antwort*); (2) words and silence.

---

117. Benedict XVI/Ratzinger, *Theology of the Liturgy*, 107.
118. Benedict XVI/Ratzinger, *Theology of the Liturgy*, 267.
119. Benedict XVI/Ratzinger, *Theology of the Liturgy*, 267.
120. Benedict XVI/Ratzinger, *Theology of the Liturgy*, 106.
121. Benedict XVI/Ratzinger, *Theology of the Liturgy*, 267.

Word and Response

Ratzinger explains the "Word and response" structure of the liturgy with his Augustinian and Bonaventurian illumination theory, which we discussed extensively in chapters 2 and 3. In his analysis of the "Word and response" structure of the liturgy of the word, Ratzinger says, "This structure of Word and response, which is essential to liturgy is modelled on the basic structure of the process of divine revelation, in which Word and response, the speech of God and the receptive hearing of the Bride, the Church, go together."[122] We have discussed in the fourth section of the current chapter how Ratzinger's understanding of the process of Revelation consists in the illumination of the revealed Word by Christ, which takes place historically in the responsive interpretation of the Church. The liturgy mirrors the structure of divine illumination: "The responsive acclamation (the Amen, the Alleluia, and the *Et cum spiritu tuo*) confirms the arrival of the Word and makes the process of revelation, of God's giving of himself in the Word, at last complete."[123] The same *Logos* who speaks in the proclaimed Word, interiorly illuminates the believers by the light of faith, so that they may understand and ascend to the truth. The descending movement of the analogy consists in the proclamation of the "Word," while the ascending analogy is the affirmative "response" to the truth by the believers. In both movements, light of Christ takes priority. The people are not responding to the letter of the Word but to the *meaning* of the Word. The liturgy expresses the ongoing historical process of humanity's understanding of the meaning of the words of Scripture. Revelation is still ongoing in the deepening of the meaning of the mystery, which is taking place liturgically as a process of illumination.

Words and Silence

In his *The Spirit of Liturgy*, Ratzinger indicates how the role of "words and silence" in the liturgy is analogical in the way that it underscores the similarity and dissimilarity between God and man. In the liturgy, the use of words and silence are two interconnected dimensions of the community's one ascending response to God's Word. For Ratzinger, the role of "words" and moments of "silence" correspond to the similarity

---

122. Benedict XVI/Ratzinger, *Spirit of the Liturgy*, 208.
123. Benedict XVI/Ratzinger, *Spirit of the Liturgy*, 208.

and dissimilarity between God and man: "We respond, singing and praying to the God who addresses us, but the greater mystery surpassing all words, summons us to silence."[124] Silence is the proper human response to the wonder of "the greater mystery surpassing all words." While *words*, acclamations and songs are functions of the similarity between human words and God's Word, *silence* demonstrates the greater dissimilarity between words and God. Benedict finds in Augustine a poignant expression of how silence underscores the analogical nature of words: "Saint Augustine's observation is still valid: *Verbo crescent, verba deficient*—when the Word of God increases, the words of men fail."[125] Distinct from spoken prayers, silent or interior prayer indicates a more profound recognition of the divine presence because awareness of the greater dissimilarity between us and God makes the *presence* of the divine mystery felt. Thus, in worship, silence is a gesture of interior awareness, which expresses how the greater mystery of God surpasses human words.

Ratzinger makes a distinction between "the absence of speech" and "a silence with content."[126] In the liturgy, silence is not merely absence of speech and action, or "just a pause."[127] In chapter 2, we saw how Augustine prioritizes silent prayer of the heart: "God should be sought and prayed to precisely in the silent depths of the rational soul, which is called 'the inner man.'"[128] We also saw how he uses *recollection* to explain both the verbal and interior words of prayer: "Speech serves us only to remember, since the memory in which the words inhere, by recalling them, brings to mind (*commemorare*) the realities themselves, of which the words are signs."[129] Prayer recalls to our minds a forgotten reality. Similarly, Ratzinger explains the use of silence in liturgy with the concept of recollection: "Such stillness will not just be a pause, in which a thousand thoughts and desires assault us, but a time of *recollection*, giving us an

---

124. Benedict XVI/Ratzinger, *Spirit of the Liturgy*, 209. As Robert Cardinal Sarah says, "Before the divine majesty, we are at loss for words. . . . In the presence of [God's] grandeur, our words no longer have meaning. . . . Sacred silence is therefore the only truly human and Christian reaction to God when he breaks into our lives" (Sarah, *Power of Silence*, 120–21).

125. Benedict XVI/Ratzinger, *School of Prayer*, 174; cf. Augustine, *Serm.* 288.5 (PL 38:1307); 120.2 (PL 38:677).

126. Benedict XVI/Ratzinger, *Spirit of the Liturgy*, 209.

127. Benedict XVI/Ratzinger, *Spirit of the Liturgy*, 209.

128. Augustine, *Mag.* 1.2 (CCSL 29:158). See chapter 2 (131).

129. Augustine, *Mag.* 1.2 (CCSL 29:159).

inward peace, allowing us to draw breath and rediscover the one thing necessary, which we have forgotten."[130] The silent prayer of the liturgy creates the space for an awakening or a remembering of the divine love and holiness; an interior illumination of God's presence. When Ratzinger says that the "homily should conclude with an encouragement to prayer, which would give some content to brief silence,"[131] he means that the homily should be a facilitator of *recollection*. The fruit of recollection is a meaningful reception of the Sacrament. "In the common experience of silence the inner process becomes a truly liturgical event and the silence is filled with content"[132]

Evangelization

In one of his Papal Audiences titled, *How to Speak about God*,[133] Pope Benedict XVI indicates how the patristic patrimony on "God-Talk" is relevant for evangelization of the modern contemporary world by asking the question: "How can we talk about God in our time?."[134] In chapter 1, we saw how Origen indicates that human eloquence can taint rather than proclaim the truth of God: "The greatness of the divine power may shine the more, when no taint of human eloquence is mingled with the truth of the doctrines."[135] He considers the humble and poor state of biblical words to be a validation of its fittingness for transmitting God's mystery: "for the treasure of divine wisdom is *concealed* in vessels of poor and humble words."[136] In a similar way, Benedict presents the simplicity and humility of Christ's words as a basic principle of evangelization. Prioritizing Christ's method of proclamation, our theologian comments, "Jesus, the Evangelists tell us, asked himself about [how to talk about God] as he proclaimed the Kingdom of God: *With what can we compare the Kingdom of God, or what parable shall we use for it?* (Mark 4:30)."[137] While Jesus confirms the poverty of using words and comparisons to speak

---

130. Benedict XVI/Ratzinger, *Spirit of the Liturgy*, 209.
131. Benedict XVI/Ratzinger, *Spirit of the Liturgy*, 210.
132. Benedict XVI/Ratzinger, *Spirit of the Liturgy*, 211.
133. Benedict XVI/Ratzinger, *Transforming Power of Faith*, 42.
134. Benedict XVI/Ratzinger, *Transforming Power of Faith*, 42.
135. Origen, *De Principiis* 4.1.7 (SC 268:398).
136. Origen, *De Principiis* 4.1.7 (SC 268:398).
137. Benedict XVI/Ratzinger, *Transforming Power of Faith*, 42.

about God, he also presents the simplicity of words as prerequisite for the ascent of words to God in proclamation. As Benedict says, "following God's own method" is the key to evangelization; and "God's method is that of humility."[138] By using images and parables to speak about God, Jesus manifests humility and simplicity as God's method of speaking about himself.

A strong passion for God's plan of salvation and a personal knowledge of the one proclaimed are the two most effective tools of evangelization. The measure of one's knowledge is not equal to the extent of the empirical value of one's intellectual knowledge; rather, the extent of one's personal closeness to the vision of God, which in turn makes one most purely human is the measure of one's knowledge. Ratzinger says, "For the Christian, the learned person is not the one who knows and can do the most but the one who has become most and most purely man."[139] Becoming "most purely man" is becoming most purely like Christ. The principle of simplicity and poverty in the epistemology of faith is the grounds for evangelization and God-Talk. Ratzinger recalls how Augustine's mother evangelized her son by the simplicity of her faith: "While he [Augustine], with his friends, all of whom came from the academic world, struggled helplessly with the basic problems of humanity, he was struck again and again by the interior certainty of this simple woman. With astonishment and emotion, he wrote of her: *She stands at the pinnacle of philosophy*."[140] Benedict says, "In talking about God, in the work of evangelization, under the guidance of the Holy Spirit, we must recover simplicity, we must return to the essence of the proclamation."[141] The simplicity of Christian faith manifests itself also in the unity of life. Like Cyprian, who considers the unicity of Christ's words and example to be the supreme revelation of the true mode of God-Talk, Ratzinger considers the unity of words and example to be critical for the credibility of evangelization. The credibility of speaking about God depends on the consistency between speech and example: "Our way of living in faith and charity becomes a way of speaking of God today, because it shows, through a life lived in Christ, credibility and realism of what we say with words, which are not solely words but

---

138. Benedict XVI/Ratzinger, *Feast of Faith*, 43.

139. Benedict XVI/Ratzinger, *Principles of Catholic Theology*, 341.

140. Benedict XVI/Ratzinger, *Principles of Catholic Theology*, 341; Augustine, *Ord.* 1.11.32 (PL 32:994).

141. Benedict XVI/Ratzinger, *Transforming Power of Faith*, 43.

reveal the reality, the true reality."[142] In both cases of speech and example, Christ takes primacy as the reality, while our words and deeds are signs and instruments of the reality.

Benedict emphasizes that the effectiveness of the act of talking about God in speech and deed, depends not on the sign, but on the illuminating power of the reality behind the sign. He comments,

> It is not we who can win over others for God, but we must expect God to send them, we must entreat God for them . . . speaking of God is communicating what is essential, forcefully and simply, through our words and through our life: that God of Jesus Christ.[143]

The primacy of Christ in God-Talk is both as the *content* of the reality conveyed through proclamation and the *illuminator* of the hearts of the hearers of the word: "The Revelation and the Revealer coincide in him."[144] Benedict's analysis of the nature of evangelization, which emphasizes the poverty of words relative to the reality they convey echoes Augustine's "priority of things (*res*) over signs." Augustine says, "The realities signified are to be valued more highly than their signs."[145] Augustine uses this principle of priority of things over signs to explain why Christ uses certain specific words to teach his disciples how to pray:

> Are you not concerned by the fact that the greatest Teacher of all taught us certain words to say when He was teaching the disciples how to pray? . . . That does not trouble me at all, for He did not teach the disciples words, but realities by means of words.[146]

As Justin Kizewski says, "Words do not teach, but only propose things for our consideration. The Light is the one who teaches."[147] Ratzinger's Christocentric approach to evangelization cautions against "succumbing to the temptation of success,"[148] which can exaggerate marketing and accommodation of secular culture at the expense of the work of Christ the Teacher.

142. Benedict XVI/Ratzinger, *Transforming Power of Faith*, 46.
143. Benedict XVI/Ratzinger, *Transforming Power of Faith* , 44, 47.
144. Benedict XVI/Ratzinger, *Transforming Power of Faith*, 81.
145. Augustine, *Mag.* 8.21 (CCSL 29:185; FC 59:38).
146. Augustine, *Mag.* 1.2: "Non enim verba, sed res ipsas eos verbis docuit" (CCSL 29:159; FC 9).
147. Kizewski, "God-Talk," 279.
148. Benedict XVI/Ratzinger, *Transforming Power of Faith*, 43.

Conclusion

Irenaeus's *rule of faith*, Cyprian's *priority of Christ's prayer*, Origen's *abbreviated Word*, Gregory of Nyssa's *limits of "physiologein,"* and Augustine's *priority of things over signs* are the recurring themes establishing continuity with the ancient ecclesiastical authors whom Ratzinger quotes. A synthesis of the three categories of analogy clearly emerges. Faith and reason grounds God-Talk in the the way that faith provides what is lacking in reason while reason guarantees the meaning of faith. Philosophy's recognition of the name of Being itself guarantees the reasonableness of the *Logos* of faith, by whom the believer is capable of naming God the Father, the Son and the Holy Spirit. Thus, the primacy of Christ emerges as the synthesis and the Trinitarian revelation of the biblical "I am" and the Greek naming of "Being itself." In Ratzinger's theology, "Image and participation" also grounds "God-Talk," in the way that the "image of divine speech" explains the ontology of Christian prayer, and participation analogy is the *ratio* behind how human words become worship and sacrifice.

Based on our observation that Ratzinger uses the ontological and historical dimensions of the self-transcendence of words to explain the biblical synthesis of *analogia entis* within the *analogia fidei*, we conclude that while he does not confuse analogy of being with analogy of faith, he is able to articulate how the biblical *Logos* synthesizes both analogy of being and analogy of faith.

GENERAL CONCLUSION

As we set out to summarize and evaluate what this study has accomplished, we revisit and recapitulate the essential claims of this thesis. At the beginning of our investigation, the *status quaestionis* prompted our study on two fronts: (1) the inadequate consideration of the patristic heritage in Ratzinger's primacy of Christ by Peter Fletcher and Peter Kucer; and (2) the unanswered questions on our theologian's use of analogy by Peter McGregor, Justin Kizewski, Peter Kucer, and Gabino Bilbao. Hence, our evaluation of this thesis must summarize the identified patristic patrimony in Ratzinger's thoughts on the primacy of Christ and demonstrate how this study allows us to respond to the concerns of the scholars mentioned above. We will include suggested points for further reflection, which would require further studies beyond the limits of our work.

The Patristic Patrimony in Ratzinger's Primacy of Christ

The primary aim of our thesis was to investigate the primacy of Christ in Ratzinger's theology through the lens of the patristic heritage of analogy. At the conclusion of this work, we can state without reservation that the patristic patrimony on analogy is the key to a comprehensive understanding of Ratzinger's primacy of Christ. A summary of the specific elements of *continuity* between the works of the ancient authors and those of Ratzinger validates our thesis and its method. The points of continuity hinge on Ratzinger's collective and specific references to the patrimony of the ancient authors on analogy, which we structured under the categories of faith and reason, image and participation, and God-Talk.

The Collective Referential Continuity

Ratzinger's collective references to the patristic notions of *spolia Aegyptiaca*, *Verbum abbreviatum*, *imago Dei*, and *semina Verbi* helped us introduce how our theologian's primacy of Christ builds on the early Christian writings on analogy. Firstly, what Origen and Gregory of Nyssa describe with *spolia Aegyptiaca*, Clement of Alexandria articulates as the migration of philosophy into the Hebrew faith. In Ratzinger, the analogical character of the image of *spolia Aegyptiaca* is apparent in the way in which he considers the elements of barbarian philosophical culture to be truly present in the human word with which God speaks in the Scriptures. What the Fathers and other ancient ecclesiastical writers articulate with *spolia Aegyptiaca*, Ratzinger further develops with the notion of the "inner self-transcendence of biblical words." Ratzinger describes the Word's assumption of both the historical and ontological dimensions of the self-transcendence of biblical words as "*analogia entis* within *analogia fidei*."

Secondly, another patristic formula that Ratzinger evokes in his Christocentric synthesis of the philosophical and the mystical aspects of analogy is *Verbum abbreviatum*. In the first chapter, we saw how Origen alludes to *Verbum abbreviatum* in his explanation of the "unity of the Word," which prioritizes the person of Christ in the descending and ascending movements of God's Word and human words. Ratzinger's idea that "all words refer to the Word" echoes Origen's abbreviated Word. As the abbreviated Word, Jesus is the short and essential Word of the Father who has told us all about him.[1]

Thirdly, Ratzinger's explanation of man as "image of the definitive Image" is replete with patristic heritage on the primacy of the Incarnate Word in God's decision to create. Irenaeus's and Tyconius's concepts of *image and recapitulation* are most representative of how the ancient authors use image to demonstrate Christ's primacy in God's intention to create. In his explanation of the priority of the Incarnation in God's decision to create, Ratzinger refers his readers to the Church Fathers, who speak of the unique way in which Christ is the Image. For our theologian, the Incarnation reveals in a definitive way, the original meaning of man. By revealing the primordial Adam in himself, Christ explains how the fall of Adam is in opposition with God's original intention for creating him.[2]

---

1. See Rom 9:28 (with reference to Isa 10:23); Benedict XVI/Ratzinger, *Transforming Power of Faith*, 81.

2. See chapter 4.

As the definitive Image, Christ also reveals most perfectly, the dialogical nature of man as being in reference to God.

Finally, Origen's *seeds of wisdom* and Justin Martyr's *seeds of the Word* allowed us to make the following conclusions about the appropriate relationship between the primacy of Christ and the analogy of participation between God and creatures. In Origen, the ontology of participation is a function of the primacy of reason, whereby all rational beings partake in Christ by virtue of the seeds of wisdom and righteousness implanted in them. Justin Martyr's distinction between the Seminal Word (*logos spermatikos*) and the seeds of the Word in all human beings (*sperma tou logou*) corresponds with the distinction between the primacy of Christ and participation analogy. The Seminal Word is *Logos* in a primordial way while the seeds of the Word in all human beings is the reality of our participation in that *Logos*. Between Origen's notion of the seeds of wisdom and Justin Martyr's seeds of the Word, the patristic *semina Verbi* emerges in our study as the description of how all creatures participate in Christ the Word by the mediation of the light of reason. Ratzinger uses this ancient notion of *semina Verbi* to clarify how the nature of the dialogue between the ancient religions and Christianity is not an interreligious dialogue but an interphilosophical one. An interphilosophical dialogue presupposes a preliminary knowledge of God or seeds of Reason in other religions. Christ did not bring the message of the Gospel to a world without any knowledge of the Word.

The Specific Referential Continuity

Our survey of Ratzinger's specific references to Justin Martyr's primacy of *Logos*, Origen's primacy of reason in politics, and Augustine's illumination theory facilitates our examination of the primacy of Christ in our theologian's analogy of faith and reason. Confronted by the modern crisis of discontinuity between Greek philosophical ontology, biblical faith, and progressive nature of history, Ratzinger finds in Justin Martyr's primacy of *Logos*, an argument for the synthesis of analogy of being and analogy of faith. The synthesis lies in Justin Martyr's consideration of the Christian conformity to the *Logos* as the true philosophical search for God. As the true philosophy, Christian faith considers faith and philosophy to be the two distinct but analogous ways of participating in the Supreme Being. On the basis of this analogy between faith and reason, the God of philosophy is the God of faith. Yet, in the tension between the transcendence and relationality of God, the Christian philosophical notion of "person" exposes the limitation of the philosophical notion of *logos* and contributes to the history of thought. Ratzinger claims that in the Christian argument, God who is pure act is equally pure relativity, and philosophy finds in the biblical dialogical person of Christ, a transformation of *relation,* from an accidental to an *original* form of being. Our theologian's identification of the Son as the revelation of the dialogical notion of person, echoes Augustine's *imago Trinitatis*, which we shall explain shortly.

Meanwhile, in his investigation of Origen on the primordial role of reason in faith, philosophy, and politics, Ratzinger uncovers Origen's primacy of God in the reasonableness of politics. For both Origen and Ratzinger, it is the role of faith and philosophy to hold the state responsible to the law of reason. In his criticism of the modern political myth that promises a false sense of absolute freedom, our theologian echoes Origen's primacy of God in politics by insisting on the Creator as the only source of the meaning of true freedom. In other words, freedom is analogical, and the light of the *Logos* is primary to the criterion for determining the reasonableness of any political ideology of freedom.

In the tension between divine transcendence and man's capacity for truth, goodness and beauty, Augustine's primacy of the Light of Christ facilitates our understanding of Ratzinger's epistemology of faith and reason. Augustine's illumination theory, which emphasizes the limits of unaided use of reason and the necessity of the authority of faith helped us to explain Ratzinger's insistence on the objectivity of truth and the mediation of the Church in man's participation in the truth. For Augustine, participation in the Good is a function of *anamnesis* of the original goodness present in Christ the primordial man. The objectivity of *anamnesis* constituted by the collective memory of the Church, then grounds the moral illumination of an individual's conscience and curtails the situation of an erroneous conscience. The guilt of acting from an erroneous conscience consists in the neglect of *anamnesis* that illuminates the internal promptings of truth. Augustine's primacy of the form of beauty in aesthetic illumination, which was already anticipated by Origen's insights on the *piercing wound of love* influences the centrality of beauty in Ratzinger's primacy of the truth. For Ratzinger, the universe is a product of the beauty that radiates the truth of being by the piercing wound of love.

Our survey of Ratzinger's references to Augustine's *image of the Trinity* and *communion,* Origen's *resemblance,* Gregory of Nyssa's *following* (ἀκολουθία), and Maximus the Confessor's *assimilation* facilitated our analysis of Ratzinger's analogy of image and participation. To explain man's intrinsic orientation to God, Ratzinger quotes Augustine, who depicts human nature as a coin bearing the image of God that needs to be given back to God. The notion of image, which expresses the ontology of man's intrinsic orientation to God underscores the dialogical character of human nature and in turn reveals something about the relational in the inner divine life. As alluded to earlier, our theologian's identification of the Son as the revelation of the dialogical notion of person, echoes Augustine's *imago Trinitatis*. In both Augustine and Ratzinger, the Incarnation takes priority in one's understanding of the analogy between the Trinitarian dialogue and dialogical nature of man. The similitude between human speech and divine Speech explains the primacy of the Incarnation in the analogy of dialogue. The Incarnation reveals how the *Logos* assumes human speech into his eternal Speech to the Father. In transforming human speech into God's Speech, the Incarnate *Logos* confirms the existing similitude between the human word and divine Word. Ratzinger's Augustinian dialogical concept of image, which accounts for the similitude between God and man explains why our theologian considers the human soul as ontologically relational and personal.

With his Augustinian dialogical character of image, our theologian articulates how the biblical *homogenesis* exposes the limits of evolutionary definition of the historical appearance of man. Without negating the evolutionary nature of history, Ratzinger explains why the theory of evolution, which negates the metaphysical in history, cannot account for the appearance of the metaphysical reality of the *spirit* of man. His argument from history for the uniqueness of man's relationship to his Creator echoes Bonaventure's *proportionality*, which portrays image as *expressed similitude*.[3] In other words, compared to other creatures, the proportionality of man's similitude to God is expressly unique. While Bonaventure's *expressed similitude* suggests a very great analogical likeness between God and man, the analogy is in continuity with the Augustinian idea of the Fourth Lateran Council, which asserts that no matter how expressly similar the creature is to the Creator, there is always a "greater dissimilarity" between the Trinity and the image of the Trinity in man.

In the fourth chapter, we demonstrated the influence of Origen's spiritual analogy of *resemblance* in Ratzinger's epistemic image of the

---

3. See chapters 3–4.

heart. In Origen, ἡγεμονικόν describes the *Logos* as the pneumatic center of man's epistemic resemblance of God in a primordial way. Origen uses the image of the "heart" to convey how love is the cognitive mode of spiritual resemblance to God. The love of Christ, which manifests divine *agape* is the place of becoming like God. In Origen, participation is the correspondence of the "seeds of love" to "Love" itself. Like Origen, Ratzinger presents participation as the correspondence of the "believer's heart" to the "pierced Heart of Christ." The primacy of Christ's Heart reveals the appropriate mode of relationship with God. The epistemic dimension of Ratzinger's primacy of Christ's Heart consists in the univocity of Christ's knowledge of the Father as the source of the descending analogy of faith. With the epistemic image of the heart, Ratzinger presents the love of Christ as the way of knowing God. Ratzinger quotes Gregory of Nyssa's depiction of Moses' "vision of God's back" as an excellent display of participation proper to the creature, namely, discipleship. The appropriate mode of participation in God is by *following* Christ the perfect Image of God because knowing, loving, and following is one and the same in a true participation analogy.

Augustine's concept of *communio* is the primary patristic influence in the ecclesial dimension of our theologian's analogy of participation. Ratzinger's study of Augustine's ecclesiology shows how Augustine's concept of communion is a synthesis of Hilary of Poitiers's *communicatio unitatis,* Athanasius's *assumptio hominis,* and Chrysostom's Eucharistic analogy. By virtue of the Word's assumption of human nature, the Eucharistic communion in the Body of Christ effects an ecclesial participation that communicates the Trinitarian *caritas* to believers. As a corrective to the politically and sociologically driven Post-Vatican II *concilar* vision of ecclesiology of communion, Ratzinger employs his Augustinian notion of *communio* to restore the spiritual character of ecclesial communion. Using the metaphor of the heart to explain ecclesial communion, our theologian refers to Augustine's conception of the Spirit as "gift," which flows from the suffering heart of Christ as the Church. In the liturgical life of the Church, the action of God in His Son is the "principal action" in which everyone has a part; hence the primacy of Christ in the analogy of partaking or participation.[4] In the real analogy between Trinitarian Communion and ecclesia κοινωνία, the Incarnation takes priority as what shapes the human communion with fellow brethren.

4. See chapter 4.

Ratzinger employs Augustine's *Totus Christus* and Communion of Saints in addressing the eschatological nature of ecclesial communion in the suffering Body of Christ. Contrary to Patrick Fletcher's Platonic approach to the study of Ratzinger's eschatology, our focus on analogy allows us to conclude that Augustine's influence on Ratzinger's eschatology is rather a matter of dialogical personalism anchored in the analogy of participation. Ratzinger's eschatology is not concerned with the Platonic body-soul schema as much as it is concerned with the Creator-creature analogy, which involves the *whole* man and the cosmos. Augustine's *Totus Christus* (head and body) is essential to the understanding of primacy of Christ in Ratzinger's eschatology. Participation of believers in Christ, which consists in the unity of the head and the body is fundamental to the Ratzinger's ideas on the doctrine of Resurrection on the Last Day. In Christ's body, the whole of mankind and all flesh are related, and participation in the resurrection of the body involves the communion of saints as the judge of all people.

In his explanation of divinization with the analogy of assimilation, Ratzinger refers his readers to the insights of the great Byzantine theologian Maximus the Confessor. To emphasize the uniqueness of Christ's human will, Maximus refused to attribute γνώμη (deliberation) to Christ. As the Savior, Christ does not possess a hypostatic realization of nature the way we do because while ours involves deliberation in the freewill, his humanity takes priority of perfection. Like Maximus, Ratzinger upholds the primacy of Christ's human will in assimilation analogy. Making the distinction between our "fallen human will" and our "transformed human will," Ratzinger clarifies that only a transformed human will is assimilated in the divine will. The uniqueness of Christ's will consists in its ability to expose the false nature of our fallen human will in light of the original and true human will, which he reveals in his own will. In Christ's will, what is true about human nature becomes apparent, namely, that the human will is ontologically ordered to the divine will. The primacy of Christ's human will explains how assimilation analogy consists in the healing of man's post-lapsarian will and the restoration of the true human will in Christ. Our examination of the influence of Maximus the Confessor in Ratzinger's assimilation analogy enables us to say with certainty that our theologian's analogical explanation of the union of the two wills has no monothelistic tendency; rather it upholds what is consistent with the nature of the human will, namely, that the ordering of the human will to the divine will belongs to man by his original nature, which Christ came to restore.

Finally, in the last chapter, our analysis of Ratzinger's references to Irenaeus's *rule of faith*, Gregory of Nyssa's *limits of "physiologein,"* Cyprian's *priority of Christ's prayer*, and Augustine's *priority of things over signs* enabled us to present an exposition of the theme of "God-Talk," which has never been developed in Ratzinger. Given the realities of the limitation of human reason and the transcendence of God, the Fourth Lateran Council's principle of *similarity in greater dissimilarity* governs our discussion of the patrimony of the Fathers on Ratzinger's God-Talk. The primacy of the Incarnate Word remains the synthesis of the apophatic and positive theology in the patristic tradition operative in Ratzinger's God-Talk. Apophatically, "The Word, which the Incarnate and Crucified one is, always far surpasses all human words" about God.[5] However, by analogy of faith, the same light of the Incarnate Word illuminates the speech of dogma and the Creed of the Church. The descending movement of analogy of faith is what enables the dogma of the Trinity to name God. To emphasize Christ's primacy in naming God, Clement of Alexandria makes the distinction between the natural capacity of reason to *"declare about God"* and the necessity of the Son's eminent grace in naming God.[6] Echoing Clement, Benedict XVI simply says, "Jesus makes God's name known to us" (John 17:6).[7] To further articulate this positive theology of God-Talk, Ratzinger harkens back to Irenaeus's *rule of faith*, which prioritizes the *meaning* of Scripture before the biblical words. Our theologian's priority of meaning also corresponds with Augustine's principle of the *priority of things (res) over signs*. In the analogy between doctrine and Scripture, Revelation is prior to the material words referring to the Word.

In his explanation of the appropriate role of reason in how the analogy of faith enables human words to become divine, Ratzinger uses Gregory of Nyssa's *limits of physiologein* (to treat in a scientific way) to nuance the positive role of the historical critical method in exegesis. In his critique of Eunomius, who claimed the possibility of a completely satisfactory concept of God by *physiologein*, Gregory asserts the necessity of setting the limits of reason in exegesis. Following Gregory, while affirming the value of the historical critical method in exegesis, Ratzinger

---

5. Benedict XVI/Ratzinger, *Many Religions—One Covenant*, 108.
6. See chapter 5.
7. Benedict XVI/Ratzinger, *Transforming Power of Faith*, 81.

clarifies the limits of the method in the face of the transcendence of the Revealed Word. For Ratzinger, biblical words bear the capacity for an inner self-transcendence, and the study of the historical developments of traditions that shaped Scripture can intuit the higher dimension of the words, which only "analogy of Scripture"—harmony of the Old and New Testament—can adequately address. Echoing Origen's concept the *poverty of biblical words*, whereby the simplicity of the words authenticates their instrumental role for the transmission of the divine Word, Ratzinger agrees with Balthasar's claim that human words become divine by way of *kenosis*. The historical and ontological self-transcendent nature of human words are part of what the Word assumed in his *kenosis*. In doing so, the words of the Word, which are one with his actions, play a unique and formal role in the liturgical and spiritual ascent of Christian prayers. Quoting Cyprian on the *priority of Christ's prayers,* our theologian emphasizes the prayer and action of Christ as the center of the descending and ascending ladder of spiritual participation in the divine life.

Answers to the Analogy Questions in Ratzinger

In the *status quaestionis,* we identified four specific analogy questions driving our study of Ratzinger. The first question pertains to Peter McGregor, who asks whether Ratzinger uses the term "heart" in a univocal way when applied to Christ and when applied to believers. The second question concerns the need to develop Justin Kizewski's brief reference to Ratzinger's contribution to the history of analogy debate. For the third question, our concern is with the relationship between *analogia entis* and *analogia fidei* in the theology of Ratzinger. Finally, Gabino Bilbao's questions about the integrity of the human nature in Ratzinger's volitional notion of divinization, constitutes the fourth analogy question. The fruits of our investigation allow us to address each of these questions below.

Univocity and Analogy

In chapter 4, our consideration of Ratzinger's notion of the "heart" as a cognitive image allowed us to addressed McGregor's question about how our theologian applies the term to Christ and human persons. In his *God and the World* and the introductory chapter in the first volume of the *Jesus of Nazareth*, Ratzinger's comparison of Christ's unique knowledge of the Father in Matthew 11:27 and Moses' vision of God's back in Deuteronomy 18:5 confirms Christ's "immediate vision" of the Father as a univocal knowledge and the believer's knowledge of God as analogical. While Christ's vision of the Father is univocal, his articulation of his knowledge is analogous. Ratzinger's reliance on Origen's Christocentric notion of ἡγεμονικόν, which uses the image of the heart to convey how love is the cognitive mode of spiritual resemblance to God, helped us to conclude that what the heart of Christ knows univocally about God, the hearts of believers receive from his words by analogy of participation. For Ratzinger, the term "heart" is an epistemic image, which he applies univocally to Christ and analogically to believers, in such a way that it conveys the primacy of Christ's knowledge and how believers participate in that vision in a personal way. Thus, our study provides the answer to McGregor's question.

Ratzinger's Contributions to the Analogy Debate

According to Kizewski, the account of truth, the reasonableness of prayer, and the analogy of the Scriptures are the three contributions of Ratzinger to the modern analogy debate. We now explain how our thesis develops these threefold contributions of Ratzinger.

With regard to the account of truth, under the category of "faith and reason," we showed how Augustine's and Bonaventure's illumination theory influenced Ratzinger's approach to the question of truth. Ratzinger prioritizes the uncreated nature of Truth and considers man's cognitive capacity for participation in Reason as analogical. Ilumination is dependent on the fact that the truth is divine. For Ratzinger, what is at stake in the modern rejection of metaphysics is the question of truth. The moral consequence of the rejection of metaphysics is a relativized meaning of conscience. Without the mediation of the Church in preserving the *anamnesis* of man's original goodness, the objectivity of truth slips away from the question of the freedom of conscience. When there is a loss of the objectivity of truth, the meaning of creation and of history are equally at stake. The meaning of creation and of history hinges upon the harmony of Greek philosophical ontology and biblical faith. Ratzinger's attempt to reconcile the metaphysical nature of faith in creation with the historical character of the theory of evolution is with an eye to the biblical and patristic primacy of Christ. In Ratzinger, the encounter with created beauty, which confirms a creative intelligence is also capable of awakening a higher knowledge of truth in all its greatness.

Regarding Ratzinger's emphasis on the reasonableness of prayer, we explained under the category of God-Talk how his arguments is by analogy of speech and of participation. Grounded on the Augustinian analogy between the eternal Speech of God and human speech, Ratzinger prioritizes the descending movement of the Incarnate Word in the logic of prayer. In chapter 4, we explained Ratzinger's relational notion of image as a reference back to the Trinitarian dialogue. The Trinitarian analogy remains essential to the logic of prayer. To be an image of God means to be a praying being. On account of the Trinitarian analogy of communion, Ratzinger considers prayer as fundamentally ecclesial and liturgical. In the Church's collective memory, she plays a mediating role in helping her children to *remember* what it means to be a praying being. Thus, image and participation are essential to Ratzinger's argument for the reasonableness of prayer.

Finally, with regard to the analogy of Scripture, we explained how Ratzinger's insights prioritizes revelation over the words of the Bible. The priority of revelation explains how the Word remains inexhaustible by the words of Scripture. We highlighted echoes of Augustine's and Bonaventure's illumination theory operative in Ratzinger's historical and ecclesial understanding of the relationship between the Creed, dogma, and Scripture. The history of the living community of faith within which the sacred authors were inspired explains the inevitability of the self-transcendence of biblical words and begs for the analogy of faith.

"Analogia Entis" and "Analogia Fidei"

While Peter Kucer uses the influence of Erich Przywara, Gottlieb Söhngen and Hans Urs von Balthasar to account for the relationship between analogy of being and analogy of faith in Ratzinger, our study uses the patristic patrimony. In the *status quaestionis,* we noticed that while Kucer finds a similarity between Söhngen's, Balthasar's and Ratzinger's Christocentric synthesis of analogy, he neither confirms nor denies explicitly that "*analogia entis* within *analogia fidei*" is part of the constitutive elements of Ratzinger's position.[8] Unlike Kucer, our patristic approach allows us to

---

8. Benedict XVI/Ratzinger, *Beiträge zur Christologie*, 1057: "Die analogia entis in der analogia fidei." Analogy of being within the analogy of faith refers to the knowledge of the ontological similarity between God and creation by the light of divine

take a both/and position. In his synthesis of analogy, Ratzinger affirms *analogia entis* within *analogia fidei* without reducing *analogia entis* to *analogia fidei*.

In chapter 2, we showed how Ratzinger synthesizes faith and reason with the Johannine primacy of the *Logos*. Present in Ratzinger are echoes of the notion of *analogia entis* within *analogia fidei*, which we saw in Clement of Alexandria's indication of "philosophy within Scripture," Origen's and Gregory of Nyssa's *spolia Aegyptiaca*, and Bonaventure's primacy of *Logos*. In chapter 5, we discovered how Ratzinger's ontological and historical explanation of the inner self-transcendence of biblical words are claims on *analogia entis* within the *analogia fidei*. His comments on Hans Urs von Balthasar's *Christian Universalism* specifies the kenotic character of words when they become the Word of God. The kenotic transformation of words into the divine Word is one way of explaining the traditional formula of *Verbum abbreviatum*, which we saw in Origen. The poverty of biblical words enhances the instrumental role of human words in the communication of the divine Word.

However, Ratzinger does not reduce analogy of being into analogy of faith. For him, the ontological similarities between God and creature are not only known by divine revelation but also partially known by philosophy. In chapters 2 and 3, we demonstrated how Justin Martyr's primacy of *Logos*, Origen's priority of reason, and Augustine's illumination analogy helped our theologian to establish the distinction and relationship between the light of reason and the light of faith. Contrary to Karl Barth's protest against *analogia entis*, Ratzinger uses Justin Martyr's *seeds of the Logos* to defend the harmony between the Greek philosophical idea of being and the biblical concept of God. By defending the *partial* nature of the Greek philosophical knowledge of Christ, Ratzinger confirms *analogia entis* as distinct from full knowledge of Christ by *analogia fidei*. While analogy of being is better understood in the context of analogy of faith, the illumination analogy, whereby Christ is the Light, still preserves the limits and range of the operation of reason. The unique function of reason is search for the truth. Reason has the capacity for the truth because of the existing analogy between God and creature. However, in Ratzinger, the truth sought by reason cannot be produced by reason because Truth is absolute; hence, reason searches for something that can only be received, and thus finds itself prone to error. Following

revelation. See Kucer, *Truth and Politics*, 57.

Augustine, Ratzinger concludes that reason needs the authority of faith to achieve its goal. Faith keeps reason accountable to the received truth and reason needs the adequate liberty of investigation to be true to its function of searching for the truth.

Origen's priority of reason shapes Ratzinger's application of analogy of faith and reason to politics. In chapter 2, we saw how Ratzinger finds in Origen, a strong defense of the law of nature as something faith and reason share in common. With regard to the priority of reason in politics, both Origen and Ratzinger consider the law of nature to be the law of Christ such that in Christ, the objectivity of reason reigns over the myths of political law. The analogy of reason and natural law with which Ratzinger explains the correspondence of creation to God, depicts how Christ the Light and the *Logos* takes primacy in *analogia entis*.

At this conclusion of our investigation, we can say without reservation that Ratzinger's Christocentric synthesis of the analogy of faith and reason affirms *analogia entis* within *analogia fidei* without reducing the analogy of being to the analogy of faith. Like the ancient authors, Ratzinger used the priority of reason to demonstrate how being looks to Christ for its knowledge of the objective truth.

Assimilation Analogy and the Integrity of Human Nature

Our study of the influence of Maximus the Confessor's *assimilation analogy* on Ratzinger's volitional Christology rejects Gabino Bilbao's claim that divinization in Ratzinger's does not adequately preserve the integrity of human nature. We highlighted in Ratzinger how the personal assimilation of Christ's human will reveals the analogy between the Father-Son eternal dialogue and the God-man volitional dialogue. In Ratzinger, the intrinsic order of man's will to God's will constitutes what is consistent in human nature. We demonstrated how the grace of assimilation presupposes this natural order of the will. Ratzinger's Augustinian understanding of human nature as intrinsically a reference to God—*imago Dei*—is central to our argument for the integrity of human nature in Ratzinger's notion of divinization. Ratzinger's relational notion of the ontology of image, which is grounds for the grace of assimilation does not confuse grace with nature but explains nature's intrinsic reference to the source of grace, who is the *Logos*.

We also examined Ratzinger's distinction between the fallen and the redeemed human will, and demonstrated how the redeemed human will radiates more clearly what is consistent in human nature. The redemptive role of the uniqueness of Christ's human will consists in its exposure of our human fallen will in light of the original and true human will. Thus, Ratzinger's soteriological argument for the primacy of Christ's will protects the integrity of the "true and original" human nature in assimilation or divinization.

Points for Further Consideration

This thesis leaves much more for further discussion. We single out three aspects of Ratzinger's thoughts on the primacy of Christ in need of further investigation: his anointing Christology, grace and nature analogy, and Mariology.

Ratzinger's Anointing Christology

In chapter 1, we briefly commented on how Origen uses the sacrificial significance of Christ's priestly anointing to explain the analogy of participation. In our treatment of Ratzinger's Augustinian notion of "Communion as participation in suffering," one finds echoes of Origen's use of the anointing Christology to explain the paschal character of ecclesial participation. An avenue for possible further discussion is the patristic patrimony in Ratzinger's anointing Christology. In the second volume of his *Jesus of Nazareth,* Ratzinger speaks of the Cross of Christ as a fulfillment of Christ's prayer of consecration in John 17.[9] As we mentioned in the *status quaestionis,* Bilbao bemoans the lack of anointing Christology in Ratzinger's commentary on the baptism of Christ.[10] For Bilbao, the absence of a developed theology of anointing in Ratzinger's theology renders his spiritual Christology inadequate because it leaves aside the interrelationship between Christology and Pneumatology grounded in the anointing theology.[11] While our study dismisses Bilbao's claim for the absence of pneumatic Christology in Ratzinger, Bilbao's question about

---

9. Cf. Benedict XVI/Ratzinger, *Jesus of Nazareth,* 2:85–90.

10. Bilbao, "Neocalcedonismo," 84: "Qué puede estar en el trasfondo de la postura de Ratzinger, obviando el tema de la uncion?"

11. Bilbao, "Neocalcedonismo," 111.

the presence of an adequate anointing Christology in Ratzinger still needs further examination. The methodology of our study has already identified anointing Christology within the context of participation analogy, whereby the preeminence of Christ's Anointing renders the anointing of the believers a sacramental participation in Christ. A discussion on the the patristic influence on Ratzinger's theology of anointing would offer good insights to Bilbao's concern.

Grace and Nature in Ratzinger

Serge-Thomas Bonino's article on *"Nature and Grace" in the Encyclical "Deus Caritas Est"* presents Ratzinger's analogy of faith and reason as a question of grace and nature. Bonino claims, "In the treatment of the encyclical's questions, Benedict XVI uses a well thought-out and precise conception of that which is classically called "the question of the relationship between nature and grace.""[12] He identified the archetype of Benedict's analogical relationship between grace and nature as the "encounter . . . which took place at the beginning of the Christian faith and the Greco-latin culture";[13] hence, the analogy of faith and reason.

In Benedict's encyclical *Deus Caritas Est*, the meeting point between the Greek philosophical notion of *eros* and the biblical idea of *agape* finds primordial clarity in Christ the Incarnate *Logos*. Benedict describes how the natural phenomenon of "ascending love" (*eros*) and the supernatural (grace) reality of "descending love" (*agape*) are fundamentally inseparable movements of nature-grace analogies made perfectly clear in Christ.[14] An element of *agape* enters into *eros* at the moment when the ascending movement of *eros* towards the promise of happiness draws near to the other, becomes less concerned with itself and more concerned with the beloved.[15] The role of faith and reason in the analogy of love is a question of the relationship between grace and nature because the process

12. Bonino, "Nature and Grace," 231.

13. Bonino, "Nature and Grace," 232.

14. Benedict XVI/Ratzinger, *Deus Caritas Est* 7 (10–11): "By their inner logic, these initial, somewhat philosophical reflections on the essence of love have now brought us to the threshold of biblical faith. We began by asking whether the different, or even opposed, meaning of the word "love" point to some profound underlying unity, or whether on the contrary they must remain unconnected, one alongside the other. . . Yet *eros* and *agape*—ascending and descending love—can never be completely separated."

15. Benedict XVI/Ratzinger, *Deus Caritas Est* 7 (11).

whereby *eros* discovers its true rational objective in encountering *agape* of faith is precisely how grace liberates nature from its impoverishment.

Bonino identifies three characteristics of the grace-nature relationship in Benedict's encyclical. Firstly, the relationship between the divine and human order is by analogy: "First, it assumes as the very least a unity according to the analogy between the two orders. . . . If the order of grace were 'another world,' without a relationship to the historic realities of human cultures, Christianity would be reduced to a gnosis, an evasion."[16] Secondly, grace is distinct from nature because grace effects a "new" reality. The theoretical (philosophy, science) and practical (justice, politics, life) capacities of reason are distinct but analogous to the objective revelation of the Mystery of faith.[17] Finally, grace purifies nature and restores it to its integral reality. As Benedict says, "an intoxicated and undisciplined *eros*, then, is not an ascent in 'ecstasy' towards the Divine, but a fall, a degradation of man."[18] Nature's rejection of grace leads to its decay.

Bonino's consideration of Benedict's grace-nature relationship as a faith-reason analogy further instantiates an undeveloped area of the analogy faith and reason in the writings of Ratzinger.

Analogy in Ratzinger's Mariology

Based on the insights gained in this thesis, there are two main avenues for future reflection on analogy in Ratzinger's Mariology. The first avenue is anthropological while the second is biblical.

Firstly, in our consideration of Ratzinger's analogy of image and participation between God and man, we did not discuss in greater details the concrete role of the biological complementarity of the male and female identity. In his Mariology, one finds a more detailed reflection on this biological dimension of analogy. In his *Introductory Essay on the Encyclical "Redemptoris Mater,"* Ratzinger finds in the encyclical, an affirmation that "Christology does not exclude the feminine or repress and trivialize it, and conversely, that the recognition of the feminine does not diminish Christology, but that the truth about God and the truth about ourselves can appear only when the correlation of the two is correctly appreciated."[19] In Ratzinger, the concept of image does

---

16. Bonino, "Nature and Grace," 234.
17. Bonino, "Nature and Grace," 233.
18. Benedict XVI/Ratzinger, *Deus Caritas Est* 5 (8–7).
19. Benedict XVI/Ratzinger, *Mary*, 44.

not exclusively pertain to Adam but to the correlation of Adam and Eve. In the Old Testament, the biological complementarity of man and woman appears in the form of marriage because in their correlation to one another, man and woman constitute the image of God: "Marriage is the immediate 'translation' of theology, the consequence of an *image of God*."[20] As Ratzinger notes, "Genesis 1:27 had portrayed mankind from the very beginning as masculine and feminine in its likeness to God, and had mysteriously, cryptically linked its likeness to God with the mutual reference of the sex to each other."[21] The *likeness* consists in the descending analogy of God's faithful love for his people, and the ascending analogy of a faithful marriage between a man and a woman. Thus, the theology of marriage ensures the inclusion of the biological element of the analogy of image and likeness.

However, the priority is not in the sign (marriage) but in the *res* (covenant of love between God and Israel). In her title as "Virgin and Mother," Mary testifies to the priority of the covenant between God and his people over the sign of marriage. The fruitfulness of Mary's motherhood is tied to her virginity.[22] While Mary is the personal image of daughter Zion, of a chosen people, her virginity represents the primordial nature of Israel's response to God's love prior to Israel's barrage of infidelities: "Israel herself, the chosen people is interpreted simultaneously as woman, virgin, beloved, wife and mother."[23] In Mary's "Yes," one encounters the revelation of Israel's primordial response. The fruit of Mary's "Yes" is the revelation of God's love in Christ, who is Mary's son and God's Son. Hence, in the Christ-Mary relationship, whereby the God-creature relation illuminates the spiritual meaning of the masculine-feminine complementarity, Ratzinger's Mariology sheds light on the sacramental analogy of marriage. How Ratzinger uses Mariology to better articulate the biological dimension of the analogy of image needs further investigation.

20. Benedict XVI/Ratzinger, *Daughter Zion*, 15.
21. Benedict XVI/Ratzinger, *Daughter Zion*, 17.
22. According to Ratzinger, "Virginity is most intimately connected to the theological foundation of marriage; it does not stand in opposition to marriage, but rather signifies its fruit and confirmation" (Benedict XVI/Ratzinger, *Daughter Zion*, 16).
23. Benedict XVI/Ratzinger, *Daughter Zion*, 21. Ratzinger traces the Marian typology of Israel to "the image of the great maternal women and what is considered to be the proper center of the Old Testament's theology of woman: Israel herself, the chosen people is interpreted simultaneously as woman, virgin, beloved, wife and mother."

Secondly, Ratzinger's Mariology confirms his emphasis on how the analogy between the Old and New Testaments is critical to the meaning of Scripture. In his book *Daughter Zion*, he calls Mary "Mother of the Word," who "signifies that in herself Old and New covenants are really one."[24] What does not feature in our investigation on Christ's primacy is Mary's place in Ratzinger's analogy of Scripture. In other words, what is the relationship between the primordial place of Christ and the place of Mary in salvation history? What is the place of Mary in biblical God-Talk?

Conclusion

A notable conclusive claim of this study is Ratzinger's affirmation of "*analogia entis* within an *analogia fidei*" without reducing analogy of being to analogy of faith. With this claim, our study shows how the Bavarian theologian maintains his mentor's ecumenical stance while unequivocally proclaiming *analogia entis* as a matter of the primacy of Christ, rather than an invention of the antichrist. We are convinced that the method of our study keeps alive the value of our common patristic heritage in the conversations about the authentic interpretation of Scripture, interreligious dialogue, eschatology, and Christian anthropology. The impetus of Ratzinger's patristic method is quite culturally and spiritually relevant. Firstly, his primacy of truth and the necessity of the Church is a challenge to our secular culture, which alienates the God of reason and the God of faith from political discourse, and relativizes the nature of man. Secondly, his dialogical anthropology, which defines man as a praying being is an encouragement to all of us who seek to follow "Christ the New Man," whose earthly life was in constant dialogue with the Father. The contributions of our study listed above demonstrate their academic and theological relevance. If our study has achieved anything beyond its academic and theological contribution, we hope that it has moved fellow Christians to take more seriously the reasonableness of *following* Christ, and has described how the logic of Christ illuminates the truth of the human person and of all things in all ages.

"*Omnia Christus est nobis!* (To us Christ is all)."[25]

---

24. Benedict XVI/Ratzinger, *Daughter Zion*, 65.

25. Ambrose of Milan, *De Virginitate* 16.99 (PL 16:291); cf. Benedict XVI/Ratzinger, *Church Fathers*, 126.

Bibliography

Ambrose. *Hexameron, Paradise, and Cain and Abel*. Translated by John J. Savage. FC 42. Washington, DC: Catholic University of America Press, 1961.
Aquinas, Thomas. *Summa Theologica*. Translated by the English Dominican Province. 5 vols. New York: Ave Maria, 1948.
Athanasius. *Selected Works and Letters*. Vol. 4 of *Nicene and Post-Nicene Fathers*, Series 2. Edited by P. Schaff. Grand Rapids: Eerdmans, 1971.
Augustine. *The City of God*. Translated by Marcus Dods. New York: Modern Library, 1993.
———. *Confessions and Letters of St. Augustine*. Vol. 1 of *Nicene and Post-Nicene Fathers*, Series 1. Edited by Philip Schaff. Grand Rapids: Christian Classics Ethereal Library, 1974.
———. *Earlier Writings*. Edited by J. H. S. Burleigh. LCC 6. Philadelphia: Westminster, 1953.
———. "Homilies on the Gospel of St. John." In *Homilies on the Gospel of John; Homilies on the First Epistle of John; Soliloquies*, edited by Philip Schaff, 7–452. Vol. 7 of *Nicene and Post-Nicene Fathers*, Series 1. Milton Keynes: Veritatis Splendor, 2012.
———. *On Christian Doctrine*. Translated by D. W. Robertson. New York: Liberal Arts, 1958.
———. "On the Literal Interpretation of Genesis: An Unfinished Book." In *On Genesis: Two Books on Genesis; Against the Manichees; and, On the Literal Interpretation of Genesis: An Unfinished Book*, 143–90. Translated by Roland J. Teske. FC 84. Washington, DC: Catholic University of America Press, 1991.
———. *The Problem of Free Choice*. Ancient Christian Writers 22. Edited by J. Plumpe and J. Quasten. London: Longmans, Green, and Co., 1955.
———. *Prolegomena: The Confessions and Letters of St. Augustine, with a Sketch of His Life and Work*. Vol. 1 of *Nicene and Post-Nicene Fathers*, Series 1. Edited by Philip Schaff. Grand Rapids: Eerdmans, 1974.
———. *The Retractations*. Translated by Maryline Inez Bogan. FC 60. Washington, DC: Catholic University of America Press, 1968.
———. "The Soliloquies." In *The Happy Life; Answer to Skeptics; Divine Providence and the Problem of Evil; Soliloquies*, edited by Ludwig Schopp et al., 333–426. Translated by T. F. Gilligan. FC 5. New York: Cima, 1948.
———. *The Trinity*. Translated by Edmund Hill. Edited by John Rotelle. Vol. 5 of *The Works of Saint Augustine: A Translation for the Twenty-First Century*. New York: New City, 1991.

———. *The Writings against the Manicheans and against the Donatists*. Vol. 4 of *Nicene and Post-Nicene Fathers*, Series 1. Edited by Philip Schaff. Grand Rapids: Eerdmans, 1974.

Balthasar, Hans Urs von. *Cosmic Liturgy: The Universe According to Maximus the Confessor*. Translated by Brian E. Daley. San Francisco: Ignatius, 2003.

———. *Heart of the World*. Translated by Erasmo S. Leiva. San Francisco: Ignatius, 1979.

———. *Presence and Thought: An Essay on the Religious Philosophy of Gregory of Nyssa*. Translated by Mark Sebanc. San Francisco: Ignatius, 1995.

Barth, Karl. *Church Dogmatics*. Vol. 1. Edinburgh: T&T Clark, 1969.

Behr, John. *Irenaeus of Lyons: Identifying Christianity*. Oxford: Oxford University Press, 2013.

Benedict XVI (Joseph Ratzinger). *Address to the Pontifical Biblical Commission, April 23*. Vatican: Libreria Editrice Vaticana, 2009.

———. *Behold the Pierced One: An Approach to a Spiritual Christology* [*Schauen auf den Durchbohrten*]. Translated by G. Harrison. San Francisco: Ignatius, 1986.

———. "Biblical Interpretation in Crisis: On the Question of the Foundations and Approaches of Exegesis Today." In *Biblical Interpretation in Crisis: The Ratzinger Conference on Bible and Church*, edited by Richard John Neuhaus, 1–23. Grand Rapids: Eerdmans, 1989.

———. *Church, Ecumenism, and Politics: New Endeavors in Ecclesiology*. Translated by Michael J. Miller. San Francisco: Ignatius, 2008.

———. *Church Fathers: From Clement of Rome to Augustine*. San Franciso: Ignatius, 2008.

———. "Conscience and Truth." *Communio* 37 (2010) 529–38.

———. *Daughter Zion: Meditations on the Church's Marian Belief* [*Die Tochter Zion*]. Translated by John M. McDermott. San Francisco: Ignatius, 1983.

———. *Deus Caritas Est*. Vatican: Libreria Editrice Vaticana, 2006.

———. *Dogma and Preaching* [*Dogma und Verkundigung*]. Translated by Michael J. Miller and Matthew J. O'Connell. Unabridged ed. San Francisco: Ignatius, 2011.

———. *Einführung in Das Christentum: Bekenntnis–Taufe–Nachfolge*. Vol. 4 of *Gesammelte Schriften*. Edited by Gerhard Ludwig Müller. Frieburg: Herder, 2014.

———. *Eschatology*. Washington, DC: Catholic University of America Press, 1988.

———. *The Feast of Faith: Approaches to a Theology of the Liturgy* [*Das Fest des Glaubens*]. Translated by Graham Harrison. San Francisco: Ignatius, 1986.

———. *Glaube in Schrift und Tradition: Zur Theologischen Prinzipienlehre*. Vol. 9 of *Gesammelte Schriften*. Edited by Gerhard Ludwig Muller. Freiburg: Herder, 2016.

———. *God and the World: Believing and Living in Our Time, a Conversation with Peter Seewald* [*Gott und die Welt: Glauben und Leben in unserer Zeit, Ein Gespräch mit Peter Seewald*]. Translated by Henry Taylor. San Francisco: Ignatius, 2002.

———. *God's Word: Scripture, Tradition, Office* [*Wort Gottes: Schrift, Tradition, Amt*]. Translated by Henry Taylor. San Fransisco: Ignatius, 2008.

———. "The Holy Spirit as Communio: Concerning the Relationship of Pneumatology and Spirituality in Augustine." *Communio* 25 (1998) 324–37.

———. "Homiliae: Ad Motus Ecclesiales Atque Novas Communitates." *AAS* 98.7 (2006) 503–10.

---. "In the Beginning . . .": A Catholic Understanding of Creation and the Fall [In Anfang schuf Gott]. Translated by Boniface Ramsey. Grand Rapids: Eerdmans, 1995.

---. Introduction to Christianity [Einführung in das Christentum]. Translated by J. R. Foster. 2nd ed. San Francisco Communio, 2004.

---. Jesus of Nazareth. Translated by Adrian J. Walker and Philip J. Whitmore. 3 vols. New York: Doubleday and Image/Random House; San Francisco: Ignatius, 2007–2012.

---. Jesus von Nazareth. 3 vols. German. Freiburg: Herder, 2007–2012.

---. Jesus von Nazareth: Beiträge Zur Christologie, Zweiter Teilband. Vol. 6.2 of Gesammelte Schriften. Edited by Gerhard Ludwig Müller. Freiburg: Herder, 2013.

---. "Jungfrauengeburt und Leeres Grab." Deutsche Tagespost, November 11, 2004.

---. Last Testament. New York: Bloomsbury, 2016.

---. Letzte Gespräche. München: Droemer, 2016.

---. Light of the World. Translated by Adrian Walker Michael J. Miller. San Francisco: Ignatius, 2010.

---. Mary: The Church at the Source. Translated by Adrian Walker. San Francisco: Ignatius, 2005.

---. Milestones: Memoirs 1927–1977. San Francisco: Ignatius, 1998.

---. The Nature and Mission of Theology. San Francisco: Ignatius, 1995.

---. A New Song for the Lord: Faith in Christ and Liturgy Today [Ein Neues Lied für Den Herrn: Christusglaube und Liturgie in der Gegenwart]. Translated by Martha M. Matesich. New York: Crossroad, 1996.

---. Offenbarungsverständnis und Geschichtstheologie Bonaventuras: Habilitationsschrift und Bonaventura-Studien. German. Edited by Gerhard Ludwig Müller. Vol. 2 of Gesammelte Schriften. Freiburg: Herder, 2009.

---. On the Way to Jesus Christ [Unterwegs zu Jesus Christus]. Translated by Michael J. Miller. San Francisco: Ignatius, 2005.

---. Pilgrim Fellowship of Faith: The Church as Communion. Translated by Henry Taylor. San Fransisco: Ignatius 2005.

---. Popolo E Casa Di Dio in Dio in Sant'agostino [Volk und Haus Gottes in Augustinus Lehre von der Kirche]. Italian. Translated by Antonio Dusini. 3rd ed. Milano: Jaca, 2005.

---. Principles of Catholic Theology: Building Stones for a Fundamental Theology [Theologische Prinzipienlehre]. Translated by Mary Frances McCarthy. San Francisco: Ignatuis, 1987.

---. "Regensburg Lecture." In The Regensburg Lecture, edited by James V. Schall, 130–48. South Bend, IN: St. Augustine's 2007.

---. "Regensburg Lecture." In Pope Benedict XVI: A Reason Open to God, edited by J. Steven Brown, 7–19. Washington, DC: Libreria Editrice Vaticana/Catholic University of America Press, 2013.

---. Saint Paul: General Audiences, July 2, 2008–February 4, 2009. Translated by L'Osservatore Romano. San Francisco: Ignatius, 2009.

---. Salt of the Earth: Christianity and the Catholic Church at the End of the Millenium, an Interview with Peter Seewald. Translated by Adrian Walker. San Francisco: Ignatius 1997.

---. A School of Prayers: The Saints Show Us How to Pray. San Francisco: Ignatius, 2012.

———. *The Spirit of the Liturgy* [*Einführung in den Geist der Liturgie*]. Translated by John Saward. San Francisco: Ignatius, 2000.

———. "Studien zur Theologie der Kirchenväter." In *Volk und Haus Gottes* in *Augustins Lehre von der Kirche*, edited by Gerhard Ludwig Müller, 555–662. Vol. 1 of *Gesalmmelte Schriften*. Freiburg: Herder, 2011.

———. *Theological Highlights of Vatican II*. New York: Paulist, 1966.

———. *The Theology of History in Bonaventure* [*Geschischtstheologie Bonaventuras*]. Translated by Zachary Hayes. Chicago: Franciscan Herald, 1971.

———. *Theology of the Liturgy: The Sacramental Foundation of Christian Existence*. Vol. 11 of *Collected Works*. Edited by Gerhard Ludwig Müller. Translated by Kenneth Baker et al. San Francisco: Ignatius, 2014.

———. *The Transforming Power of Faith: General Audiences, October 17–February 16, 2013*. Translated by L'Osservatore Romano. San Francisco: Ignatius 2013.

———. *The Unity of the Nations: A Vision of the Church Fathers* [*Die Einheit der Nationen: Eine Vision der Kirchenväter*]. Translated by Boniface Ramsey. Washington, DC: Catholic University of America 2015.

———. *Volk und Haus Gottes in Augustins Lehre von der Kirche*. Munich: Herder, 1954.

———. "Volk und Haus Gottes in Augustins Lehre von der Kirche: Die Dissertation und Weitere Studien zu Augustinsus und zur Theologie der Kirchenväter." In vol. 1 of *Gesamnelte Schriften*, edited by Gerhar Ludwig Müller, 43–414. Freiburg: Herder 2011.

Bilbao, Gabino U. "El Neocalcedonismo De Joseph Ratzinger. Implicaciones Para La Teologia De La Uncion Y De La Voluntad Humana De Cristo." In *La Uncion De La Gloria: En El Epiritu, Por Cristo, Al Padre—Homenaje a Mons. Luis F. Ladaria, SJ*, edited by Manuel Aroztegi Esnaola et al., 81–111. Madrid: Biblioteca de Autores Cristianos, 2014.

Bonagura, David. "Joseph Ratzinger/Benedict XVI's Christology of Jesus' Prayer and Two Contemporary Theological Questions." *Nova et Vetera* 12 (2014) 287–306.

———. "Logos to Son in the Christology of Joseph Ratzinger/Benedict XVI." *New Blackfriars* 93.1046 (2011) 475–88.

Bonaventure. *Sententiarum II*. Vol. 2 of *S. Bonaventurae Opera Omnia*. Latin. Florence: Quaracchi, 1885.

———. *Sententiarum III*. Vol. 3 of *S. Bonaventurae Opera Omnia*. Latin. Florence: Quaracchi, 1887.

Bonino, Serge-Thomas. "'Nature and Grace' in the Encyclical *Deus Caritas Est*." *Nova et Vetera* 5.2 (2007) 231–48.

Carola, Joseph. *Augustine of Hippo: The Role of the Laity in Ecclesial Reconciliation*. Rome: Gregoriana, 2005.

———. "Non-Christians in Patristic Theology." In *Catholic Engagement with World Religions: A Comprehensive Study*, edited by K. Becker and I. Morali, 23–48. Faith Meets Faith. Maryknoll, NY: Orbis, 2010.

Chapman, Emmanuel. *Saint Augustine's Philosophy of Beauty*. New York: Sheed & Ward, 1939.

Colish, Marcia L. *The Stoic Tradition from Antiquity to the Early Middle Ages*. Leiden: Brill, 1985.

Corkery, James. *Joseph Ratzinger's Theological Ideas: Wise Cautions and Legitimate Hopes*. New York: Paulist, 2009.

Crouzel, Henri. *Théologie De L'image De Dieu Chez Origène*. Paris: Aubier, 1955.

Cyprian of Carthage. *Treatises*. Translated by Roy J. Deferrari. FC 36. Washington, DC: Catholic University of America Press, 1958.
Egbulefu, Charles. "The Ecclesiology of Saint Bonaventure in the Second Vatican Council." PhD diss., Universita Urbaniana, 2015.
Einstein, Albert. *Mein Weltbild*. Stuttgart: Verlag, 1953.
Fantino, Jacques. *L'homme, Image De Dieu Chez Saint Irénée De Lyon*. Paris: Cerf, 1986.
Ferri, Riccardo. *Gesù E La Verità: Agostino E Tommaso Interpreti Del Vangelo Di Giovanni*. Roma: Città Nuova, 2007.
Flannery, Austin, ed. *Vatican Council II: The Conciliar and Post Conciliar Documents*. 5th ed. Northport, NY: Costello, 1998.
Fletcher, Patrick J. *Resurrection Realism: Ratzinger the Augustinian*. Eugene, OR: Cascade, 2014.
Fourth Lateran Council. *Constitutiones*. In *Nicaea I to Lateran V*, edited by Norman P. Tanner, 230–71. Vol. 1 of *Decrees of the Ecumenical Councils*. Washington, DC: Georgetown University Press, 1990.
Granados, Jose. *Los Misterios De La Vida De Cristo En Justino Martir*. Rome: Gregorian University, 2005.
Gregorios, Paulos M. *Cosmic Man—The Divine Prescence: The Theology of St. Gregory of Nyssa*. New York: Paragon, 1988.
Gregory of Nyssa. *The Life of Moses*. Translated by Abraham Malherbe and Everett Ferguson. Classics of Western Spirituality. New York: Paulist, 1978.
Guardini, Romano. *Christliches Bewußstsein*. German. 2nd ed. Munich: Verlag, 1950.
Hand, Thomas A. *St. Augustine on Prayer*. Westminster, MD: Newman, 1963.
Harrison, Carol. *Beauty and Revelation in the Thought of Saint Augsutine*. Oxford: Clarendon, 1992.
Heim, Maximilian H. *Joseph Ratzinger: Life in the Church and Living Theology*. Translated by Michael J. Miller. San Francisco: Ignatius, 2005.
Horn, Stephan. "Creation and Evolution." In *A Conference with Pope Benedict XVI in Castel Gandolfo*, edited by S. O. Wiedenhofer, 271–77. San Francisco: Ignatius, 2007.
Irenaeus of Lyons. *Proof of the Apostolic Preaching*. Ancient Christian Writers 16. New York: Newman, 1978.
Ivánka, Endre von. *Plato Christianus: Übernahme und Umgestaltung des Platonismus Durch die Väter*. Einsiedeln: Johannes, 1990.
Jeremias, Joachim. *"Abba": The Prayers of Jesus*. London: SCM, 1967.
John Chrysostom. *Homilies on Galatians, Ephesians, Philippians, Colossians, Thessalonians, Timothy, Titus, and Philemon*. Vol. 14 of *Nicene and Post-Nicene Fathers*, Series 1. Edited by Philip Schaff. Grand Rapids: Eerdmans, 1969.
Justin Martyr. *The First Apology; The Second Apology; Dialogue with Trypho; Exhortation to the Greeks; Discourse to the Greeks; The Monarchy of the Rule of God*. Translated by Thomas B. Falls. FC 6. Washington, DC: Catholic University of America Press, 1965.
Kasper, Walter. "Das Wesen Des Christlichen." *Theologische Revue* 65.3 (1969) 182–88.
———. "A Friendly Reply to Cardinal Ratzinger: On the Church." *America* 184.14 (2001) 8–15.
———. "Theorie und Praxis Innerhalb einer Theologia Crucis: Antwort auf J. Ratzingers 'Glaube, Geschichte und Philosophie.'" *Hochland* 62 (1970) 152–57.

Kizewski, Justin J. "God-Talk: The Patristic Patrimony of Medieval Analogy in Theology." PhD diss., Gregorian University, 2016.
Krieg, Robert. "Cardinal Ratzinger, Max Scheler, and Christology." *The Irish Theological Quarterly* 47.1 (1980) 205–19.
Kucer, Peter S. *Truth and Politics: A Theological Comparison of Joseph Ratzinger and John Milbank*. Minneapolis: Fortress, 2014.
Lam, Joseph C. Quy. *Joseph Ratzinger's Theological Retractations* New York: Peter Lang, 2013.
———. *Theologisches Verwandtschaft: Augustinus von Hippo und Joseph Ratzinger/ Papst Benedict XVI*. Würzburg: Echter, 2009.
Louth, Andrew, ed. *Genesis 1–11*. Vol. 1 of *Ancient Christian Commentary on Scripture: Old Testament*. Edited by Thomas C. Oden. Downers Grove, IL: InterVarsity, 2001.
Lubac, Henri de. *Catholicism: Christ and the Common Destiny of Man*. Translated by L. C. Sheppard and E. Englund. San Francisco: Ignatius, 1988.
———. *History and Spirit: The Understanding of Scripture According to Origen* [*Histoire et esprit: L'Intelligence de L'Éscriture d'après Origène*]. Translated by Anne Englund Nash. San Francisco: Ignatius, 2007.
Maximus the Confessor. *On the Cosmic Mystery of Jesus Christ: Selected Writings from St. Maximus the Confessor*. Translated by P. M. Blowers and R. L. Wilken. Popular Patristics Series. New York: St. Vladimir's Seminary, 2003.
———. *On the Difficulties in the Church Fathers: The Ambigua*. Translated by N. Constas. Vol. 1. Cambridge, MA: Harvard University Press, 2014.
———. *Selected Writings*. Edited by John Farina. Classics of Western Spirituality. London: SPCK, 1985.
McGregor, Peter J. "Heart to Heart: The Spiritual Christology of Joseph Ratzinger." PhD diss., Australian Catholic University, 2013.
McLeod, Fredrick G. *The Image of God in the Antiochene Tradition*. Washington, DC: Catholic University of America Press, 1999.
Merriell, Donald J. *To the Image of the Trinity: A Study in the Development of Aquinas's Teaching*. Toronto: Pontifical Institute of Medieval Studies, 1990.
Nash, Ronald H. *The Light of the Mind: St. Augustine's Theory of Knowledge*. Lexington: University Press of Kentucky, 1969.
Newman, John Henry. "Letter to the Duke of Norfolk." In vol. 2 of *Certain Difficulties Felt by Anglicans in Catholic Teaching*, by John Henry Newman, 175–78. London: Longmans, Green, and Co., 1900.
Origen. *Commentary on the Gospel according to John, Books 1–10*. Translated by Ronald E. Heine. FC 80. Washington, DC: Catholic University of America Press, 1989.
———. *Homilies 1–14 on Ezekiel*. Translated by T. P. Scheck. ACW 62. New York: Paulist, 2010.
———. *Homilies on Genesis and Exodus*. Translated by Ronald E. Heine. FC 71. Washington, DC: Catholic University of America Press, 1982.
———. *Johannescommentar*. Vol. 4 of *Origenes Werke*. Die Griechischen Christlichen Schriftsteller der ersten drei Jahrhunderte. Berlin: Griechischen Christlichen Schriftsteller, 1903.
———. *On First Principles* [*De Principiis*]. Translated by G. W. Butterworth. Gloucester, MA: Peter Smith, 1973.
Osborn, Eric. *Clement of Alexandria*. New York: Cambridge, 2005.
———. *Irenaeus of Lyons*. Cambridge: Cambridge, 2001.

Philo of Alexandria. *The Works of Philo*. Peabody, MA: Hendrickson, 1993.
Pohlenz, Max. *Die Stoa: Geschichte einer geistigen Bewegung*. Göttingen: Vandenhoeck and Ruprecht, 1948.
Powell, Samuel. *Participation in God*. Minneapolis: Fortress, 2003.
Przywara, Erich. *Analogia Entis, Metaphysics: Original Structure and Universal Rythm*. Translated by John R. Betz and David Bentley Hart. Grand Rapids: Eerdmans, 2014.
Rahner, Hugo. *Symbole Der Kirche: The Ecclesiologie der Väter*. Salzburg: Müller, 1964.
Rahner, Karl. *Foundations of Christian Faith: An Introduction to the Idea of Christianity*. New York: Crossroad, 1978.
Sakowski, Derek. *The Ecclesiological Reality of Reception Considered as a Solution to the Debate over the Ontological Priority of the Universal Church*. Rome: Gregorian, 2012.
Schall, James V. *The Regensburg Lecture*. South Bend, IN: St. Augustine's, 2007.
Silvas, Anna M. *Gregory of Nyssa: The Letters—Introduction, Translation, and Commentary*. Leiden: Brill, 2007.
Söhngen, Gottlieb. "Bonaventura als Klassiker Der Analogia Fidei." *Wissenschaft und Weisheit* 2.2 (1935) 97–111.
———. *Die Einheit in Der Theologie: Gesammelte Abhandlungen, Aufsätze, Vorträge*. München: K. Zink, 1952.
Tanner, Norman P., ed. *Decrees of the Ecumenical Councils*. 2 vols. Washington, DC: Georgetown University, 1990.
Tyconius. *The Book of Rules*. Translated by William Babcock. Atlanta: Scholars, 1989.
Vega, Angel C. *Saint Augustine, His Philosophy*. Translated by Denis J. Kavanagh. Philadelphia: Peter Reilly, 1931.
White, Thomas J., ed. *The Analogy of Being: Invention of the Antichrist or the Wisdom of God?* Grand Rapids: Eerdmans, 2011.

Index

Ambrose of Milan, 38–39, 40, 252n173
Antiochus of Ascalon, 20n13
Aquinas, Thomas, 138, 148, 156n99, 173
Aristophanes, 166
Aristotle, 40, 41, 156
Athanasius, 95, 102–4, 115, 194, 240
Augustine, 1, 3, 5n27, 6, 10, 11, 68, 77–88, 89, 90–94, 95, 96, 104, 105, 107–16, 123, 125, 128–32, 135, 137, 139, 139n21, 140, 141, 142, 144, 150, 156, 157, 159, 160, 161, 163, 167, 171, 172, 175, 179, 185, 186, 190, 194, 195, 196n114, 197, 199, 204, 205, 208, 213, 221, 223, 230, 232, 233, 234, 237, 238, 239, 240, 241, 242, 244, 245, 246

Balthasar, Hans Urs von, 10, 12, 40, 119–20, 121n221, 122n226, 128n254, 181n51, 201n137, 220, 243, 245, 246
Barth, Karl, 2, 3, 139n18, 149, 169, 246
Basil, 36, 40, 64, 80
Behr, John, 31n65
Betz, 3n11
Bilbao, Gabino U., 7–8, 11, 14, 171, 202, 235, 243, 247, 248, 249
Boethius, 156

Bonaventure, 10, 11, 12, 94, 135, 137–48, 154, 157, 163, 167, 175, 223, 239, 244, 245, 246
Bonino, Serge-Thomas, 249, 250

Carola, Joseph, 42, 70, 71n13, 110n183, 112n188, 114, 151n80, 152n82, 153n85, 199n128
Chapman, Emmanuel, 81n58
Chesterton, 136
Clement of Alexandria, 18–23, 24, 25, 26, 28, 33–34, 35, 40, 43, 59–60, 61, 154, 180n46, 209, 236, 242, 246
Colish, Marcia L., 44n127
Corkery, James, 4, 6, 8
Crouzel, Henri, 35n81
Cyprian of Carthage, 123, 124–26, 131, 132, 212, 228, 232, 234, 242, 243

Darwin, Charles, 176

Egbulefu, Charles, 138n17
Einstein, Albert, 164
Eunomius, 62, 64, 127, 216, 242

Fantino, Jacques, 30
Ferri, Riccardo, 94n111
Flannery, Austin, 221n82
Fletcher, Patrick J., 6, 11, 14, 89n93, 171, 173n10, 173n16, 185, 187n77, 190n91, 204, 235, 241

Granados, José, 44, 45, 67
Gregorios, Paulos, 101
Gregory of Nyssa, 12n44, 27–28, 36n87, 52n154, 60–65, 66, 89–90, 94, 95, 100–102, 108, 123, 125, 126–28, 129, 132, 154, 179, 183, 184, 189, 190n91, 209, 216, 234, 236, 239, 240, 242, 243, 246
Gregory the Wonder-worker (Thaumaturgus), 24
Greshake, Gisbert, 187n77
Guardini, Romano, 189

Hand, Thomas, 131
Heidegger, Martin, 149
Heim, Maximillian Heinrich, 191n97
Heraclitus, 24n37, 70
Hilary of Potiers, 95, 104–7, 109, 195, 240

Irenaeus, 29–33, 35, 40, 46–47, 52–54, 59, 66, 123–24, 129, 132, 146n58, 171, 176, 182, 208, 224, 234, 236
Ivánka, Endre von, 96, 181n51

Jaspers, Karl, 149
Jeremias, Joachim, 204
Joachim of Fiore, 135, 136, 145
John Chrysostom, 37, 38n93, 40, 95, 104, 106, 109, 195, 240
John Paul II, 84n73
Justin Martyr, 24, 26, 41–46, 47, 49, 51, 65, 66, 67, 68–71, 88, 152, 153, 158, 237, 246

Kant, Immanuel, 150n73
Kasper, Walter, 4, 5n24, 8, 192n98
Kizewski, Justin J., 9–10, 11, 12, 17n1, 17n2, 19n10, 21, 22, 24, 31, 33, 37, 38, 39, 42n116, 42n119, 51–52, 53, 54, 56, 57, 59n194, 60, 61, 62, 64, 65, 77, 91, 107–8, 117, 124n233, 136n6, 138, 180n45, 233, 235, 243, 244
Krieg, Robert, 5–6
Kucer, Peter S., 10, 11, 139n18, 140, 150, 168, 221, 235, 245, 246n156

Lam, Joseph C., 5, 6
Lohfink, Gerhard, 187n77
Lombard, Peter, 136
Lubac, Henri de, 26n47, 89n91, 98, 99
Luther, Martin, 149

Marx, Karl, 168
Maximus the Confessor, 95, 117–23, 132, 179, 201, 239, 241, 247
McGregor, Peter J., 4, 5, 6, 8, 9, 11, 14, 171, 179, 200, 204, 225, 235, 243, 244
McLeod, Fredrick G., 30, 33
Merriell, Donald J., 91n101, 92, 172n3

Nash, Ronald H., 78n43, 79n45, 80n51, 81n57, 82, 83n66, 161
Nazianzen, Gregory, 121n222
Newman, John Henry, 162n132

Origen, 24–26, 27, 28, 34–36, 47–50, 51, 54–59, 62, 65, 66, 68, 71–77, 88, 95–100, 108, 129, 132, 154, 158, 160, 163–64, 169, 179, 181, 182, 190, 205, 220, 224, 231, 234, 236, 237, 238, 239, 240, 243, 244, 246, 247
Osborn, Eric, 19n13, 20n13, 22, 23, 30, 31, 32n69, 33, 34, 40, 41, 46, 54n167

Philo of Alexandria, 22, 23, 33, 35n81, 198, 199
Pius XII, 8
Plato, 22, 23, 24n37, 40, 41, 71, 83n66, 86, 193

Przywara, Erich, 2, 3n11, 10, 17n2, 97n123, 171n1, 245

Richard of Saint Victor, 156

Sakowski, Derek, 192n98
Sarah, Robert Cardinal, 230n124
Schall, James V., 136, 207n6, 208n10
Scheler, Max, 5
Seewald, Peter, 136, 180
Patriarch Sergius, 121n222
Silvas, Anna, 36n87
Socrates, 70

Söhngen, Gottlieb, 2, 3n11, 10, 12, 138, 139n18, 150, 245

Tanner, Norman P., 136n3
Tyconius, 39–40, 66, 112, 171, 176, 236

Varro, 85, 159
Vega, Angel C., 87n84

White, Thomas Joseph, 2, 3n12
Whitmore, Philip, 201n136

www.ingramcontent.com/pod-product-compliance
Lightning Source LLC
Chambersburg PA
CBHW071247230426
43668CB00011B/1627